FUTURE GIRL

FUTURE GIRL

YOUNG WOMEN IN THE
TWENTY-FIRST CENTURY

ANITA HARRIS

ROUTLEDGE
NEW YORK AND LONDON

Published in 2004 by
Routledge
29 West 35th Street
New York, New York 10001
www.routledge-ny.com

Published in Great Britain by
Routledge
11 New Fetter Lane
London EC4P 4EE
www.routledge.co.uk

Routledge is an imprint of the Taylor & Francis Group.
Printed in the United States of America on acid-free paper.

10 9 8 7 6 5 4 3 2

Library of Congress Cataloging-in-Publication Data

Harris, Anita, 1968-
    Future girl : young women in the twenty-first century / Anita Harris.
        p. cm.
Includes bibliographical references and index.
    ISBN 0-415-94701-4 (hardcover : alk. paper) — ISBN 0-415-94702-2
(papercover : alk. paper)
    1.   Teenage girls—Social conditions. 2.   Teenage girls—Attitudes. 3.
Teenage girls—Economic conditions. 4.   Identity (Psychology) 5.
Success in adolescence. I.   Title.
    HQ798.H357 2004

                                        305.235—dc21
                                        2003013080

This book is for Gill,
Kevin, Michael,
Racia, and Scottie.

CONTENTS

ACKNOWLEDGMENTS

The following organizations and individuals generously provided permission to reprint images: Australian Army and Defence Force Recruiting, BMG Music, Bonne Bell, British Ministry of Defence, Caitlin Cahill and the Fed Up Honeys, Getty Images, Lisa Hamilton Management, and Tim Wright. Some small portions of this book have been published in a different form in the *International Journal of Critical Psychology* 4, 2001, and in *Feminist Review* 75, November 2003, and are used here with permission from Lawrence & Wishart and Palgrave.

This book was written with the assistance of a Monash University research fellowship, along with several Monash small grants. I am appreciative of the support of all my colleagues in the School of Political and Social Inquiry at Monash University, particularly in the Centre for Women's Studies and Gender Research, where I held my research fellowship, and in sociology, where I now work. Special thanks to John Arnold, Jan van Bommel, Denise Cuthbert, Maryanne Dever, Richard Devetak, Michael Janover, Pete Lentini, Jane Maree Maher, Kirsten McLean, Paul Muldoon, Marnie Neal, Phil Oakley, Andrew Singleton, Ron Smith, Sue Stevenson, Paul Strangio, and Lesley Whitelaw. Ceridwen Spark's thorough research helped me get started, and Meredith Sherlock's incredibly efficient proof work enabled me to finish. At Routledge I owe thanks to Ilene Kalish for encouragement as well as cheerful and razor-sharp editing and to Salwa Jabado for answering so many questions and helping with permissions.

I am lucky to know so many smart and generous people who have helped shape this project. The book is far better for their input, although, inevitably, my incorporation of their excellent ideas and suggestions has been imperfect.

I am enormously grateful to the colleagues and friends with whom I have shared years of reading, writing, talking about, and doing youth studies. Thanks in particular to Sinikka Aapola, Peter Dwyer, Marnina Gonick, Roger Holdsworth, Liz McDonnell, Adreanne Ormond, Anne Marie Tupuola, and Johanna Wyn. Thank you also to those youth activists, writers, and artists who have given their time and energy to help me with my research, especially Michelle de Cean and Yvette Pusser. I began developing a framework for this project while I was a visiting scholar in the Social/Personality Psychology subprogram at the City University of New York Graduate Center. I feel blessed to have found a place there in a community of scholars and activists who continue to inspire and challenge me. Thank you to April Burns, Caitlin Cahill, Sarah Carney, Bill Cross, Katie Cumiskey, Michelle Fine, Tracy McFarlane, Yasser Payne, Rosemarie Roberts, Martin Ruck, and María Elena Torre.

I am thankful to Chilla Bulbeck, Chris Griffin, Valerie Hey, and Angela McRobbie for reading versions of some chapters and providing me with excellent and useful feedback. Michelle Fine, Michael Ure, and Johanna Wyn read and commented on the manuscript in its entirety and have my heartfelt gratitude for undertaking this arduous task. They have been enthusiastic supporters and wonderful critics, and their insights and suggestions have been invaluable.

The greatest debt is closest to home. Deepest thanks to Michael and Scottie for the *Mitfreude*.

INTRODUCTION

This book explores the idea that in a time of dramatic social, cultural, and political transition, young women[1] are being constructed as a vanguard of new subjectivity. They are supposed to offer clues about the best way to cope with these changes. Power, opportunities, and success are all modeled by the "future girl"—a kind of young woman celebrated for her "desire, determination and confidence"[2] to take charge of her life, seize chances, and achieve her goals. The abundance of books about girls' voices, webpages for their issues, and goods and services geared to a girl market indicates how young women are made visible in more and more places to exemplify this new way of being. Such a proliferation of sites to see and hear young women suggests that we are very interested in applauding but also scrutinizing their lives and that we have created more ways for this to happen. I suggest that this new interest in looking at and hearing from girls is not just celebratory, but is, in part, regulatory as well. There is a process of creation and control at work in the act of regarding young women as the winners in a new world. In holding them up as the exemplars of new possibility, we also actively construct them to perform this role.

What does it mean to say that young women and girlhood itself are constructed or regulated to demonstrate how we all might prevail today? In *Act Your Age!*, her brilliant study of the cultural construction of adolescence at the end of the nineteenth century, education scholar Nancy Lesko argues that

> adolescence became a social space in which to talk about the characteristics of people in modernity, to worry about the possibilities of . . . social changes, and to establish policies and programs that would help create the modern social order and citizenry.[3]

Lesko suggests that a new modern political and civic order was being created in the United States and the United Kingdom at the time, one that was

1

preoccupied with nationalism, "civilization," and racial progress. The behavior, attitudes, and development of adolescents were all monitored closely in the interests of producing rational, patriotic, and productive citizens for a modern nation-state. In the late nineteenth century, therefore, the state, scientists, and the community paid considerable attention to young people's social and moral development because they were meant to embody the ideals of national progress. If educators "got it right" with youth, then nations themselves would have their futures secured. Young people were expected to personify modern civic values, such as responsibility, strength, and sacrifice, and model the new style of nation-defending citizenship.

I suggest here that this kind of attention to and construction of youth as integral to the successful transition to a new social order has reemerged in important ways. However, it is young women, rather than youth in general, who are now the subjects of this scrutiny and regulation. Displaying, extolling, and inquiring into young women and girlhood, rather than adolescence, serves many of the same purposes in a contemporary context. Young women today stand in for possibilities and anxieties about new identities more generally. At the beginning of the twenty-first century, the creation of the contemporary social order and citizenship is achieved in part within the space of girlhood. That is, the appropriate ways to embrace and manage the political, economic, and social conditions of contemporary societies are demonstrated in the example of young women, through the ideal of the future girl. She is imagined, and sometimes imagines herself, as best able to handle today's socioeconomic order.

The focus on adolescents at the *fin de siècle* and the attention paid to young women today thus serve similar interests. Girlhood operates now as adolescence functioned then, as a space for "worries about unknown futures, about ability to succeed and dominate in changing circumstances, about maintenance of . . . hierarchy in changing social and cultural landscapes."[4] While these anxieties also confront contemporary social orders, what is different today is the kind of state/civil society relation that is constructed in this space. In the modern period of the late nineteenth century, youth were disciplined directly by the state and its agents so that they would develop slowly, under close supervision, to serve a unified and progressive nation. Late modern times, however, are characterized by dislocation, flux, and globalization, and demand citizens who are flexible and self-realizing. As we shall see, direct intervention and guidance by institutions have been replaced by self-governance; power has devolved onto individuals to regulate themselves through the right choices. The social and economic logic of late modernity compels people to become self-inventing and responsible citizens who can manage their own development and adapt to change without relying on the state. To understand this shift and its implications for youth in general and young women in particular, we need to explore the socioeconomic features of late modernity more closely. First, I want to provide some description and definitions of *late modernity*, focusing especially on the concepts of risk and individualization, as they are central to understanding the world in which future girls live. Although there are many national and cultural differences, I want to make some general claims about what late modernity means for young women across a range of Western nations.

Late Modernity

Before exploring how young women and girlhood in contemporary Western societies are represented as the future, it is important to understand the circumstances and characteristics of late modernity that have given rise to anxieties about the direction of social and economic life. Only then can we interpret the significance of investments in young women as both carriers of and defenders against social change. Put briefly, as youth sociologists Andy Furlong and Fred Cartmel argue in their book *Young People and Social Change*, "Young people today are growing up in a different world to that experienced by previous generations—changes which are significant enough to merit a re-conceptualization of youth transitions and processes of social reproduction."[5] This "different world" is marked by both social and economic characteristics that have forced a fundamental reassessment of the material with which young people are able to craft their identities and forge their livelihoods. Put simply, the late modern era is distinguished by its economic and social break with industrial modernity. This previous era was characterized by a system of industrial capitalism built around manufacturing; strong centralized government; enduring social ties based on shared identifications with community, class, and place; and, in the post-war era, the development of both liberal welfare states and robust social justice movements.

By contrast, late modernity is defined by complex, global capitalist economies and a shift from state support and welfare to the private provision of services. The key feature of late modern economies is deindustrialization—the contraction of large-scale manufacturing and the expansion of global communications, technology, and service industries. Across these and other industries, full-time ongoing employment has been replaced by part-time, casual, temporary, and short-term contract work. Markets, corporations, and production are increasingly globalized, a process fueled by the information revolution, the capacity to move capital and information around the world instantaneously, and changes in national regulations about trade, ownership, movement of capital, and offshore production. Along with this trend nation-states have retreated from industrial regulation of both transnationals and small businesses, and public policy often employs the language of individual responsibility and enterprise bargaining to fill the gap left by deregulation. The economic impact of these conditions has been an increase in family and child poverty, and greater polarization between rich and poor, both within states and between North and South.[6]

The new focus on enterprise, economic rationalism, and individualization has social as well as economic effects. These include a sense of change, insecurity, fragmentation, and discontinuity within communities and nations, as well as a new emphasis on the responsibilities of individuals. Economic rationalism has been accompanied by a shift to a new brand of competitive individualism, whereby people are expected to create their own chances and make the best of their lives. The social theorists Ulrich Beck and Anthony Giddens suggest that the idea of predictability that was a feature of modern times has been replaced by a new sense of danger and contingency. Late modernity has been defined by Beck in his groundbreaking book *Risk Society: Towards a New Modernity* as generating the foundational conditions of what he describes as "risk society," wherein global insecurities and economic unpredictability are combined with weakening collective ties and identities. This feeling of risk, and a sense of the loss of what was known and enduring, are generated by real or perceived broader global trends towards a world sped up and in flux. Mass movements of migrants and refugees; the visibility of civil, religious, and ethnic conflicts; worldwide health threats; economies whose fortunes appear dependent on arbitrary and foreign forces; and global human security concerns all contribute to a real sense of living in a risk society. Alongside these experiences late modern individuals may also feel they have lost significant connections with others, for example, through the diversification of the family unit, the transience of neighborhood populations, and the fragmentation of social movements.

With the falling away of collective ties and longstanding social relationships that helped us know our place and identity, risks must be negotiated on an individual level. This means that people are required to make choices and create life trajectories for themselves without traditional patterns or support structures to guide them. They must develop individual strategies and take personal responsibility for their success, happiness, and livelihood by making the right choices in an uncertain and changeable environment. From one perspective this process of individualization creates opportunities for forming oneself independently of the traditional ties that have previously been so instrumental in structuring life trajectories. It carries with it the promise of choice, freedom, and real autonomy. However, apparent opportunities for self-invention and individual effort exist within circumstances that remain highly constrained for the majority of people. Sociologist Steven Miles suggests that the image of subjectivity generated by risk society is

> one of increased independence, self-determination and self-realization. But as discussions of risk illustrate, the conditions within which these apparently positive developments are occurring are actually taking place in a world which in some respects is quite possibly less secure than it has ever been.[7]

This insecurity is manifested in unpredictable chances for employment and other avenues for livelihood, the shift from production to consumption as a framework for making meaning and identity (which in turn depends on the capacity to generate income), the rollback of nation-states' accountability for the social rights of their citizens, and the replacement of strong social bonds with momentary identifications. Furthermore, whereas once obstacles to maximizing one's life chances could be understood through analyses of structured social inequality and addressed through political collectivities, the collapse of these collectivities means that today these can only be remedied through more strenuous self-invention and self-transformation.

These conditions and the requirement of individuals to now "make themselves" in order to survive and perhaps even flourish have generated considerable anxiety about the future of youth, who are imagined as the inheritors of this somewhat frightening world. It is young people who must try to forge their futures by mastering the anxieties, uncertainties, and insecurities conjured up by unpredictable times. As youth studies theorist Peter Kelly argues, "Processes of individualisation . . . visit new forms of responsibility on young people and their families to prudently manage individual 'reflexive biographical projects' in increasingly uncertain settings."[8] In other words, young people are newly obliged to make good choices for themselves and set themselves on a path toward success with little support or security outside the private sphere. In a risk society their circumstances and opportunities seem more precarious than ever. However, as the future-girl phenomenon suggests, youth are also imagined as those who may be best able to prevail, having grown up with unpredictability as their only reality. After all, young people are taking up the opportunities of late modernity, particularly in technology and communications, in ways that many of an older generation find admirable.

In the late nineteenth century youth were constructed as highly dependent and were expected to take guidance from experts to become citizens in the development of a larger social plan for national homogeneity and progress. The features of the ideal young person were clearly prescribed. Today, they are supposed to become unique, successful individuals, making their own choices and plans to accomplish autonomy. The benchmark for achieving a successful identity is no longer adherence to a set of normative characteristics, but instead a capacity for self-invention. This means that they are the focus of a different kind of attention from the state, service providers, educators, and advertisers. Young people in modern times were governed by experts who would overtly direct and then reward or punish appropriate behavior. The new watchfulness in youth research, policy, and popular culture seeks to shape conduct through perpetual everyday observation and to elicit self-monitoring in youth themselves. They are not only obliged to manage their own life trajectories, but are enticed to display this management for the scrutiny of experts and observers. The obligation for youth to become unique individuals is therefore constructed as a freedom, a freedom best expressed through the display of one's choices and projects of the self. The current focus on placing young people in school, workplaces, and appropriate recreational centers, and in hearing from them, for example, in youth citizenship debates, can be understood as related to this trend toward exhibition of one's biographical project.

Why Young Women?

Young women have taken on a special role in the production of the late modern social order and its values. They have become a focus for the construction of an ideal late modern subject who is self-making, resilient, and flexible. But why is it young women and not youth in general who have been invested in, symbolically and materially, in these ways? I answer this question in two ways. First, changed economic and work conditions combined with the goals achieved by feminism have created new possibilities for young women. Successful campaigns for the expansion of girls' education and employment have coincided with a restructured global economy and a class/gender system that now relies heavily on young women's labor. Second, new ideologies about individual responsibility and choices also dovetail with some broad feminist notions about opportunities for young women, making them the most likely candidates for performing a new kind of self-made subjectivity.

The transformations in women's status throughout the Western world have been strongly felt in the sectors of education and employment. Women's participation in both areas has increased significantly since the 1960s and 1970s. Changes in laws, policies, and social mores have all made this participation possible and desirable for women. State-sanctioned discrimination which once privileged men in education and at work has been largely eliminated, and the assumption that women do not need careers because they derive their livelihood from a man, as well as a complete identity from the heterosexual nuclear family, has been fundamentally challenged. Young women have been promised equal access to all educational programs and are encouraged by educators and others to pursue meaningful work that aligns with their interests and skills.

At the same time that feminism was ensuring these entitlements, the world of education and employment was changing dramatically for young people, and young women in particular. With the collapse of the full-time youth job market, the rise of the service and communications sectors, and the fragmentation of both workplaces and work trajectories, young people are now expected to stay in education longer to train for flexible, specialized work in a constantly changing labor market. There has been an enormous increase in part-time work for women in the flourishing industries,[9] as well as a departure of men from some professional and managerial spheres in favor of better-paying options in the new finance or technology sectors of the global economy. These conditions create opportunities (although not always good ones) for young women's work participation. Thus, the feminist push to dismantle the barriers keeping women out of education and employment has coincided with a broader socioeconomic need for young women to take up places in the new economy. As education scholar Jill Blackmore argues, "The new global work order has offered girls the types of opportunities that feminism and their education have well prepared them for, giving them both the skills and desire to take up new subject positions."[10]

Further, education and employment have become increasingly important to the standing of young women in terms of the new class/gender structure of late modernity. This is particularly so for the middle classes. Whereas once a comfortable middle-class position was attained or sustained through marriage, today this process is much less assured. The family wage that was once paid to men on the assumption that they had a wife and children to support has largely disappeared. Regulations and protections around pay rates are no longer the norm, and men's incomes are less secure, particularly in the industries employing the lower and middle classes. In addition, the expansion of consumer capitalism and the connection between consumption and middle-class status mean that two incomes are required to sustain a family's appropriate class lifestyle. Finally, the changing nature of the labor market has seen an expansion of "women's work," such that there is sound economic logic for middle-class families to depend on women's wages. Middle-class young women can no longer rely on marriage to secure their economic status or social standing. These young women must become successful and income-generating in their own right, and this means doing well academically and professionally.

Along with changes to education and employment have come reforms to legislation and a shift in attitudes regarding relationships, marriage and divorce, reproduction and sexuality, harassment and sexual assault, and many other dimensions of what had previously been seen as the realm of the personal. Feminism has often been described as a program for change to allow women freedom of choice regarding their bodies, work, family, and relationships—and personal, autonomous responsibility for these choices. These changes have enabled the current generation of young women to see themselves, and to be seen, as enjoying new freedoms and opportunities. They are far more at liberty to make choices and pursue lifestyles independently of their families, the state, and men in general. Young women have been encouraged to believe that "girls can do anything" and "girls are powerful."

These ideas about choice and freedom are central to contemporary notions of individuality. In today's risk society individuals are expected to be flexible, adaptable, resilient, and ultimately responsible for their own ability to manage their lives successfully. One's own life becomes a personal project much like a do-it-yourself assemblage or what Ulrich Beck calls a "choice biography"[11] that can be crafted as one desires, rather than a fixed set of predictable stages and experiences. These are key ideas in differentiating late modern young people's identities from modern, late-nineteenth-century adolescence. As Peter Kelly argues, today, "youthful subjects are constructed as responsible for future life chances, choices and options within institutionally structured risk environments. . . . The subject is compelled to prudently manage . . . his or her own DIY [Do-It-Yourself]-project of the self."[12] These features of the late modern self pick up on key elements of some general feminist principles about young women's new opportunities for choice, individual empowerment, personal responsibility, and the ability to "be what you want to be." Young women are thus doubly constructed as ideal flexible subjects; they are imagined as benefiting from feminist achievements and ideology, as well as from new conditions that favor their success by allowing them to put these into practice.

By interrogating the new visibility of young women and focusing specifically on the idea of girls' success as a publicly displayed, mainstream experience, we can see how "making it" in new times appears to be contingent on personal responsibility and effort, the kind of effort best illustrated by the way all girls are now apparently leading their lives. The popular story is that girls as a whole are performing brilliantly and are the great example and hope for the future. Educated, young, professional career women with glamorous consumer lifestyles appear to be everywhere. This scenario is a reality for a small number, but the image also functions as a powerful ideal that suggests that all young women are now enjoying these kinds of lives and that this is what it means to be successful.

There are, however, many young women who are not living in ways that match the image of success. Their situation results from the same conditions that produce the future girl, that is, a changed labor market, economic rationalization, and a devolving of responsibility—a "responsibilization"—onto individuals. In order for the popular story to prevail, however, the consequences of the sexual and economic exploitation of these young women are not confronted, and the socioeconomic benefits delivered by them are not acknowledged. Instead, their circumstances are labeled "failure," and this is attributed to poor choices, insufficient effort, irresponsible families, bad neighborhoods, and lazy communities. In the move to cultivate young women as the new success story for our times, the struggles, disappointments, and barriers experienced by many young women are put to one side as the aberrant experiences of a minority of youth. Set in the context of the late modern Western world, this book therefore argues that there is another story behind the representation of young women as the winners in rapidly changing societies. I suggest that young women are living more complex lives than the dominant images of girls' freedom, power, and success suggest and that class and race inequalities continue to shape opportunities and outcomes. Because young women are supposed to embody the new flexible subjectivity, analyzing their experiences, practices, and political engagements can illustrate more broadly the dangers and opportunities of late modernity for its self-inventing subjects.

Organization of the Chapters

I build my argument by making connections between current representations of young women, the material conditions within which they live, and the new ways they are able to challenge both of these. The intense interest in young women as the vanguard of the late modern social order has resulted in an expansion of the places they are seen and heard. The problematic effect of this move has been an increase in the regulation of their lives through a proliferation of sites where their biographical projects can be observed. Young women's roles in the class/race system of globalized capitalism are secured through this new kind of regulation. However, this public focus on young women has also generated new strategies for social critique. Many express resistance to their part in the production of the new socioeconomic order through an activism that works by evading surveillance. I argue that many young women respond to their visibility with skepticism; they seek new kinds of political engagement and communities to confront the seductive lure of unlimited self-making and to develop a critique of the future girl.

Chapter 1 demonstrates how and why young women have emerged as the central subjects of discourses about how to prevail in a late modern world. They have come in for particular kinds of attention through two new contrasting narratives, one about girls' power and the other about the difficulties they encounter. These discourses position young women as either "can-do" or "at-risk" girls. They show how success, personal effort, and self-invention have become linked together in the project of surviving in a risk society. Through these discourses young women are disciplined into creating their own successful life trajectories and taking personal responsibility if they fail. I explore the can-do and at-risk positions in relation to young women as workers, consumers, and mothers. I demonstrate how a normative image of the girl for our times both relies on and shores up class and race stratifications that persist despite the discourse of meritocracy.

Chapter 2 looks more closely at the construction of young women as successful in education and employment. It examines the impact of the loss of the full-time youth labor market and the new emphasis on flexibility and skill development for young women. The chapter argues that young women are often perceived as beneficiaries of the new world of work and training but that this picture changes radically when a diverse range of young women's experiences is taken into account. I demonstrate the enormous expectations placed upon them to seize all the opportunities offered by deindustrialized and globalized labor markets, and how only a small minority of young women are structurally located in ways that make this possible. The economic shifts that characterize late modernity have had deeply divisive effects on young women, particularly in the world of work. This stratification has enormous benefits for the new economy, as it has enabled differently advantaged young women to take up positions that must be filled at opposite ends of the labor market. At the same time the accompanying narratives about choice, self-invention and, opportunity ensure that stratification and disadvantage become reconfigured as merely individual limitations of effort or vision, to be addressed through personal strategies alone.

Chapter 3 explores the ways in which young women are invested in as symbols of ideal citizenship at a time of profound change. I argue that as a consequence of globalization, new patterns of migration, the retreat of the state, the shift toward privatization and marketization, and a sense of uncertainty, notions of citizenship are increasingly in flux. Young women are constructed as the ideal new citizens to manage these conditions when they are imagined as economically independent, as "ambassadresses" for their nations, and as successful consumers. The neoliberal discourse that has accompanied deregulation and deindustrialization merges well with a version of girlpower that emphasizes self-invention and individual economic empowerment.

Chapter 4 explores some of the most significant spaces in the lives of young women. It suggests that even while they appear to be everywhere, the spaces they are expected to occupy have become more regulated. Schools, workplaces, and centers of leisure are all central to young people's constitution of self in late modernity. In these sites new kinds of surveillance and vigilant attention are used to construct educational, professional, and consumer success as normal and possible for all young women and to manage and punish failure as individual inadequacy, through such means as at-risk programs and new policing regimes. In addition, I argue that another significant space for young women in late modernity is the overhauled welfare and justice systems that use new punitive measures to discipline them for "failure."

Chapter 5 examines the idea that young women are not only perceived to be seen everywhere, but heard everywhere as well. I discuss the proliferation of research, texts, policies, and programs concerned with girls' voices. I explore the possibility that this new emphasis on eliciting young women's voices constitutes a kind of surveillance. I consider the ways in which young women's private selves and their "authentic voices" are made subject to display and regulation through a renewed interest in enhancing youth participation and eliciting youth opinions. Young people are encouraged to speak up and be heard, but this process often fails to result in enduring political change. The chapter explores what French social theorist Michel Foucault describes as the "incitement to discourse"[13] as it is played out in a confessional culture that encourages young women to speak out. The conventional approaches to young people's participation and the strategies undertaken to encourage youth involvement are also analyzed from this perspective. I suggest that both youth voice and youth involvement have become strategies for the regulation of young women.

The overmanagement of the spaces of girls' lives, the incitement to display their life projects, and the appropriation of their discourses have serious implications for young women's capacity to enact alternative, more complex, and critical subject positions beyond success and failure. These increased regulatory practices surrounding young women have made it difficult for them to express political resistance in conventional ways. Chapter 6 explores young women's new possibilities for making community, evading surveillance, and building activism. I explore how young women find new places and strategies for politics that undermine and challenge investments in and uses of girls. As we shall see, young women have complex and ambivalent relationships to the normative discourses and practices about their success and power. Shaping and legitimizing the future girl is a constant struggle, the site of which is young women's subjectivities, and the outcome of which is far from guaranteed. What is thus partly at stake in this investment in and regulation of girls is the consent of young women who may be critical of the effects of economic rationalism and individualization on their lives, particularly in terms of the negative consequences for their labor market opportunities, family arrangements, and community and civic engagement. Their ability to find other ways and other places to develop such a critique, in spite of the compelling nature of the discursive space of success (and its flipside), is therefore also an important part of the story that this book has to tell.

CHAPTER 1

THE "CAN-DO" GIRL VERSUS THE "AT-RISK" GIRL

The new generation has arrived. Meet the Can-Do girls:
confident, optimistic and enthusiastic.
—Liz Deegan, "Girls with the World at Their Feet"

Welcome to the new teen generation—Alienated, Cynical, Experimental
and incredibly Savvy. Members of the ACES generation
lose their virginity at 13, start smoking and taking drugs
about the same age and are binge-drinking at 15.
—Tina-Marie Morrison, "Teen Angels Bite Back"

Since the early 1990s young womanhood has become a topic central to debates within Western societies about cultural and economic change. Popular culture, public policy, academic inquiry, and the private sector are now interested in young women in ways that are quite unprecedented. Recent times have seen a fiery generational contest within feminism, sociological interest in young women as the new professionals (and speculation about consequent changing family patterns), criminological concern with girls' violence, health alerts about their sexual behavior, and educational discourse and policy preoccupied with girls outperforming boys. Teenage girls are supposed to be more confident and resilient than ever before; they have "the world at their feet."[1] At the same time research, journalism, and popular debates suggest increasing fears about young women's low self-esteem and risk behaviors. The Body Shop–sponsored U.K. research report entitled *Can-Do Girls* finds that young women who do not expect to succeed in life manifest their low ambitions in mental health problems such as depression and eating disorders, and are more likely to become teen mothers.[2] The construction and separation of these two kinds of girlhood occurs around some key motifs. The "girls with the world at their feet" are identifiable by their commitment to exceptional careers and career planning, their belief in their capacity to invent themselves and succeed, and their display of a consumer lifestyle. They are also distinguished by a desire to put off childbearing until "later." The others are more likely to suffer from what youth researchers Barbara Schneider and David Stevenson describe in *The Ambitious Generation* as "misaligned occupational ambitions," a lack of a sense of power or opportunity, and inappropriate consumption behaviors, for example, of drugs or alcohol. These young women are also more likely to become pregnant at a young age.

How are we to make sense of these opposed positionings of young women as exemplars of both success and failure? The issues facing young women are deemed to be new and specific to their historical location. In both of these images, young women's fortunes are linked to the particular historical circumstances of their generation. That is, in both cases it is the features of current times that render young womanhood a site of either new possibilities or problems, that fill young women with confidence and optimism or, conversely, leave them alienated and self-destructive. The shifting labor market, the expansion of higher education, cultural and economic globalization, and changing notions of female identity, the family, citizenship, and the state create new choices for them. These opportunities and challenges are now available to enhance the life chances of those who can seize them. However, at the same time that young women's fortunes are seen as intricately interwoven with late modernity, the fortunes of late modernity are equally interwoven with young women. This intense interest in them, and, specifically, the new depictions of girls as either can-do or at-risk, suggests that what it means to prevail or lose out in these new times has become bound up with how we understand girlhood. Their public presence indicates that both actual young women and the symbolic value of girlhood have been deeply invested in and that they have come to stand for a number of hopes and concerns about late modernity. As noted girls' studies scholar Angela McRobbie argues, " 'Girls,' including their bodies, their labour power and their social behaviour are now the subject of governmentality to an unprecedented degree."[3] This chapter explores why the regulation of young women has come to matter in quite the way it does currently and how this is enacted through the construction of the can-dos and the at-risks.

Investing in Girls

There has been a series of historical moments when this same phenomenon of symbolic and material investment has occurred in relation to youth in general. Nancy Lesko argues that from its invention at the turn of the century, the notion of adolescence as a life phase has become "institutionally ordained and reduced to stereotypes, commodified and malleable as a sign of futures, pasts, fears and hopes."[4] As has been well documented, young people have become the focus for a variety of moral panics during social change and economic crisis. Paradoxically, they have also been traditionally perceived as "the future" and held up as fearless pioneers who will show the way forward in uncertain times.[5] Young people have also been invested in materially, insofar as their labor has always been important in maintaining and reproducing class relations. For some commentators the emergence of youth as a recognized life phase can be mapped onto the emergence of industrial capitalism.[6] The need for young people to take up their appropriate roles in the labor market has generated particular images of youth. For instance, the invention of "juvenile delinquency" occurred at a time when young working-class men were gaining power and threatening to disrupt the socioeconomic order by moving out of their class positions.[7] However, these kinds of symbolic and material uses have more typically been applied to young men, or youth in general, than young women.

It is far less common that young women *as a category* have been the subjects of these kinds of investments. This is not to say that the construction of young femininity has not mattered to the social order. Growing up "right" has always been a highly managed process for girls in order for particular forms of gender relations to be maintained. Female adolescence has typically been represented as a risky business that must be carefully navigated, usually with the help of professionals, to ensure that girls make a successful transition to normative adult womanhood.[8] However, young women of quite specific populations have been used symbolically: particular kinds of young women have been constructed as a problem for society, namely young mothers, the sexually active, and Black and Indigenous girls.[9] Others again, such as the well-integrated and upwardly mobile migrant, have been used as symbols of social success.[10] Material investments in young women have also been deeply class and race stratified. The work performed by young working-class women, both paid and unpaid, has received little recognition, although it has always been the subject of a great deal of social control. Similarly, colonizing societies including the United States, Australia, Canada, and New Zealand/ Aotearoa have established their nations on the indentured labor of young Indigenous and enslaved peoples, both women and men, although this is little discussed.[11] By contrast, the emergence of white, middle-class young women as workers, as the "New Women" or "New Girls" of the early twentieth century, was heralded as a moment of important cultural change.

However, the idea that young women in general and young womanhood itself actually hold the key to imagining the social and economic future is new. As Angela McRobbie suggests in her book *Feminism and Youth Culture*, "Young women . . . have replaced youth as a metaphor for social change . . . [and] are now recognised as one of the stakes upon which the future depends."[12] This is evidenced by the investments in them as new kinds of workers, consumers, and citizens. Their relationship to the labor market, their patterns of consumption, and their sexual lives are all of increasing interest to the state, the private sector, researchers, and the media. They are imagined to be those most able and likely to prevail and succeed in a risk society. However, the emphasis on the resilience and achievements of young women is matched by a concern, even a moral panic, that at least some of them are not succeeding as they should be. This dual focus on young women is played out in the attention to and regulation of their attitudes and behavior. The construction of the can-do girls and the remaindering of the others in the at-risk category is the purpose of this regulation. In the rest of this chapter, I will explore these two categories of contemporary young womanhood through the issues of work, consumption, and motherhood. I discuss the normative ways in which young women are expected to relate to these experiences. These new ways of being a worker, a consumer, and a mother are supposed to show how young women are best able to enact the subjectivity required by late modernity. Successful achievement of these new subject positions is constructed as a mainstream experience for young women, and failure is deemed to be the consequence of an individual limitation. Although the socioeconomic conditions of late modernity have created unequally distributed opportunities and impediments for young women, it is the idea that good choices, effort, and ambition alone are responsible for success that has come to separate the can-dos from the at-risks.

Meet the Can-Do Girls

As we have seen, the ideal late modern subject is one who is flexible, individualized, resilient, self-driven, and self-made and who easily follows nonlinear trajectories to fulfillment and success. Young women play a critical role in this remaking of subjectivity. As argued by scholars in the field, flexibility and self-actualization are now expected of young women because they are perceived as those most confident, resilient, and empowered of all the demographic groups affected by risk.[13]

Girlpower

One of the most important words in the new lexicon of young female success is *girlpower*. The concept of girlpower has been highly significant in the image of young women as independent, successful, and self-inventing.

Originally, girlpower or *grrrlpower* was the catchword of an underground young radical feminist movement that advocated for the improvement of girls' lives.[14] Emerging in the early 1990s as a blend of punk and feminist politics, it became the first powerful youth movement or political subculture to be organized entirely around young women's concerns. The rewriting of the word *girl* into *grrrl* was intended to communicate anger (the *grrr* stood for growling) and rejection of patronizing attitudes toward young women. Those using this word and driving the movement were largely involved in alternative music cultures in the United States, the United Kingdom, and to a lesser extent Europe, the Asia-Pacific region, and elsewhere, and used music and writing to develop a political platform for younger feminists. However, its punk philosophy of DIY (do it yourself) and individual responsibility for social change lent itself easily to its transformation into a discourse of choice and focus on the self. Since this reinvention, it has become a catchphrase for young women's new style of display and attitude. This is a sexy, brash, and individualized expression of ambition, power, and success, neatly captured, for example, in the image of Britney Spears.

This kind of girlpower constructs the current generation of young women as a unique category of girls who are self-assured, living lives lightly inflected but by no means driven by feminism, influenced by the philosophy of DIY, and assuming they can have (or at least buy) it all. The evidence for these new ways of being is drawn from a wide range of areas: girls' educational success; their consumption, leisure, and fashion practices; apparent rejection of institutionalized feminism; sexual assertiveness; professional ambitions; delayed motherhood, and so on. Nowhere is girlpower more evident, though, than in popular culture, particularly in the promotion of certain pop stars, comic book heroes, TV and film characters, and advertising icons. Girlpower celebrities include such diverse subjects as Lara Croft, Tank Girl, Buffy the Vampire Slayer, Courtney Love, and the Spice Girls (whose own girlpower heroine was, famously, Margaret Thatcher). They are deemed to embody girlpower because they are outspoken, not afraid to take power, believe in themselves, and run their own lives. Cultural studies theorist Susan Hopkins argues that " 'girlpower' is a provocative mix of youth, vitality, sexuality and self-determination. The story on offer here is one of power through and control over one's own identity invention and re-invention."[15] The idea of girlpower encapsulates the narrative of the successful new young woman who is self-inventing, ambitious, and confident.

Success at Work

Can-do girls are notable for their high ambitions with regard to their employment and their commitment to elaborate planning for success in their careers. They seize the opportunities made available within the new economy and make projects of their work selves from an early age. New resources and efforts are required for young people to succeed in the new economy, and these can-do girls are represented as particularly able in applying themselves to maximize their future chances in the changing world of work.

In *The Ambitious Generation* Schneider and Stevenson discuss the importance of young people developing a plan, with the help and support of family and school, to realize their professional ambitions. They describe the case of "Elizabeth," the child of professional, highly educated parents, attending a well-regarded school in a Northeastern U.S. town, who planned for a career in journalism or politics from her early school years. In high school she took higher-level science and mathematics classes (in spite of disliking these subjects) as well as extra university-level classes in economics and history at a competitive private institution. She was fluent in French, edited the school newspaper, was selected for the decathlon and debating teams, and held various leadership positions in the school. She completed a college course in government studies at a highly competitive summer school and worked for several summers as an intern for a local senator. She prepared intensively for college entrance exams and applied to fourteen prestigious institutions. At her college of choice she maintained an A average, worked for the Department of Justice, learned Danish, and undertook a traveling scholarship to Paris. She says, "In terms of having created the tools for success in the workplace I am confident about them. . . ."[16] "Elizabeth" is clearly on track to realize her professional ambitions through these extraordinary efforts to work on herself to maximize opportunities for success. She is an example of a can-do girl in her ability to fold in together ambition, professional intentions, success, and her DIY project of the self.

Angela McRobbie's discussion of young women's place in the "new meritocracy" illustrates the ways in which new modes of young femininity have been bound up with success and striving for success, particularly in the context of work. She argues that in the United Kingdom, the Labour government has built a campaign about bright prospects for success and generation of wealth in the new economy almost exclusively around the potential of girls. With the stripping away of gender-based barriers to participation in education and the labor market and the development of a more open, meritocratic system, young women are perceived to have risen quickly to the top in terms of educational attainment, aspirations, and job prospects. The signs of their success are glamorous careers and luxurious consumer lifestyles, financial independence, and high standards of physical beauty and grooming. She suggests that political, media, and advertising interests have converged in the construction of young women as "standard bearers for the new economy, as creators of wealth."[17] Government policy and agenda setting is squarely focused on young women's economic independence by placing them on a path of success at school and then at work, in the process creating docile good girls who can uncomplainingly participate in meeting the needs of the marketplace.

Government, nongovernment organization (NGO), or community initiatives that attend to these goals for girls thus tend to attract strong corporate sponsorship. This is well illustrated in the United States, where millions of dollars of private and public funding are poured into programs like Take Our Daughters to Work Day, which aims to initiate girls into the world of the successful woman worker. This program was developed by the Ms Foundation and a communications strategist who felt "that the *workplace* was the place for girls to begin to hold on to their sense of identity and power."[18] Although this initiative was driven by a broadly feminist objective, its interpretation of success as corporate opportunity saw it lose its political edge, and it was soon taken over by powerful sponsors, for example Merrill Lynch, Deloitte and Touche, and IBM. Feminist commentators Jennifer Baumgardner and Amy Richards note that girls participating in the program commonly leave workplaces with sample bags of company branded products rather than a "real workplace experience," and cite the example of MTV's support of this scheme in the form of a careers talk by a supermodel.[19]

Logically, advertisers can benefit considerably from this new glamor-worker mode of feminine subjectivity, bound up as it is with products, accessories, self-presentation, and lifestyle, all now available to those with increased disposable income (and desired by those without). And the media celebrates this image of success enthusiastically, with magazine, television, and newspaper features on girlpower, investment advice for women, and profiles of female role models of glamor and wealth. Susan Hopkins cites a feature on modeling in the Australian girls' magazine *Dolly* that offers advice about breaking into "star" careers. She says, "The dream on offer combines beauty *and* brains, love *and* money, glamour *and* power—no wonder girls are held in thrall."[20] These magazines, whose content is largely advertisements, trade in a glamorous heterosexual imperative combined with a pseudoliberatory new consumerism.

As Angela McRobbie notes, while media and advertising have always focused on feminine success in relation to body and appearance, what is new is that this is now connected to success at work. The processes of working on the self and competing with others, especially other women, to be perfect in self-presentation have been extended so that improving oneself is necessary to success in the labor and consumer markets. Youth studies scholar Harriet Bjerrum Nielsen finds in her research with young, middle-class Norwegian women that focusing exclusively on appearance without engaging with the project of success at work is no longer appropriate. According to her cohort,

> Traditional femininity is *shameful*—something which is seen in these girls' pronounced contempt for "ordinary girls" who are absorbed in fashion and exaggerated dieting. Such girls, they consider, also choose low-paid women's jobs instead of developing their skills and abilities. . . . Gender is something that befalls "the others"—and this leads to a somewhat suspicious attitude towards those girls who are not as successful as them in becoming individualized. Have they really made an effort?[21]

McRobbie suggests that what we are witnessing is "a new right vocabulary which celebrates female success in the market place, which punishes failure as individual weakness and which boldly advocates competitive individualism as the mark of modern young womanhood."[22] This vocabulary is widespread and persuasive, combining as it does laudable attention to the potential and entitlements of girls with a more problematic promotion of success as achieved through personal effort alone and as measured by labor market accomplishments and material gain.

Consumption

Success in the workplace has therefore become linked up with the display of a consumer lifestyle. Social theorist Lisa Adkins argues that "consumption skills . . . are the essential preconditions for . . . economic power and are central for . . . professional success in the cutting-edge economic sectors of late capitalism: the lifestyle, marketing and image industries. . . ."[23] With the construction of young women as those most likely to be successful and prosperous in the new economy comes their emergence as a key consumer group, and campaigns to capture this market have not been so aggressive since the 1950s.[24] As the editor of *Dolly* says, "Ten years ago we were the only teen fashion and lifestyle magazine on the market, now there are more magazines because people realise the importance of this market."[25] The spending power of twelve- to seventeen-year-old British girls has been estimated at £1.3 billion. In Australia, eleven- to seventeen-year-olds' collective income is AUS $4.6 billion, and in the United States, young women aged eight to eighteen are deemed to be worth $67 billion.[26] These figures do not even include the family purchases they influence.

What is interesting, however, is that young women not only constitute an important consumer group as their disposable income increases, but also that the image of successful, individualized girlhood itself is one of the most profitable products being sold to them and others. An advertising trade journal article subtitled "The Shopping Power of Generation Y" claims that "the new trend is about Girl Power—a celebration of femininity and individualism."[27] It is now cool to be a girl. Some products, brands, and line are marketed directly through the terminology of girlpower; for example, the Spice Girls have endorsed many items including deodorant, a soft drink, and snack foods. Girlpower has also been used directly to promote clothes (the Australian fashion label Sportsgirl's Girlpower line), dolls (the all-girl pop group Barbie doll set, the Get Real Girls dolls), cosmetics, and so on. It has been used to sell clothing and accessories such as underwear, handbags, jewelry, hats, and "baby doll" (that is, small and tight-fitting) T-shirts with provocative slogans, ranging from the fairly tame "girl power" or "girls rule" to "babe," "slut," and "bitch."

With the use of girlpower as both a slogan and a concept, Jill Blackmore argues that "consumer capitalism and the media depictions of feminism have . . . cultivated for many girls a sense that they have made it."[28] The image of the successful and assertive girl in control of her own destiny has become central to the entertainment industries, a trend which arguably started with Madonna, who continues to peddle this image into her forties (with a 2000 single entitled "What It Feels Like for a Girl"). Particular kinds of female solo artists, groups, and celebrities who trade on this representation of assertive, self-inventing girlhood have dominated music sales charts, magazine covers, and "Who's In?" lists. The profit potential of girlpower is thus undoubtable. Of course, young, attractive women have always been used to sell products, and marketing to girls has always been a matter of constructing the latest, coolest kind of femininity. Now, however, a particular kind of young, assertive, and sassy woman selling particular kinds of girlpower-inflected products or services has become enormously important in constructing and then tapping the (presumed to be universal) consumer power of young women.

There are now thousands of websites for girls which are supported by a huge amount of advertising and which sometimes double as market research companies. Successful and independent young women are constituted as an all-powerful market, both in terms of their own purchasing power and their influence over family consumption and lifestyle patterns, including grocery, clothing, holiday, and home décor choices.[29] However, they are also invested in as the style makers and trend shapers of late modernity, and "successful girlness" has become the revitalizing force in marketing. Figure 1.1 depicts the 2002 lip gloss campaign of teen cosmetics brand Bonne Bell. It features the face of a beautiful young white woman, across which is written "I know I will succeed." Next to this image is a checklist stating "I have a brain, I have lip gloss, I have a plan, I have a choice, I can change my mind, I am a girl." Success and young femininity are connected through notions of choice, versatility, beauty, and clever-

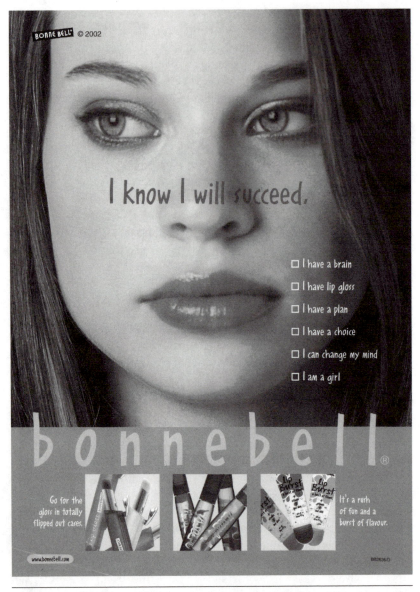

Fig. 1.1 "I know I will succeed" Advertisement for Bonne Bell Lip Burst. Reprinted with permission.

ness. Cultural studies theorist Rosalind Gill cites the example of the production of T-shirts by the London School of Economics proclaiming "LSE Babe," and she suggests that being sexually attractive, smart, and savvy—and declaring this through consumption and display—is the new package of young female success.

Delayed Motherhood

The achievement of labor market accomplishments and a glamorous consumer lifestyle are premised on the idea of an unencumbered individual who can devote herself to full-time paid work. An intrinsic element of the can-do experience is thus the delaying of motherhood. Young women with professional prospects are putting off having children into their thirties and forties, choosing to have only one or two children, or opting for childlessness altogether. There is a great deal of social and economic support for these pathways, although this has required a reshaping of traditional conservative family values around mothering to accommodate the neoliberal agenda that calls for young women to function as high-status workers. From a conservative perspective reproduction has been under threat since second-wave feminism, but this concern is now coupled with anxieties about the loss of a maternal feminine identity in the new emphasis on work. Consequently, motherhood is repackaged so that it is consistent with a glamor-worker subjectivity but also in ways that reinscribe the maternal. Can-do girls are encouraged to delay childbearing until their careers are established but not to renounce motherhood altogether. McRobbie notes that the U.K. government has begun to focus on easy access to contraception and the morning-after pill as a priority area for maintaining the well-being of school-aged young women. In the United States the social control of young women's reproduction has been well established.[30]

These measures are increasingly related to the disciplining of the bodies of privileged young women. Critical psychologists Valerie Walkerdine, Helen Lucey, and June Melody argue in their book *Growing Up Girl* that

> the regulation of feminine sexuality for middle-class girls has to be understood as part of a wider regulation of their achievement and academic success. Nothing is allowed to obstruct the academic path—certainly not motherhood, which is seen as the ultimate failure.[31]

They find that the linking of success with delayed motherhood is taken extremely seriously by young women on the can-do track, who perceive young motherhood as an unthinkable waste and tragedy. The families of young women who are high-achieving also tend to be committed to the regulation of their daughters' sexuality. Cultural anthropologist Signithia Fordham finds in her study of African-American high school students that

> there is virtually no time during the day when the mothers of the high-achieving girls do not know where their daughters are. Most of the girls, who are either seventeen or just short of that age, are not allowed to date or their dating is relentlessly controlled.[32]

However, the more traditional requirement for women to have children at some point still comes to bear on these girls. They are simultaneously told that they must pursue careers and at the same time factor in children before it is "too late." New concerns about falling birth rates and young women renouncing childbearing altogether have led to state intervention in the lives of young professional women in unprecedented ways. In Australia the Infertility Prevention Clinic for Young Career Women was launched by a major IVF facility in 2002. Its purpose is to provide information and advice in the form of a program for these young women to ensure they are able to have children at the "appropriate" stage of their careers. Contraception is now marketed differently to young women, with an emphasis on fertility enhancement rather than disease or pregnancy prevention. In Australia condoms are advertised with the slogan "they can help you get pregnant too." That is, they are not merely contraceptives, but they prevent infertility caused by sexually transmitted diseases such as chlamydia. Fertility is something that must be preserved in order to be used later.

Motherhood has been repackaged as a profitable and attractive choice for the career woman in her mid-thirties. Various government policies and private programs in a range of Western countries demonstrate the ways this is sold to young women. Paid maternity leave and baby bonuses that favor the professional and already privileged are often a feature of these new programs. The classed nature of these opportunities is evident in that, for example, paid leave can only be operationalized in workplaces that are regulated by industrial law or where one has enough power to negotiate. In Australia a baby bonus has been instituted to compensate only the highest-earning women for lost income during maternity leave.

In terms of popular culture, certain kinds of motherhood are represented as desirable: in particular, the sexy and glamorous mom. For example, in the popular press, Uma Thurman declared motherhood to be "the sexiest thing I've done!" The promotion of particular kinds of wealthy and attractive celebrity mothers is evident throughout women's magazines and television shows. These are women who have established their careers, made an enormous amount of money, and have capped it off with a child or children produced in their late twenties to early forties. Increasingly, it is celebrity adoptive mothers who are featured in the media. Adoption is evidence of a deep desire for the maternal experience, and the promotion of this phenomenon suggests how important it has become to map an eternal feminine instinct for mothering onto the professional, glamorous, successful woman. Importantly, these women have not foregone their sexiness and sassiness in having children, but rather this experience at this stage of their lives underscores these qualities.

Delayed motherhood is pitched as a cool and sexy endeavor, something that can be done without forfeiting beauty, fun, or work. New maternity wear represents pregnancy as fashionable and an opportunity to show off a temporarily rounded belly in an otherwise toned body. Celebrities show how extra pregnancy pounds can be lost quickly and the preferred body shape easily restored. Children are important accessories to the successful can-do life, so long as they are planned to come along at the right time. Can-do girls are thus encouraged to delay motherhood until their careers are established; then they can treat it as both an essentially feminine moment of fulfillment and a consumer lifestyle experience that enhances an image of success.

Young Women "At-Risk"

Alongside the production of these can-do girls who excel in star careers, glamorous consumer lifestyles, and delayed motherhood is the construction of another kind of young female identity. While can-dos are optimistic, self-inventing, and success-oriented, other young women's behavior has become a focus for a more general moral concern about juvenile delinquency, nihilism, and antisocial attitudes. Not only are these girls unlikely to be middle class, but they are also generally of particular ethnic minorities. These young women are often seen as those either most at-risk or those most likely to be risk takers. It is through the designation of "at-risk" that another kind of female subjectivity is produced, that is, the girl as failure. At-risk youth are those who are seen to be rendered vulnerable by their circumstances—living in poverty, in unstable homes, in communities known for violence, drugs, and crime, and so on. If these conditions are identified early, young people can be tagged and closely observed in an attempt to keep them on track. However, these situations tend to become the only lens through which these youth are seen, and this then invites surveillance and intervention. As youth studies scholars Peter Dwyer and Johanna Wyn explain, the at-risk category is a problematic one, for although it is usually intended as a framework for helping young people in difficult circumstances, it tends to dramatize and individualize their problems.[33] While it seems to provide an early-warning system to alert authorities to young people's potential difficulties, it also quickly problematizes the complex experiences of youth and sets them up as failures in the making.

The problems of the at-risk are often seen as endemic to the communities they come from, and individual families and cultural groupings are held to blame for the lack of success of their youth. Incompetent parenting is often erroneously associated with unsafe neighborhoods, which are in turn linked to crime, poverty, and an ethnic demographic. This is what the urban family research team headed by Frank Furstenburg describes as "the myth of bad neighborhoods/bad parents."[34] Structural disadvantage is recast as poor personal choices, laziness, and incompetent family practices.

At-risk and risk-taking youth are then frequently seen as inheriting bad attitudes, which trickle down through their communities. Through this categorization they are constructed as likely failures. Young women who are deemed to be at-risk are cut off from the imagined majority of successful girls, and their problems tend to become the ways in which they are universally defined. As Dwyer and Wyn suggest, "They become defined as a potential underclass and are then treated as an underclass."[35] This construction of an underclass of the at-risk occurs through a range of social processes and social institutions, but it tends to start at school and fans out into broader concerns regarding the school-to-work transition. The at-risk category operates in a particular way in relation to young women, for they are imagined as both the passive victims of circumstances beyond their control, and also as willful risk takers who use girlpower to their own (self-) destructive ends.

Risking the Future: (Girl)power Failure

The production of some young women as failed subjects is achieved by an uncritical analysis of their circumstantial disadvantage as well as an attribution of personal incompetence or willfulness. The at-risk framework does little to tackle their material environment; instead it focuses on improving competencies and attitude. State, community, and school authorities therefore implement early intervention through support and special programs. What is deemed to be of particular concern is that these young women are on a track that leads to early school leaving and poor employment prospects. This is depicted as partly a consequence of their particular home situations and partly the result of their limited ability to plan properly for the future. As Peter Kelly notes, "Youth, as it is constructed in at-risk discourses, is at-risk of jeopardising, through present behaviours and dispositions, desired futures. The discourse of youth at-risk mobilises a form of probabilistic thinking, about certain preferred or ideal adult futures. . . ."[36] That is, the concept of at-risk contains an implicit ideal of a good future. Failing to understand or subscribe to this ideal means failing at the future entirely. By contrast with the can-do girls, those at-risk are deemed to suffer from what Schneider and Stevenson call "misaligned ambitions." In other words they do not know either what job they would like to do or how much education would be required to be qualified for their job of choice. They cannot construct plans for meeting their career goals because they lack knowledge about the relevant educational pathways. They do not readily see "life events as sequentially organized," and they cannot engage in "strategic effort."[37] These failings are attributed to a combination of family, community, and personal limitations.

The example offered in *The Ambitious Generation* of a young woman with misaligned ambitions is "Rosa," a Mexican-American girl living in a poor and dangerous Southern California neighborhood with her unwell single mother. She had harbored a desire to become a medical doctor since she was a child, but she lacked specific knowledge about what this work entailed or how to achieve her goal. Her mother preferred the idea that she become a secretary. Her academic performance was uneven, owing to absences and a self-declared lack of interest in study at the critical period of her junior year in high school. She was regularly taken out of school to help her mother in a cleaning job. She was not involved in any extracurricular activities that were skill-enhancing. By her senior year she had replaced a science class with art and was hoping simply to complete her high school diploma. She stated, "Well, if I have the chance, I hope that I graduate."[38] She was unsure about college admission requirements or the training procedure for acquiring a medical degree. Unlike "Elizabeth," the can-do girl with aligned ambitions, "Rosa" had little family support and lacked a network and resources to help her engage in a strategic effort to realize her professional wishes. The likelihood of her becoming a doctor seems low indeed.

Although "Rosa" is not specifically described as at-risk, her situation demonstrates well how this attribution can be made so that a lack of success is constructed as an individual, family, and community failing. In her case risk factors become associated with personal family circumstances, lack of will, and an inability to educate herself or strategize with a long-term plan in mind. Success is deemed to elude her because she cannot effectively apply herself and because she is insufficiently supported by her family. However, what is not taken into account, as Frank Furstenburg and his colleagues found in their study of the success or failure of urban youth, is that "many parents simply [don't] have adequate knowledge of the middle-class world to guide their children in how to succeed, and they rarely [have] the resources to subcontract with those who [do] have that knowledge."[39] For Schneider and Stevenson, however, the key difference between "Rosa" and "Elizabeth" is not the chasm between them in terms of their material and cultural resources, but their degree of effort and their families' commitment to their success. The state of at-risk is depicted as a set of personal limitations that can be overcome through sufficient effort. However, it also acts as a warning to all young women that failure is an ever-lurking possibility that must be staved off through sustained application. Seemingly small decisions, such as doing art instead of science for a year, are imagined to have massive ramifications for future prospects. "Rosa" is supposed to illustrate the way in which small bad decisions can become major life mistakes, as her potential profile seems closer to "drop-out" than "pre-med college student." Failure is thereby produced as individual choice.

For youth in general, but young women in particular, academic success has become the key to safeguarding the future. It is not only considered essential to securing an appropriate adult professional and consumer lifestyle, but it is also touted as the most effective weapon against disaffection, criminality, and disenfranchisement. Doing well at school is vital for good citizenship. For example, in a report entitled "Female Offenders: An Emerging Crisis," the U.S. Office of Juvenile Justice and Delinquency Prevention declares that "the most significant risk factor relating to early onset of delinquency is poor academic performance."[40] Academic success is even promoted as a cure for the "disease" of delinquency, which itself is perceived as a rising problem among at-risk girls.

Delinquency and Disordered Patterns of Consumption

While can-do girls are lauded for their role as active consumers in the girlpower market, young women in the at-risk category have different and much more troubled relationships to consumption. As youth researcher Dorothy Bottrell notes, for some girls everyday participation in popular culture or common recreational pursuits is redefined as offending.[41] The distinction between leisure and crime is frequently determined by where the activity takes place and who is partaking. Critical psychologist and youth scholar Chris Griffin suggests that while consumption has become more important to the constitution of contemporary young femininity, only some young women are deemed to get this right. She argues that many are instead identified as having "disordered" patterns of consumption, broadly defined. She writes:

> Our concept of consumption needs to include more than material goods and services and the various symbolic meanings associated with particular consumption patterns. . . . Young people's use of substances such as illegal drugs, alcohol, tobacco and food extend[s] the notion of consumption into the domains of health, medicine and therapy. It is important to consider how various groups of young women . . . are represented in specific contexts as consumers, and especially as disordered consumers, and the ways in which such representations and the associated regimes of management and treatment are gendered, sexualized, racialized and class-specific.[42]

Griffin's extended definition of consumption thus includes a market of drugs, sex, and leisure activities in which many young women are participating. These kinds of consumption are deemed to represent new and problematic patterns for some girls. There are new concerns that some young women are becoming more "laddish" in their behavior; for example, they smoke and drink more, they use illegal drugs, they are more violent, they exhibit more masculine qualities on the streets like carrying weapons, fighting, and forming gangs, and they take sexual risks.[43] Increased debate, more research funding, and new styles of punishment and rehabilitation are evident in relation to girls' involvement in crime (especially gangs and violent crime), sexual behavior (particularly teen pregnancy and sexually transmitted diseases), dropping out of school, and drug taking.[44]

Periodically, the media report on extraordinary acts of violence committed by young women, such as torturing and even murdering other youth, as though this is the beginning of a new crime wave. Panic over increased alcohol and recreational drug use, especially Ecstasy, has led to claims of the emergence of a generation of self-styled bad girls. Prominent feminist Germaine Greer suggests that "the career of the individual bad girl is likely to be a brief succession of episodes of chaotic drinking, casual sex, venereal infection and unwanted pregnancy, with consequences she will have to struggle with all her life."[45] Such young women are frequently represented and treated as risk takers who are increasingly disinhibited in their actions and must be monitored not simply for self-destructive behavior, but for potential harm to others.

Young women are thus taught that while girlpower is about being confident and assertive, it should not be taken too far. The fears for girls as the new risk takers are often discussed around this idea that they have misunderstood girlpower. The Australian *Herald Sun* newspaper declares under the headline "Girl Danger: Attacks Rise on Modern Power Teens" that "experts say the youngsters are putting themselves at-risk in the mistaken belief 'girlpower' will protect them."[46] Girlpower is intended to provide young women with the tools for mainstream success, and those who stray from this path are constituted as delinquent risk takers. Young women who are involved in gangs, commit crimes, or act violently are often depicted as the byproducts of girlpower out of control. In the words of the U.K. newspaper *The Independent*, "The dark side of girl power means that young women are increasingly turning to violence."[47] Interestingly, however, privileged young women who act assertively in public, hang out with their girlfriends, and take self-defense classes are lauded for their spirit and confidence. For example, an Australian newspaper article entitled "Girls with Attitude and a Right Hook" celebrates "North Shore schoolgirls"—that is, from one of the wealthiest areas in Sydney—who are learning tae kwon do and boxing.[48] In the same month the New Zealand/Aotearoa paper *The Dominion* includes a report entitled "Young Girl Thugs Bash for the Thrill of It," naming "vicious teenagers of Niuean descent"—an underprivileged Pacific Islander migrant population—as representative of dangerous young women increasingly involved in girl gangs that commit mindless violence.[49]

The notion that there exists a new cohort of bad girls indulging in disordered consumption is another strategy by which some young women are produced as failures. Unlike the can-do girls, who know how to successfully engage in the market, these other young women make poor consumption choices and enact the gains of feminism in problematic ways. Their consumer failures, as demonstrated through drug use, gang membership, criminal activity, and early sexual relationships, are depicted as a consequence of bad choices. It is this idea of willfulness and agency that makes an attribution of self-selected failure straightforward. Young women are imagined as having a range of good choices before them, and therefore those who choose poorly have no one to blame but themselves. The structural conditions that in fact limit their choices are generally only taken into account to demonstrate how families and communities model inappropriate lifestyles to their youth. Their so-called failure seems not only inevitable, but freely chosen and therefore warranting little sympathy.

"Disordered" patterns of consumption have led to new kinds of policy and procedural responses, particularly in relation to the management of female juvenile detention, the imposition of court orders, and increased state-sanctioned public and private intervention into girls' sexuality.[50] The new "regimes of youth regulation,"[51] including political, legal, and procedural strategies, have brought about circumstances of increased surveillance of young women, much of which is constructed as protection, either *of* them, or, as is more likely, of society *from* them. The objective is to "get tough" on those who choose bad behavior, and the outcome is the production of a subject whose failure is perceived as a matter of personal will.

Teen Mothers

Griffin notes that young women's consumption of sex takes on distinct meanings in relation to at-risk girls. The panic over teen motherhood is a prime example of the regulatory focus on a disordered pattern of consumption and the personalizing of failure. Motherhood in the teen years, especially if the woman is single or partnered but unmarried, is marked as inherently fraught, the cause of lifelong social problems and the end of opportunity. Even if planned (and sometimes especially if it is planned), it is always read as a mistake. It is often described as "children having children,"[52] with the implication that young women, by nature of their years, are insufficiently mature to handle the responsibility of children. It is the most prominent example of the dire consequences that will befall them if young women fail to plan properly and indulge in disordered leisure. In spite of considerable evidence to the contrary, young motherhood is repeatedly represented as an epidemic and a crisis.[53] It is frequently and simplistically correlated with certain class and race characteristics in ways such that Blackness and poverty, for example, are seen to somehow cause young women to be willful, wanton, and stupid.

The symbolic value of teen motherhood as wasteful, destructive, and a drain on social resources has been well mined. Social commentator Mike Males suggests that in the United States, "The teenage mother became a relentless destroyer of her own and future generations. . . . The peak of absurdity came with former Surgeon General Jocelyn Elders' claim that 90 per cent of all violent criminals were born to unwed teenage mothers."[54] The British Home Secretary of the same era, Michael Howard, made similar claims about these mothers breeding criminals.[55] Sometimes young mothers are depicted as criminal themselves, in that substance use, status offenses, and deviance are added on to their profile.[56] They are often also accused of plotting pregnancies to obtain extra social security payments or subsidized housing, or to selfishly create a more positive identity for themselves with no regard for the child's welfare.[57]

McRobbie describes teenage mothers in the United Kingdom as the "bad girls of the New Labour sociality."[58] This could be equally extrapolated to all Western societies that hold to these New Labour principles, namely, where social and educational policies are driven by the needs of the market. The new economy is dependent on young women taking up new positions in the workforce and delaying childbearing, and the teenage mother defies this position and persists in drawing attention to the dwindling welfare state. Vilification and punishment of teenage motherhood serve in the recruitment of young women to good-girl behavior, and justify the reduction of social security on the basis that opportunists must be denied their handouts, and the so-called cycles of poverty and dependence must be ended. Given that young mothers are distinguished by their socioeconomic disadvantage,[59] it stands to reason that, as McRobbie argues,

> having a child in these circumstances horrifies government because of the future costs it must bear in supporting the mother into reasonably well paid work, helping her also with childcare, and then providing sufficient state support for the child or children to make them job-ready in years to come.[60]

This has certainly been the case in the United States, where the rollback of support to poor mothers was a feature of the Clinton administration's attack on welfare.

Accordingly, governments are putting in place a variety of regulatory measures to reduce teenage pregnancy. The most dramatic and draconian of these are to be found in the United States. "Behavior modification" is tied into welfare provision, such that the receipt of government assistance for child support can be made conditional on mothers being implanted with the contraceptive Norplant or being sterilized.[61] In many states young mothers who are charged with offenses can be contracepted as a probationary or parole condition.[62] As local government researcher Stephanie Reich reports, pregnancy prevention measures include initiatives like the Baltimore City campaign to distribute Norplant to low-income students through school clinics.[63] Those with drug problems are especially targeted by these interventionist regimes. Lobby groups such as CRACC (Children

Requiring a Caring Community) step in to support these measures in vigilante ways, by paying drug-addicted women to be sterilized. The language used today to manage young mothers is less about protecting them from men, and more about reining in their sexual desires and misguided tendencies. Put starkly, the regulation of teen mothers operates so that young women at risk of being failures will stop breeding and start earning. This construction of the teen mother generates its own economy; that is, alongside products marketed to the "girlpowered" are profit-making services catering to disordered patterns of consumption. In this instance, what is being commodified are the actual bodies of young women, which are subject to pharmaceutical and surgical interventions, costly therapies, incarceration in detention centers and prisons, residential treatments, and educational programs.[64]

The Production of Success and Failure

Success and failure are constructed as though they were dependent on strategic effort and good personal choices. These qualities then seem instrumental in categorizing young women as either can-do or at-risk. However, these designations have much more to do with economic and cultural resources than personal competencies. It is because of these resources that can-do girls are rarely able to fail, while other young women have few opportunities to succeed. While there are plenty of can-do girls who are inexplicably feeling that they can't do, they are relentlessly managed back onto a success track. Expectations of some young women are now so high that a great deal of attention is being devoted to fixing those potential can-dos who do not live up to the fantasy of girls reveling in unconstrained opportunity. An unprecedented number of programs and campaigns is in place to tackle this curious problem of young women who suffer psychological conditions that prevent them from being their best. These obstacles tend to be constructed as individual and intrapsychic, and they are treated through therapeutic methods. One key problem that has been identified is girls' lack of self-esteem. Other mental health issues, including eating disorders, self-harming, depression, anxiety, and increased suicide attempts, have also been highlighted.[65] Thus it is not that can-do girls are imagined as problem-free, but rather that their problems must be quickly dealt with to ensure their success.

The issue of achievement-oriented girls derailing from their fast track to success was perhaps first identified by human development theorists and educators Carol Gilligan, Nona P. Lyons, and Trudy J. Hanmer in their 1990 book, *Making Connections*, about a privileged girls' school in the United States, but it was brought to public attention by the guidance manual–type book *Reviving Ophelia*, by the U.S. therapist Mary Pipher.[66] Both of these books posit the idea that young women "lose their voices" when they reach adolescence; that is, as they are enculturated into adult femininity, they sometimes lose ways to express themselves freely and to be independent and strong. What must be done, according to Pipher's subtitle, is to "save the selves of adolescent girls." This in turn has become somewhat of an industry. Parents, teachers, doctors, counselors, and young women themselves are enlisted in the surveillance of girls who may be at risk of crises of identity and self-esteem, or who exhibit suicidal or depressive behaviors. Jennifer Baumgardner and Amy Richards document how this mission "spawned books and movies for and about girls in crisis, which in turn spawned magazines and games and more money allocated to girls' programming,"[67] that is, yet another niche in the girl market.

It is not the case then that the sufferings of many young women are disregarded or left untreated. However, in this attention to the personal problems of can-do girls, a broader and more systemic analysis of young women's circumstances is lost. The primary focus of this concern about girls' self-esteem is white, middle-class young women who are supposed to succeed, or who are perceived to have everything and yet cannot overcome psychological obstacles to their own guaranteed success.[68] The problem is defined as their personal, psychological barriers to feeling confident and optimistic, being able to achieve, and developing internal resilience, strength, and self-belief. Accordingly, strategies for overcoming these problems are generally therapeutic and individualizing in approach, and they take the young woman as the unit of analysis and the project that must be worked on and regulated back into success. As Baumgardner and Richards argue in relation to the plethora of books for and about girls in crisis,

> They are still chock-full of workbook things you can do to improve yourself—
> in much the same way that the maligned teen magazines are—and they all start
> from the supposition that girls need fixing. The literature of the girls' move-
> ment might not be saying "you're not thin enough or pretty enough" but it is
> saying "you're not strong enough or confident enough."[69]

What is constructed here is the never-good-enough girl who must perpetually observe and remake herself.

The purpose of this work on the self is to get or keep can-dos on track for academic and employment success. As Walkerdine, Lucey, and Melody suggest, emotional or psychological troubles are a problem insofar as they interfere with maintaining high levels of achievement. They say, "A middle class girl . . . who has any kind of problem with academic success is typically presented with a number of costly therapies to allay the problem and produce or sustain the required success."[70] Chris Griffin cites the examples of specialty schools and residential programs for "troubled teens" in the United States as more institutionalized forms of intervention and regulation that claim to bring these youth back onto the path of success.[71] Similarly, McRobbie perceives the new political concern with and response to young women's mental health problems, particularly eating disorders, as a technique of governmentality. She argues that these issues have become of national importance in the United Kingdom and require top-level intervention because so much is at stake in the success of young women, including lowering the cost of social welfare and maintaining a skilled and acquiescent workforce for the new economy.[72]

Thus the potential for failure is central to the regulation of can-dos insofar as problems must be quickly dispensed with so that failure itself can be displaced and cast out onto other young women. The construction of these others as at-risk or as risk takers leads to close attention from the state and its agencies, or, increasingly, private services in employment, education, training, incarceration, and health care that have taken over state functions and seek to profit by them. Unlike middle-class young women, whose resources allow them to find private solutions to crises and whose circumstances do not permit them to fail, at-risk young women are more likely to be treated as a problem for the police, government, or law courts to deal with. They are pathologized or criminalized when they do not succeed, and they are at the mercy of stigmatizing institutional interventions. This is in stark contrast to those therapized middle-class young women whose families are more likely to be paying for professional services to help with problems primarily identified as related to self-esteem. If they are subject to more rigorous and punitive programs, these tend to be private and client-servicing. As Griffin notes in the case of schools for problem youth in the United States, these "are predominantly residential, fee-paying and frequently recruit their clientele via approaches to affluent parents through advertising."[73]

The U.S. Office of Juvenile Justice and Delinquency Prevention acknowledges that African-American, Asian, and Latina girls who are poor and addicted are more likely to be incarcerated than referred for treatment, while white girls are more likely to be referred to mental health facilities than juvenile justice agencies.[74] And Mike Males elaborates:

> A visit to a state youth prison . . . reveals a sea of black, Hispanic and Asian adolescents. A trip to the ward of an upscale adolescent psychiatric hospital reveals a sea of white inmates running insurance-paid tabs of $1000 per day or more.[75]

Further, disadvantaged young women's failures are less likely to be attributed to low self-esteem; rather, they are constructed as individual bad choices consciously taken up through unruliness and defiance.[76] These other young women are not imagined as suffering a temporary loss of self-esteem but are instead depicted as inherently bad, or as being in such dire circumstances that their cause is more or less lost. What is shared, however, in the approach to both of these groups is the necessity of surveillance and management, and the understanding that whatever problems they may suffer are personal in cause and solution. The result of these interventions is to construct a normative trajectory of young women's success. Privileged girls who derail can then be assisted to get back on track, and the others can be split off, stigmatized, blamed, and punished for failure.

The newly emergent discourses of can-do and at-risk demonstrate a cultural fascination with girlhood and with the market value of young women. They succeed in papering over the enduring and perhaps deepening inequalities generated by class and race stratification in current times. These discourses are deployed such that young women's success at being a can-do rather than an at-risk is made out as largely a question of personal effort. In a world of DIY youth projects of the self, can-do and at-risk are almost never articulated as classed and raced positions. They are also infrequently understood as serving material purposes. The examples of "Elizabeth" and "Rosa" demonstrate how success in education, employment, consumption, and in life generally seems to depend on good strategies for working on oneself as a project. What is not highlighted, but is fundamentally important here, is that the material resources and cultural capital of the already privileged are required to set a young woman on the can-do trajectory. Instead, good or bad families, neighborhoods, and attitudes are held to account. The construction of the at-risk category serves to house a diversity of marginalized youth whose problems are rarely named as structural. It suggests that failure is both a matter of personal choice and at the same time the unintended consequence of an unfortunate individual biography. Either way, solutions are not the province of social and economic policy.

Conclusion

This chapter has demonstrated how and why young women have emerged as the central subjects of discourses about how to prevail in current times. Girls have come in for particular kinds of attention within both a story of power and a narrative of youth risk. These constructs show how success and self-invention have become linked together in the project of surviving in a risk society. Through these discourses young women are disciplined into creating their own successful life trajectories and into taking personal responsibility if they fail. Dwyer and Wyn discuss the ways in which a dominant discourse about success is sustained by the fiction that there exists a large majority of successful youth and only a small minority of at-risk young people.[77] This is reflected in youth policy that is geared toward the imagined successful mainstream, and the at-risk minority is then treated as an aberration, of concern chiefly because it constitutes a threat to society. This minority can then be marked as different from the norm and pathologized, criminalized, and punished. As we see from the discussion here, however, there are many young women who are not succeeding, both those who are structurally disadvantaged by poverty and racism, as well as those who are far more privileged and yet cannot cope with the enormous pressure on them to achieve. Both groups are monitored closely, with the latter more likely to be therapized and managed back toward the path of success, while the former are blamed and split off as a small minority destined to fail in any case. In this way the dominant narrative of the can-do girls is sustained, and success can be attributed to confidence, flexibility, good choices, and work on the self. In the next chapter I turn to the ways that this is played out in the context of employment in the new economy.

CHAPTER 2

JOBS FOR THE GIRLS?
Education and Employment in the New Economy

Success and self-invention have become key projects for young women in the current world of work. New industries, new kinds of training, new modes of work, and the need for new kinds of workers have had an enormous impact on young women's participation in education and the labor market. Young women are a vital labor force within the restructured and globalized market. They are the latest models of overachieving professionals, as well as making up the ranks of those part-time, flexible workers required by emerging and changing industries. In unregulated factories or homes, where the manufacturing industry has largely shifted, it is young women who produce the majority of the world's consumer goods for multinational corporations. And in shopping malls around the world, it is young women who constitute a vital consumer market for these products. There is little doubt that young women matter to globalized capital as both a labor force and a market. Stratified forms of their labor are required in the new economy. At the same time feminism has been seen to produce ambitious and flexible subjects who can adapt quickly and willingly to changing labor conditions.

It is thus in the reconceptualization of work that the discourse of the can-do girl operates so powerfully, because young women are imagined as the ideal flexible subject of the new economy. Walkerdine, Lucey, and Melody speak of this as the "remaking of girls and women as the modern neoliberal subject; a subject of self-invention and transformation who is capable of surviving within the new social, economic and political system."[1] The requirement to make "choice biographies" shapes most young people's relationships to education and employment, but as I will argue, it is young women in particular who are meant to prevail in these circumstances, making successes of themselves through the right choices. At the same time class and race structures continue to shape their opportunities for livelihood. Ideas of individual responsibility or the inherent risk factors within a girl's personal biography are mobilized to obscure these structures. These ideas, based as they are on personalizing responsibility for success, also conceal the investments of global capitalism in the maintenance of systemic inequality.

Young People, Work, and Flexibility

As we have seen, globalization, information technology, and a shift to a casual, flexible labor force have fundamentally changed employment practices and opportunities. These conditions have had particular effects on young people right across the socioeconomic scale. Most basically, deindustrialization and deregulation have brought massive, global youth unemployment and underemployment. The full-time youth job market has effectively collapsed throughout the Western world. Many argue that young people are those most vulnerable to contemporary labor market vicissitudes.[2] The once-sure route from school to a guaranteed job has become much less certain. Youth who leave school without qualifications find that any kind of work, let alone a full-time position, is extremely difficult to secure. Consequently, participation in education has increased dramatically, and a range of certifications and qualifications has been introduced to keep nonacademic young people in education rather than unemployed. This skills training has become essential to young people's job prospects right across the industries, without actually guaranteeing success. As Furlong and Cartmel note, "Changing labour market structures have not simply provided positive incentives for young people to improve their qualifications; the sharp decline in opportunities for minimum-aged school-leavers in many areas has produced an army of reluctant conscripts to post-compulsory education."[3] Many countries have added other incentives to stay in school or join a training program by cutting unemployment benefits and other welfare measures for those under eighteen.

Tertiary education has also expanded along with other kinds of postsecondary training. In many instances credentialing and training have become eternal transit zones for youth who once would have commenced permanent full-time work directly out of school. Middle-class youth, who may have always gone on to tertiary education or professional training of some sort, are encountering circumstances where no amount of credentialing seems enough. All young people are finding that this emphasis on credentials and lifelong learning of transferable and flexible skills does not actually translate into security of employment. In their book *Youth in Society: The Construction and Deconstruction of Youth in East and West Europe*, youth researchers Claire Wallace and Sijka Kovatcheva say that "the outcome of education and training is uncertain, unemployment is a risk and the proliferation of routes and opportunities through education and training has resulted in a very complex and rather open-ended situation for young people."[4] This is a finding consistent throughout the United States, the United Kingdom, Australia, Canada, and elsewhere.[5]

A critical ideological shift has accompanied these massive changes to youth education and employment. This ideology seeks to construct a new subject for these circumstances. Traditional ways of being a worker, being young, or being a student are no longer relevant. Deindustrialization, globalization, and widespread labor force insecurity require new ways of speaking, thinking, and acting for youth. Most importantly, the current market demands young people who are not only highly skilled, but are also flexible. This notion of *flexibility* carries a range of meanings: that the person can easily change work locations unencumbered by family or other commitments; is untroubled by flux such as downsizing, irregular hours, or retraining; will negotiate individual rates of pay and conditions without union or award interventions; and will perform a variety of tasks not limited to a traditional job description and duties list. Clearly, those most able to succeed in this climate are young people who can turn tremendous insecurity into freedom and autonomy. These are youth who are qualified, skilled, and well-supported enough to secure highly paid work (or create their own businesses) in new, risky industries, survive company collapses, and reinvent themselves as markets and industries shift.

Unsurprisingly, they are also likely to be middle-class youth, who can rely on their families for a home, financial support, career modeling, professional contacts and advice, and even investments in their businesses. They can also draw on their status as well as their social circles for cultural capital, self-esteem, and support. For those youth without these kinds of resources, flexibility is more difficult to operationalize. As the European Group for Integrated Social Research points out,

> In terms of the heterogeneity of the phenomenon of young adults according to social origin, educational level and employment situation, we . . . might distinguish between young people following "choice biographies" . . . and those who are marginalised through education and labour market processes and have . . . [no] prospect of achieving . . . an autonomous life-project.[6]

In spite of this, the discourse cuts across class and is equally applied to and required of all youth. Public policy and its ideological underpinnings are perhaps less attentive to class than they ever were, and youth are currently very much understood as a monolithic, generational category, sharing the same flexible relation to the dynamic labor market, and presumably the same self-generated opportunities for success.

How young people are encouraged to imagine their futures under these circumstances is telling. Flexibility, choice, freedom, and opportunity are all emphasized in the new versions of becoming an adult worker. Openmindedness and adaptability are assets under these conditions, for the new flexible worker may have to change industries and jobs, retrain or acquire new skills, and even move cities several times in a single career. Consequently, young people are advised to account for change in their future plans. The new rhetoric of choice and the DIY self is closely aligned with this requirement of changeability. It refigures the state of insecurity and risk in which they live as simply an opportunity to make good choices. It allows young people to articulate themselves as being whatever they want to be, as self-made, picking through a range of options, and personalizing their decisions. In this way success or failure can be explained by personal attributes and choices rather than structural conditions. Walkerdine, Lucey, and Melody suggest that "if we think about the end of jobs for life and the production of a culture of uncertainty, self-invention through a discourse of limitless choice provides a way to manage . . . potentially unruly and disaffected subjects."[7] Certainly, this discourse has proved to be a very powerful one; it has been central in creating and limiting the ways young people can talk about their circumstances and opportunities. This is demonstrated particularly in the case of how young women's labor market opportunities in the new economy are represented.

Young Women in the New Economy

It is overwhelmingly young women who are perceived as the real beneficiaries of the new economy, and it is young women who are constructed as those most capable of seizing its opportunities. In reality, however, young women experience both the best and worst of these conditions: they are to be found on the fringes of the formal economy, in part-time, casual, insecure, and unprotected labor; they are also found among the highest levels of the new professions, enjoying the very flexibility that limits many others of their generation. Labor sociologists Belinda Probert and Fiona Macdonald demonstrate how young women have felt the impact of full-time job losses caused by the changing labor market much more than young men.[8] However, from another perspective education and employment opportunities have grown enormously for young women. With few remaining formal barriers in their way, they are free to pursue a wide variety of education, training, and work possibilities. The success of young women in out-performing young men in school and attaining high positions in the work-place has often been noted as evidence that they are the real winners in a changed economic world.

Young women have been seen as quick to adapt to the new training re-quirements, and some of them have left some boys behind in educational achievements and employment rates. This in turn has provoked an intense debate about boys' underachievement, a crisis in masculinity, and femi-nism "gone too far."[9] Considerable anxiety, as well as celebration, has been generated about this new cohort of high-performing young women. These issues aside, it is a fact that young women's educational standards and par-ticipation in the labor market have been increasing rapidly. Claire Wallace and Sijka Kovatcheva note that across Western, Central, and Eastern Eu-rope the trend for young women's participation rates in secondary and higher education is to match and even overtake young men's. This finding is supported in research throughout the Western world.[10]

Youth researchers Ali Rattansi and Ann Phoenix suggest that the possi-bilities of the changed labor market create greater self-confidence and in-dependence in young women.[11] Young women are often represented as simply more capable of adjusting to change than are young men. For ex-ample, noted youth studies scholar Lynne Chisholm argues that

> there is a good deal of evidence from cultural contexts as diverse as Finland, Italy and the Netherlands to suggest that not only are the majority of reflexivity losers male, but the majority of those equipped to cope positively with the challenges of risk society and cultural postmodernity are . . . young women—if by no means all, then at least some of them.[12]

This has been supported by a wide range of researchers in the field.[13] Dwyer and Wyn have found that young women are better able to incorpo-rate change and redirection into their life plans.[14] They are seen as more psychologically robust and able to both adapt and "grow up" more quickly. Life-course theorist Helga Krüger has found that within new transitional processes, "girls tend to be much more resilient than boys in coming to terms with the structures of opportunity and disillusionment."[15] Young women tend to leave home earlier and are less likely to return once they have made this break. They are sometimes perceived to be more ambitious than young men. Other research has found that they are also more opti-mistic about their futures generally and about their employment prospects in particular.[16]

Unlike previous generations of women, young women today expect a life of paid work in the form of a career that is personally fulfilling.[17] Dei-dre Wicks and Gita Mishra, directors of the Women's Health Australia

(WHA) project, a large-scale Australian research project involving 14,804 young women, found that 75 percent of those surveyed aspired to more educational qualifications (with only 7 percent stating they definitely would not want this), and 91 percent aspired to paid work (with the majority desiring full-time work); 92 percent wanted children by the time they were thirty-five with 60 percent desiring full-time paid work at the same time, and only 4 percent desiring no paid work outside the home at the same time. Feminist theorist Chilla Bulbeck has reflected some of these results in her important comparative research looking at how young Australian women in 1970 and today imagine(d) their future lives. She has found that today the majority of young women imagine entering higher education and then having a lifetime of paid work. They are fairly optimistic about combining work and motherhood. However, in 1970 the majority of young women did not mention having a job or progressing to higher education when discussing their aspirations.[18] Similarly, in *The Ambitious Generation* Schneider and Stevenson point to the vast differences in employment and educational ambitions between young American women of the 1950s and those of the 1990s. Specifically, the expectation that fulfilling work ought to be balanced with raising a family seems one of the most significant, almost universal findings in the contemporary literature on young women's hopes and plans for the future.

What kind of employment do young women aspire to? Schneider and Stevenson note that today young people in general have extremely high occupational ambitions. Sociologists E. Dianne Looker and Pamela Magee have found in large-scale Canadian research with a diversity of respondents that young women have somewhat higher expectations than young men, stating more frequently that they realistically expect to enter fairly high-status positions. The vast majority expect to go into professional, semiprofessional, or managerial jobs; 21 percent anticipate a service or sales job; very few expect to end up in unskilled or low-status jobs. The Australian WHA study reflects these findings, establishing that 65.8 percent of young women desire professional, paraprofessional, or managerial work, and a further 17.8 percent aspire to a sales job.[19] Interestingly, while the Canadian research inquired about what they "realistically expect," the Australian study asked what work the respondents would like. The similarity in response rates suggests that young women expect to get what they hope for. Education scholar Linda Hughes-Bond's qualitative research with working-class, rural, Canadian young women rounds out this picture. She says, "They want jobs which they enjoy, and which offer them the opportunity for creativity, skill development, financial autonomy and stability, and an expanding degree of responsibility and power."[20]

Education researcher Tehmina Basit's study of working-class, British-Asian, Muslim young women offers some insights into the specific nature of a preferred career. She says the participants in her research "aspired to a wide range of lucrative careers with high status. Some mentioned the jobs of doctors, lawyers, accountants and pharmacists. . . . A few girls wanted to start their own businesses, and one girl wished to be a pilot."[21] Class, ethnicity, and rurality do not cut across these aspirations in straightforward ways. As Walkerdine, Lucey, and Melody note, while more privileged young women may have access to knowledge about the requirements of professional work, and expectations of higher rewards, structural disadvantage does not mean one "could not hope for a secure and interesting job."[22] So, while family migration experiences might strengthen aspirational resolve,[23] or geographical isolation might make prospects more traditional,[24] it seems that a diverse group of young women in a range of locations imagine themselves to have better work options than previous generations, and they take employment seriously as part of their identity work.

Young women's desire and capacity to pursue education and find employment in the higher echelons of the labor market in unprecedented numbers today is not an historical accident. It is a consequence of hard-won feminist gains, but this phenomenon also dovetails with the feminization of certain kinds of work and the disappearance of others, a dramatic restructuring of the labor market, and the requirement of a different kind of worker for this market. Deindustrialization has brought about the collapse of traditional male work in the manufacturing industry, while also creating new opportunities for professional men to shift into the finance and technology sectors. Consequently, young women are now able (and needed) to fill spaces in the professions as well as to take up new positions in more typically female service and communications work. Labor sociologist Jennifer Johnson argues that

> These changes have produced two classes of women workers: low-paid service providers . . . who do the cooking, cleaning, and caring-for-others work that has always fallen to working-class women, and well-paid professional women who have joined men in high-income professional and managerial jobs.[25]

However, young women are universally encouraged to aim for the latter, and as we shall see, when their aspirations come up against labor market realities, the full effects of the discourses of choice, risk, and responsibility can be felt.

Young women are frequently described as more confident, assertive, self-assured, and keener to seize all of life's opportunities than either their male peers or their foremothers. There is a sense in which feminism is seen to have done its job in empowering this generation to succeed and in creating positive, ambitious, can-do girls. McRobbie argues that the neoliberal discourse of individual responsibility and self-invention deliberately taps into feminist language. She says, "The aim is to modernise and rejuvenate the political right by articulating ideas of success, wealth and individualism with those of female empowerment and even 'women's rights.'"[26] This use of feminism within a new agenda is certainly borne out in the generalized representations of a monolithic generation of overachieving, ambitious, confident, and psychologically resilient young women ready to embark on careers in the brave new world of work.

The flexible, self-made worker is the kind of subject young women are imagined and encouraged to be. Flush with the gains of feminism, embarking on new education and career paths, young women are perfect candidates for a subjectivity built around self-invention, dynamism, and capacity for change. The promotion of professional and work life over family commitments also picks up on new possibilities for young women's life choices. However, the difficult reality of merging a flexible, professional work life with a (deferred) role as parent results in ambivalence and contradiction, as we shall come to see. The requirements of the new economy thus also rely on a rhetoric that evokes, although thoroughly liberalizes, feminist principles. Feminism encourages young women's freedoms and opportunities, including making individual choices and pursuing nonstereotypical life trajectories. Education and employment within the new economy also seem to be offering a range of choices and giving young women the chance to break out of traditional roles. However, the aspirations that are encouraged simply cannot be met in a labor market that demands that most young women be less than they would like. Again, it is at this point—where the idea that "girls can do anything" meets the reality of not enough of the good jobs to go around—that stories of responsibility and risk are so well utilized.

As Walkerdine, Lucey, and Melody point out, in the U.K. context at least, class remains the most reliable indicator when it comes to establishing exactly which young women are successful and which are not. However, material advantage intersects with race and culture in different ways according to context. Those overachieving schoolgirls and new professionals who are represented simply as the "next generation of young women" are predominantly middle class and of the cultural majority. Their less-privileged counterparts are subject to the same discourses about flexibility, choice, and opportunity, and the same circumstances of uncertainty and flux, but they reap few of the economic rewards. In other words, the can-dos are constructed as a mainstream cohort, but in fact they constitute a class elite. Next, I want to consider where differently classed and raced young women are actually to be found in the new economy and to understand the impact of enormous socioeconomic changes on their circumstances and aspirations.

Which Young Women?

It is not difficult to see how young women are constructed as those most ready and able to flourish in new economic times. However, a slightly different picture emerges when we look at how they are actually located in this new configuration of training and employment. As we have already seen, young women are pursuing education and entering the workplace in unprecedented numbers. But what does this really mean, and where exactly are they going? One way to understand what is happening for young women is to see them in terms of three broad groupings: first, young women from economically secure, professional, and successful families; second, those from the lower-middle to working classes; and third, those in lower-working-class or "underclass" circumstances.

The purpose of this three-part framework is to disturb some of the assumptions of the neat categories of can-do and at-risk. First, it shows that young women are not simply divided between a successful mainstream and a minority of failures or that any such divisions might be constructed simply according to effort and good choices. Further, it demonstrates that monolithic categories of race and culture are not useful ways for understanding young women's opportunities. Material circumstances have much to do with employment outcomes. Second, it demonstrates the constructed nature of these categories by drawing attention to a large number of young women who are not clearly in either camp.[27] Their attempts to live up to the can-do publicity reveal most clearly its limited capacity to accurately reflect the lives of all young women. Third, by closely examining the most disadvantaged group, those typically perceived as at-risk, it becomes apparent that the real risk factors in their lives are generated by socioeconomic inequalities rather than individual behaviors or inappropriate community lifestyles.

All of these young women are subject to the same work problematic: they must obtain qualifications in order to secure employment. All of them are also subject to the same popular and persuasive narratives about being part of a monolithic new generation of confident and able young women well poised to make the most of the opportunities before them. This narrative dovetails with older ideologies about personal effort as the key to success. For example, Signithia Fordham argues that young whites and African Americans are equally taught "the American dream," that is, of meritocracy.[28] The impact of material resources, cultural capital, and racism is erased in this image of opportunity for those who work hard. However, the ways in which youth are able to negotiate these conditions and articulate these discourses meaningfully differ enormously, and these differences are largely generated by class and race inequality. In seeing how they accomplish these negotiations, we can also understand how stratified groupings of young women have come to matter very much to the smooth running of new economies, how enduring structures of inequality ultimately determine who can-do and how ideas about responsibility and risk obscure both of these realities.

The Privileged

The picture painted earlier of the high-achieving schoolgirl who goes on to a well-paid, successful, professional career is indeed a reality. There has been a significant transformation in the levels of success young women can expect to achieve and an expansion and upgrading of the kinds of work they can pursue. Young women are entering traditionally male professions such as law and medicine, earning high salaries, and enjoying their disposable income with a consumer lifestyle that would have been unimagined a generation ago. However, this kind of biography is only available to a tiny minority of young women: specifically, those from economically prosperous families with the range of resources and capital to make this trajectory possible, meaningful, and successful for their daughters. Walkerdine, Lucey, and Melody state that "girls from professional, managerial and wealthy families are now performing well at school, and in fact are going on in large numbers to do well at university and enter the professions. In that sense something has changed."[29] What has not changed is the reality that these kinds of young women would always have been successful in some way. Today, however, the measures of young women's success are tertiary qualifications, professional careers, and high salaries. Youth researcher Debra Roker's U.K. study indicates how success for middle-class girls in private education is carefully planned out by themselves, their parents, and their schools from a young age.[30] Career planning commences by the age of thirteen, and a girl's subject preferences are channeled into the highest possible educational and professional goals. Unsurprisingly, Roker found that the rate of university acceptances and desired career achievement was very high for this cohort. These young women were effectively able to bypass the constraints of the local youth labor market situation by plugging directly into an elite network of national and even global education and employment opportunities. Elite schools are chosen for privileged young women precisely because they offer these kinds of advantages. For example, educational ethnographer Amira Proweller found in her research at a private girls' school in the United States that parents selected the school because of future work opportunities generated by such networks.[31] Parents spoke about the value of their daughters mixing with peers who would become "very, very important people."

It is not surprising, then, that with these elaborate support structures in place, as youth researcher Jaana Lahteenmaa argues in the Finnish context, "High-achieving schoolgirls are responding admirably to the demands made upon young people to acquire the qualifications and skills that are required by highly advanced economies."[32] This kind of young woman is likely to receive excellent qualifications and pursue a professional career in a traditionally male sector (law, medicine, management), or find a well-paid place for herself in new industries (information technology, corporate finance), or even become a self-employed entrepreneur with her own start-up or small business. Roker found that the privileged young women she researched tended to believe that these kinds of opportunities were open to anybody, as reflected in the view that "the level that an individual reached in the occupational hierarchy was dependent primarily on such factors as individual ability and effort."[33] Education theorists Jane Kenway and Lyn Yates both cite similar findings among students at elite schools in their Australian studies.[34] These opinions are also prevalent in the U.S. context, where more established discourses about self-making and the American dream blend easily into newer ones about flexibility, good choices, and success in a risk society.[35]

This emphasis on making one's own opportunities, and the idea that success is due to personal effort rather than structural circumstances, is consistent with the requirement of flexible individualism that accompanies the new economic order. Sociologist Ivar Frønes states that "young educated girls and students from a middle class background are most representative of those who want a professional career with an emphasis on freedom, challenge, self-realization, and travel—that is, what could be termed modern post-industrial values."[36] The promise of flexible hours, locations, and conditions; enterprise bargaining; travel; multispecialization; and retraining can only be added advantages to these kinds of working lives. The Australian *Age* newspaper reports on this new kind of career for young women, illustrating the case of "Cynthia," a twenty-four-year-old lawyer who has just been "wigged and robed." She speaks three languages, finished her degree overseas, and spent a year traveling before beginning her articles. She is excited by the opportunities for travel, combining a range of expertise and interests, and the professional support that are available to her as a result of this career choice. She says,

> There's the double degree phenomenon—so many young people have combined law and commerce or law and science degrees—and the fact that so many want to do the London thing as well, to travel. [Also] it's traditionally a place for mentoring; that's part of the culture of the law.[37]

Part of the attraction of this career is flexibility, opportunities for in-service training, travel, and a support structure for the cultivation of her professional future.

These new possibilities constitute an exciting and radically different future than could have been imagined by young women even thirty years ago. What is troubling, though, is that these daughters of wealthy families have become the postergirls for their generation, implicated in the fiction that all young women can be self-inventing, high-flying, and ideally placed to seize power in the new economy. Deindustrialization, along with feminism, has opened up new employment possibilities for some young women, but only these few are structurally positioned to take advantage of them. Further, the advantages of the new features of professional employment quickly become disadvantages in the context of semi- or unskilled work. What must also be acknowledged is that the heady heights of success that are often portrayed as young women's entitlements remain elusive, with a very slow rate of change at the top levels of all the professions and high-status jobs in terms of gender balance and a female-friendly culture.

What is also little discussed are the costs to young women for whom this trajectory is not merely an option, but, increasingly, a requirement. Walkerdine, Lucey, and Melody write of the enormous anxieties experienced by the privileged young women in their study, who were always conscious of not doing enough or being enough. Physical and emotional manifestations of these anxieties among their participants included hair pulling and eating disorders. They say that

> despite evidence of their success, the feeling of not being good enough was endemic among the young middle-class women. This anxiety typically surfaced as an individual pathology, an indication that the young women had internalized this failure as a personal one that could only be overcome by working harder and harder.[38]

The case of "Elizabeth," the *Ambitious Generation* example of a privileged young American woman who is able to sustain a strategic effort to realize her ambitions, throws some light on how working harder and harder can operate. To overcome the perceived problem that college was easier than she had expected, she busies herself with achieving not just high marks, but perfect ones. She says, "The difference between an A and an A minus is often enough to keep me well-occupied."[39]

The sense that one can never rest and can never be good enough is also found in German research on young women attending the privileged *Gymnasiastinnen*—schools for the university bound. In Germany, where the school system is rigidly streamed, the pressures on youth in the schools that award the *Abitur*, the diploma that is a ticket to a professional future, is considerable. German culture theorist Mareike Herrmann's research on young women in *Gymnasiastinnen* is revealing of these pressures. She says,

> What matters in school is achievement and good performance, and these girls felt they were under intense pressure there to prove themselves. When I asked about their fears for the future, Mareike (thirteen) quickly stated, "I am afraid of doing something wrong," and her sister Annika said she was afraid of "obstructing her future" through bad choices in school; Gesa expanded on this theme, sharing that she was afraid of "life as a test." These fears indicate that the girls are not allowed much room for experimentation or for making mistakes.[40]

Schools and families work together to regulate these young women's lives so that errors are minimized, and spontaneity may also be sacrificed. Even their daily schedules, which are supposed to provide a good mix of educational, cultural, and physical activities, can seem somewhat regimented. Education theorist Julie McLeod writes of the "busyness" of such a life, suggesting that these kinds of regimes "give some insight into the pressures involved in becoming a successful middle-class young woman—accomplished in many fields, with a fully-rounded personality."[41]

The high expectations of the family and the maintenance of its class position is also felt by privileged young women in their striving for success. At a time when the class system seems to be in great flux and privilege must be secured anew, doing well becomes a family project of the greatest importance. Johanna Wyn argues that "educational success is also a form of 'straitjacket,' often a product of anxiety about individual performance and carrying the weight of concern by middle-class families about securing middle-class futures for their daughters."[42] To some extent then, these daughters are utilized as defenses against fears of a downward slide during times of change. The anxieties that are the result of the loss of guaranteed privilege are focused on hopes for their children.

The emotional and financial investments made by families can be considerable. Private tutors, schooling coaches, and other kinds of supplementary teaching, increasingly used by privileged families to "cut the risk of receiving less than a B in an advanced-level course"[43] are all expensive. This is quite apart from the normal expenses of private school tuition, college applications, and university costs. Family support in the form of help with homework, visits to the school, construction of study schedules, and the provision of private tutoring can all be felt as enormous pressure. The high-achieving schools themselves are also deeply invested in such young women doing well, and their obligations to the pastoral care of their students, particularly in mental health service, can be overlooked as a result. Psychological problems such as anxiety, stress, and depression interrupt academic success, and in some instances they are made out to be a personal problem of no concern to the school, one that ought be managed by the young woman privately.[44]

The other significant issue for young women who are expected and even obliged to seize these new opportunities for high-flying careers is motherhood. As McRobbie suggests somewhat provocatively,

> If ruthless female individualism prevails, then it might also come up against its own limits. This, I would hazard a guess, will occur at that point, when in their thirties these new young women either decide to have children, or as is increasingly common, decide not to have them.[45]

There is some considerable evidence that this is already occurring among the prototype of the can-dos: the ambitious, Generation-X women who are now reaching their thirties and discovering that they cannot have it all because of diminished fertility.[46]

We have already seen how can-do girls are encouraged through popular culture and public policy to delay motherhood. This message has been taken seriously by many young women. Some of them remain optimistic about being able to combine work and children at this later stage, but at the same time they use deferral as a device to avoid thinking through the complexities of this scenario. Others simply cannot imagine how children could fit into their lives at all. The Australian WHA research found that just over 9 percent of those aspiring to professional, paraprofessional, or managerial jobs did not want children by the age of thirty-five. A further 66 percent wanted only one or two.[47] Specifically, it is the realities of the time and energy commitment required by the new world of work that often makes motherhood difficult to think about. For example, a twenty-one-year-old, white, middle-class participant in the *Growing Up Girl* study says,

> I don't know actually (when I'll have children). It would be nice to have them soon because I don't want to be too old when I have them, but looking into the future, I can't see that they'd happen within the next five or six years at least, because simply with the demands of the job, I mean. Because the next two years after I qualify I'll be working, like, 150 hours every week kind of thing. You can't have kids then.[48]

If anticipated childlessness is still a minority experience, the notion of career first, family later is common to young women who aspire to successful professional lives. This is not only because these careers require a commitment that excludes other priorities, but because professional status must be secured before taking any time out, and money must be saved to pay for child care and housekeeping when they reenter the workforce. These young women are responding to well-grounded fears of a ruthless labor market that will shut them out as soon as their attention is divided, as well as industrial and family policies that remain inadequate for women's needs. The media scare stories of executive women conducting international teleconferences while giving birth send a strong message to the can-dos that career and motherhood are compatible, so long as the career is made paramount. The real possibilities for active engagement in the pleasures and responsibilities of raising children while maintaining a satisfying work identity seem remote indeed.

Lower-Middle and Working Classes

As we have already seen, it is not just this privileged minority who make up the huge numbers of young women in senior secondary and tertiary education. While it is this group earning the most prestigious degrees and finding the best work, an enormous number of lower-middle-class and working-class young women are also entering further education. After all, in the current climate, they have little choice. Whereas once they may have completed secondary school and found secure work fairly easily, today they cannot be competitive without credentials. As Dwyer and Wyn note, in Australia at least, it was work traditionally done by young women that was the first to disappear in the new economy.[49] Training and education have now become necessary steps to employment. However, this group is far less able than their more advantaged counterparts to convert these qualifications into successful, high-paying careers. This is partly due to the types of educational courses that are available to them, the kinds of other social and economic resources they lack, and the sorts of jobs that are actually obtainable with these credentials.[50]

Wallace and Kovatcheva have found that while young women spend longer in education, they are concentrated in specific, feminized sectors, leading in turn to lower-paid, feminized jobs. This pattern was found in all the European countries they investigated. They say that

> whilst women were some of the main beneficiaries of educational reforms, particularly in former communist countries, they do not necessarily benefit from this in the labor market. This tendency has been reinforced with the move towards market economies in post-communist countries.[51]

The fact that young women are now so strongly represented in education does not translate into employment success, particularly in the case of those from ethnic minority backgrounds.[52] U.S. Labor Department data indicate that for every matched year of education, men earn far more than women, and Black women with some college education earn only slightly more than white, male high-school drop-outs.[53]

Seen in this light, the acclaimed education participation rate for young women is not the triumphant step forward it may initially appear to be; it is merely a basic strategy for survival. Even university degrees are no guarantee of labor market success. Dwyer and Wyn cite a Canadian study that has found that three years after graduating from university, only 33 percent of young women were in full-time permanent careers.[54] This knowledge is anxiety-producing for young women who are already disadvantaged by a lack of economic and cultural capital. Sonja, a working-class, rural, young Canadian woman in Hughes-Bond's study says,

> I'm hoping for stability in my job, whatever it is. Just know my job's there and it will be for a while. They say our generation's going to change jobs three times, three major careers. . . . I don't want to do that.[55]

It is this large group of lower-middle-class and working-class young women who have been "hit hard by credential inflation"[56] and who have had to keep training and then scramble for positions in the sales, service, and communications industries, albeit often reluctantly. As Furlong and Cartmel note, "The tendency for young women to remain in full-time education . . . is partly explained by the demands of service sector employers for educated female workers."[57] In other words, it is labor market demands, rather than career preference, that is keeping these young women in certain kinds of training and dictating their subsequent employment choices. Invited into the same narrative about professional success and girls' freedom to be anything, they often find their desires do not match up with the reality of the limited job market. As the WHA project researchers point out, "The possibility of these aspirations being realised assumes an employment market where the desired sorts of jobs, in the desired number, will be available to these young women. At present, the indications for jobs growth are not optimistic."[58] Wicks and Mishra researched three age cohorts of Australian women and found that it was "instructive to compare the aspirations of the young cohort with the occupational realities of our mid-life cohort. For instance, while 23.8% of our mid-life cohort are working as clerks, only 3.5% of the young cohort want to be clerks."[59] In spite of this, a good number of the young cohort will probably at some stage work in clerical positions, simply because their preferred work is not available.

Once class is taken into account, the picture becomes even more stark. In the WHA study, a clear majority of young women from high-income households aspire to professional, paraprofessional, or managerial work (82 percent), and as we have seen, they can feel reasonably confident of achieving this aim. However, 67 percent of the young women from low-income households also held this aspiration, but they must attempt to fulfill this desire in the same competitive market without any of the matching resources or support. Similarly, Basit found that all of the working-class, British-Asian, Muslim young women in her study aspired to occupations "which were unambiguously middle class," in defiance of their current class location. She says, "They appeared to be totally incognisant of the discrimination they were likely to face in the labour market" in terms of racism, sexism, and classism. A one-year follow-up found all but one in education. She says, "The qualifications that they pursued ranged from GCSE [General Certificate of Secondary Education] retakes to A-levels and vocational courses."[60] These young women were following the recommended pathways through education toward professional success, but the likelihood of them realizing their middle-class occupational aspirations must be interpreted against the backdrop of the segregated labor market. As Dwyer and Wyn argue, "What [such youth] are not told and what they [do] not therefore take into account in ambitioning professional careers [is] that the realities of the labour market [do] not fit the imagery surrounding them."[61] In other words, the myth of the open and expanding knowledge society does not match the fact that massive job creation has been overwhelmingly in the service industries.

Various agencies once served a cooling-out function in light of this inevitable mismatch between ambition and opportunity. The term *cooling out* was generated by B. R. Clark in the context of U.S. schools encouraging some people to choose less ambitious paths in ways that made these choices appear to be their own. Education theorist Alison Jones shows how this process has functioned in reshaping class-based ambitions for young women. Citing examples of careers talks in the New Zealand/Aotearoa girls' school she studied, she demonstrates how working-class Pacific Islander students are encouraged to think carefully about their futures, but in ways that direct them to low aspirations. She asks,

> Could it be in New Zealand too, that in order to minimise the possible anxiety and disappointment caused by the gap between the ideology of "chances" and the reality of lack of chances, the school must reduce the "failing" girls' expectations of success to a "realistic" level?[62]

Today, while young women are still very much encouraged to see themselves as making their own choices, cooling out has been to some extent replaced with an even more rampant discourse of opportunity. That is, the expansion of tertiary education and the language of feminism implies that now more than ever all young women today can get what they want, as long as they proceed with further training. Nonachievement is thus personalized to a greater extent than before. These young women are faced with taking responsibility for their choices and failures, lowering their expectations, and attempting to secure work where they can find it. This is most likely to be in the new service and communications industries, where employment tends to be casual, part-time, temporary, or contract-based; pay and conditions are unregulated; and most staff are overqualified for their positions. From this perspective, flexibility does not carry the advantages it might within the professions or other kinds of well-paying careers.

Equally, ideas about choice and flexibility in terms of career plans take on different meanings for this cohort. Hughes-Bond finds that the young working-class women in her study emphasize the importance of flexibility in mapping out their occupational futures. She says,

> Lack of certainty seems to be viewed as a positive. Sandra defines plans that are "very foggy" as allowing for "doors (that) are opening everywhere"; Tina interprets a lack of goals as an opportunity "to pick and choose." Sharon sees fixed career plans as detrimental to future success.[63]

In these ways, these young women have picked up on the language of the choice biography and have rightly identified the disappearance of the job for life. However, whereas privileged young women are encouraged and able to interpret choice as meaning the power to carefully create one's own life plans for success, working-class girls are offered the discourse without the resources.

Lower-Working- and Underclasses

The third group of young women constitutes those from lower-working-class or "underclass" circumstances who are on the fringes of the education system and the labor market. Unlike both the privileged young women being educated for professional careers and the middle group participating in training courses, certificates, diplomas, and degrees merely to compete in the new industries, this last group is un- or seriously underqualified and struggles to achieve a livelihood. Walkerdine, Lucey, and Melody suggest that the most serious concern in deindustrialized economies is precisely these "working class girls with few or no qualifications. It is these uncredentialed young people who are most likely to enter and remain in the most vulnerable, insecure and poorly paid sectors of the labour market."[64] Similarly, Chisholm draws on French research to argue that "whilst poorly qualified young people from working class backgrounds are at greater risk of vulnerable transitions, the risk is particularly marked for young women with these attributes."[65] These young women often leave school before graduating or do not manage a sustained progression through school, which makes further education inaccessible. They sometimes participate in obligatory government training programs that do not often translate into ongoing employment, or they are in and out of the welfare system in other ways. They are obliged to take work where it can be found, but they are seriously disadvantaged by a labor market that requires qualifications for almost any work and by the dismantling or deregulation of traditional industries where they may have once found jobs.

Young women who leave school early are identified as being those most at-risk of failing in the labor market. Employment outcomes for female non-graduates are extremely limited.[66] Johanna Wyn notes from her Australian research that part of the motivation to leave school comes from a mismatch between these young women's own priorities and interests and their perceptions of secondary education and training programs as too focused on specific skills. However, young women's reasons for dropping out of school, which is often perceived as one of the first steps down a path to failure are infrequently taken into account in developing policy solutions. As school researchers Robert Stevenson and Jeanne Ellsworth have found, dropping out is rarely seen as a problem with schools or society. Rather, it is instead attributed to "personal deficiencies and/or family or cultural deprivation."[67] This attribution is made possible by an at-risk analysis that focuses on the individual's poor choices and the responsibility of a family and community that are perceived as inherently inadequate. However, as Wyn suggests, dropping out of school reveals much more about the limitations of schools and curricula in the new knowledge societies. She says,

> The narrow vocationalism of the new education agenda, with its emphasis on (ungendered) skills and competencies appears to be especially irrelevant to the perspectives of many young women. They valued education and training, but they also valued other aspects of their lives: independence from their families, establishing and maintaining a home for themselves, and making a contribution by using their skills in the workplace.[68]

The problem, of course, is that these young women find themselves unable to fulfill these other aspects of their lives without participating in the education and training they find so narrow in focus, by which stage it is often too late or too difficult to reconstruct that other biography.

Young women who have not found work or a place in further education after finishing high school, whether they leave before graduating or not, are increasingly subject to compulsory youth training schemes. These are intended to provide skills and credentials to young people vulnerable to labor market marginalization, as well as to introduce a mutual obligation framework to youth social welfare. The role of training schemes has been a controversial issue in managing the livelihood opportunities for these young women. For many commentators, compulsory training schemes fail to provide young people with real opportunities and are more useful for the subsidized businesses that run the programs or employ the youth (often only temporarily) afterwards.[69] Claire Wallace has found that in both the United Kingdom and Germany they also tend to reproduce a gendered division of labor by funneling youth into gender-stereotypical schemes, and they produce different outcomes accordingly, with young women more likely to end up with diminished aspirations and in stagnant jobs.[70] Youth scholars Gill Jones and Claire Wallace cite U.K. research that shows how misleading this training can be, giving the example of "girls who undertook schemes in design [who] were highly motivated because they wrongly imagined that the scheme would lead to a glamorous career."[71] Ethnic youth issues researcher Esther Gregory found in Australian research with young unemployed women from refugee and non-English-speaking backgrounds that almost none had received career counseling and, consequently, the young women held "unrealistic expectations that completion of vocational or occupational courses or training would ensure their employment prospects."[72]

An often traumatic process of adjustment is required once young women understand the grim realities of their labor market prospects and the role of training in focusing their aspirations on these. Youth researcher Inge Bates's U.K. study of sixteen- to eighteen-year-old young women who ended up in training as caregivers for the elderly because they did not get into preferred courses or find other work illustrates this process. What is particularly interesting is the enduring narrative of choice and self-invention, even for these trainees who had aspired to far different occupations but who found themselves being trained in low-skilled, stressful, dirty, and exhausting work. Bates suggests that "reflexive individualism [can] facilitate . . . a re-invention of ambitions in line with labour market prospects." In other words, concepts such as being able to do anything or making the right choices for oneself structure the ways all young women are able to talk about their career trajectories, even those whose options are extremely limited by circumstances entirely beyond their control. Bates found repeated instances of "re-writing of personal biographies in terms of choice, for example, through the 'discovery' of vocation," which enabled these trainees to feel they had agency in their circumstances, as well as feeling well suited to the only kind of work they could get.[73]

Of course, it is possible for some young women who leave school without qualifications to bypass training schemes and find work. However, this work tends to be insecure, low in pay, and unstimulating. Walkerdine, Lucey, and Melody found that of the uncredentialed nongraduates in their research,

> The overwhelming majority of working class young women in paid employment were employed at the lower grades within their organisation. . . . [H]alf of this number could not expect to achieve a promotion, an increase in pay or an improvement in job security if they remained in their current post.[74]

These young women generally work in unskilled positions in the service sector.[75] In Canada, 84 percent of fifteen- to nineteen-year-old female workers occupy service, clerical, or sales jobs.[76] Furlong and Cartmel note that in the United Kingdom in 1991, nearly 76 percent of young women aged eighteen and nineteen working in the service sector were in lower-tier services, such as fast-food chains.[77] The expansion of the service sector and the contraction of manufacturing has had particular implications for young unskilled women from non–English-speaking backgrounds in Anglo countries. The requirement of English-language proficiency in this sector without a concomitant provision of programs to these women has left them seriously disadvantaged in the new labor market.[78]

These positions are characterized by poor working conditions and little job security. They are generally casual, short-term, or temporary jobs, often without basic protections, and do not provide a living wage. Unionization, leave provisions, occupational health and safety regulations, minimum wage enforcement, legally binding contracts, and avenues for promotion are all virtually nonexistent. Given their inability to compete equally in the labor market, young working-class women are often afraid of losing their jobs and are thus vulnerable to exploitation. Much research has documented the nature of the exploitation that takes place in this sector, which includes sexual harassment and bullying, unfair dismissal, nonprovision of breaks or enforcement of irregular shift lengths to allow employers to avoid paying for breaks during shifts, underpayment and illegal pay docking, unpaid probation or training periods, and union banning.[79] The competition for this kind of work is depressingly fierce. Uncredentialed nongraduates school-leavers must compete for these jobs not only with other youth in their circumstances, but with young people who are undergoing further education and seeking work at the same time. In Australia, it is this latter group who actually hold 70 percent of available jobs.[80] Also in the competition are older unskilled or semiskilled workers who may be returning to the workforce after retrenchment or child rearing and are willing to take work for which they are overqualified.

The restructured economy and the rollback of youth welfare provisions put enormous pressure on nongraduates to take work where they can find it. Deregulation and globalization have also created splintering and stratification within local economies, so that those who are not competitive or employable in the formal economy are squeezed downward into informal, under-the-counter, and criminal economies. It is increasingly common for young working-class women to work across these sectors in order to build up a living wage. One expanding industry that cuts across these economies is the manufacturing of clothing, footwear, and textiles. It is overwhelmingly young disadvantaged women who work in this sector, cutting and sewing garments for the subcontractors of multinational corporations. As garment industry researcher Steve Nutter explains in the case of sweatshops in Los Angeles, "The typical garment worker is a young, non-English speaking immigrant woman with no prior sewing skills."[81] Sometimes these women are direct employees of the subcontractors, working in small factories or sweatshops, and sometimes they form a hidden workforce, whereby their mothers are the official employees, but other members of the family perform the labor alongside her in an outsourced context in their home.[82] Owing to the unpredictability of the volume of work and the tight schedules for completion, women are often assisted by their children, generally their daughters, to finish large batches of garments on time.

The women in garment work are thus, for the most part, refugees or migrants who are rendered vulnerable by punitive immigration policies, language barriers, lack of recognition of former skills and training, poverty, dislocation and trauma, and inadequate integration programs. Pay and conditions in this sector are dismal, but the work is often perceived as the only option available to those who are otherwise completely marginalized by the labor market. This scenario also emerges in other industries, such as agriculture. Multicultural literature theorist Barbara Kaoru Ige notes that in the United States, girls and young women constitute a significant proportion of seasonal or migrant farm workers who harvest, process, or pack crops for major American companies. Just as with garment making, the bulk of this farm work is performed by migrants, the vast majority of whom have legal citizenship status.[83] This work is physically exhausting and constitutes a major health risk owing to pesticide exposure. It is characterized by long hours, low pay, few or no protections, and no insurance. As with sweatshop work, its conditions are made possible by the new economy, and it is particularly exploitative of the young women who are most disadvantaged by economic restructuring: the poor, uncredentialed, and unsupported.

For these young women, alternatives to these kinds of jobs are few. Welfare provisions for those under eighteen have been eliminated throughout the Western world. Long-term unemployment is a reality for many disadvantaged youth who do not find a job quickly after leaving school, but unemployment benefits are increasingly difficult to secure, even for those older than eighteen. These young people face the prospect of never having a career as such, and they must attempt to get by through a combination of meager and intermittent government support, insecure work opportunities, and forays into the informal and criminal economies. These are youth surviving in the most precarious circumstances, having fallen through the gaps of school, training, and work; they become statistically absent as a consequence. Youth researcher Howard Williamson describes these youth as "status zer0," because they are outside mainstream transition routes, and they appear to "count for nothing and [are] going nowhere."[84]

Young women are particularly vulnerable to these circumstances.[85] Labor market analysts Alison McClelland, Helen MacDonald, and Fiona

Macdonald have found that in Australia, eighteen- to nineteen-year-old females are those least likely to be participating in education and training, and young women who are social security recipients are more likely to be receiving an additional benefit for homelessness.[86] At their most desperate or resourceful, young women who are status zer0 survive through the criminal economy and in many cases through prostitution.[87] This then brings them into the regulatory circuit of the state and the law, which tends to pathologize their experiences and attributes much to the risk factors apparently inherent in the communities from which such young women come. Structural disadvantage is thus reworked as at-risk, such that young women, their families, and communities can be held responsible for outcomes that are socioeconomic in nature.

The Stratification of Young Women within the New Economy

Understanding where and how a wide range of young women are participating in education and employment puts a slightly different spin on the image of this generation of girls as the new high flyers. While it is true that more young women are remaining in secondary education and participating in training or tertiary education, this is not leading to better jobs or more satisfying or secure modes of livelihood for most of them. In fact, *Growing Up Girl* suggests that the situation today is possibly worse than it was in the 1960s and 1970s, in spite of the expansion of higher education for girls. The arrival of some successful young women in the professions and their capacity to take advantage of new labor market conditions is a step forward. However, alongside them are many more who have found flexibility and choice biographies to actually translate into insecurity, uncertainty, and poor prospects owing to their circumstances of structural disadvantage. The fact of an increase of young women in the labor force does not reveal the detail: that this is largely the result of the expansion of part-time, low-skilled positions in the new service and communications sectors.

Overall, young women are still to be found in more gender-stereotypical industries, and in less-skilled jobs. They make up the vast majority of the part-time workforce and are clustered into a narrow band of occupations. They still earn less than their male counterparts. The majority of young women have been deeply affected by the collapse of the full-time youth job market, but some far more than others; for example, in Australia, nearly 50 percent of both Indigenous young women and young women from non–English-speaking backgrounds work part time, and not by choice.[88] This collapse and the accompanying scramble for credentials has also had profound implications for young women living in rural and remote communities, where youth unemployment, particularly young women's, is skyrocketing. Health sociologist Lynne Hillier and colleagues found that 80 percent of the young Australian rural women they surveyed intended to leave their towns in the hope of finding work or study opportunities in the city.[89]

In reality, then, it is only a small minority of young women who live up to the image of girls as the new occupational success story. The vast majority of young women struggle to find personally meaningful and financially sustaining work in the new economy. Probert and Macdonald cite Australian research that demonstrates the growing class-based polarization of women's employment patterns. In tracking labor force participation trends from 1976 to 1991, the research demonstrates that

> by 1991, the probability that a woman would be employed if she lived in the top 5 per cent of SES [socioeconomic status] neighbourhoods was 78 per cent more than if she lived in the lowest 5 per cent SES areas.[90]

What this more variegated picture also reveals is that the labor market stratification of young women is a critical element in the transition to deindustrialization. The success of middle-class young women in the professions is partly a consequence of these areas being vacated by men, who in turn have moved on to even more prestigious and better-paying employment. Walkerdine, Lucey, and Melody argue that "women are thus being allowed to enter the professions at precisely the time when these professions are being devalued and high-flying men are going elsewhere."[91] Researchers in postcommunist countries make a similar argument about the feminized professions in these places.[92]

The influx of lower-middle-class and working-class young women into the service and communications sectors also indicates the ways in which the new economy relies on young female labor. These new industries have feminized work in the wake of the contraction of manufacturing, and they require unskilled and semiskilled workers for their part-time, flexible positions. Key elements of the restructured manufacturing industry also depend on the labor of young women, having shifted from national plants to subcontracted piecework in homes and sweatshops. Migrant labor is particularly important in these sectors, as discussed earlier.[93] Under these conditions companies are able to pay their workers the very least and provide minimal protection. Thus, at all levels of social class, young women have a critical part to play in the smooth functioning of the new economy. While the discourse of girls' success suggests that now they all have the opportunity to take advantage and be the winners, in fact it is necessary for many young women to effectively fail. These failures are the ones who will fulfill the increasing need for low-skilled and poorly paid labor.

This discourse devolves responsibility for success and good choices onto young women themselves, in spite of their own structural positionings and the uncertain and limited labor market they are operating within. They must take personal responsibility for success or failure because the choices appear to be all before them; thus, they must work hard to stave off failure and assign personal blame when this is not accomplished. It is not surprising to find that with the introduction of individualized lifestyles to post-communist countries, young women show a significantly higher level of depression, uncertainty, and anxiety associated with these changes than do young men.[94] Other researchers have drawn links between "autonomous subjects willing to reinvent themselves and high rates of mental illness."[95] It is no wonder that money and employment are key stressors for young women.[96]

In the new economy, it is difficult to see how a diverse population of young women will be able to realize their professional ambitions, in spite of the press about their sky's-the-limit opportunities. It is also difficult to see how they will sustain narratives about blending occupational success and motherhood as it is currently presented to them through the can-do story. Work and motherhood debates and policies tend to focus on balance and choices, but to what extent can these be realized in such a stratified labor market? After all, this economy depends on some young women delaying motherhood for professional advancement and on others working the part-time, unskilled jobs that are frequently all that is available to those who have children earlier. Neither of these scenarios really presents a good balance of work and family, and both indicate the failure of social and industrial policy to accommodate young women's aspirations. Probert and Macdonald document the emergence in Australia of a "polarisation of work and parenting experiences around class and education lines."[97] That is, young women who are structurally disadvantaged tend to have children earlier and experience difficulties entering the labor market and pursuing education. On the other hand, young women who are structurally advantaged tend to want to delay motherhood in order to achieve professional success. Similarly, sociologist Roger Penn speaks of a bifurcation emerging in the United Kingdom between

> full-time career professionals who will either have one, or increasingly, no children and a majority of women located in part-time employment, often of a relatively mundane and unrewarding nature, who will continue to have two (and occasionally more than two) children.[98]

The choice between having children earlier and working part-time and pursuing a career path and having no children or only one at a later stage is perhaps the key choice that separates the can-dos from the others. It is also fundamentally a choice shaped by class, and in this sense, as Probert and Macdonald argue, it is not really a choice at all. The issue of work and family thus reveals the structural underpinnings of the can-do category. We have already seen how the vilification of young and especially teenage mother-hood serves the purpose, in part, of keeping can-do girls on the success track. Delayed motherhood is the only good choice for those who are seri-ous about pursuing a career. However, we can begin to observe here how the economic requirements for young women to be operating at different levels in the new labor market also generate a logic about who has children when. The stratification of young women within this market is increasingly occur-ring along the lines of those with children versus the childless.

Conclusion

This chapter has shown how young women are positioned in the new economy in terms of education and employment opportunities. It has demonstrated that there are enormous expectations placed upon them to personify the ideal flexible worker of the future and to seize all the oppor-tunities offered by contemporary labor markets. However, only a small mi-nority of young women are structurally located in ways that make this kind of success possible. The socioeconomic and ideological shifts that characterize risk society have had deeply divisive effects on young women. This stratification has enormous benefits for the new economy, as it has enabled differently advantaged young women to take up positions that must be filled at opposite ends of the labor market. At the same time, the accompanying narratives about choice, self-invention, and opportunities for girls ensure that stratification and disadvantage become reconfigured as merely individual limitations of effort or vision, to be addressed through personal strategies alone. In the next chapter I will examine how the expectation that all young women can be can-dos is also borne out in constructions of a new youth citizen.

CHAPTER 3

CITIZENSHIP AND
THE SELF-MADE GIRL

The construction of girls as those most able to adapt, along with a sidelining of those who fail to do so, is also borne out in new constructions of youth citizenship. As I will demonstrate here, citizenship for youth is constituted around responsibilities rather than rights, managed forms of participation, and consumption. Young women are presented as well positioned to take up these three dimensions of the new youth citizenship. They are depicted as better able to secure their social rights without relying on the state, they are often utilized as symbols of the nation, and they are the new consumers *par excellence*. Beneath these constructions of young women as defense against threats of globalization and migration, or as winners in the new socioeconomic order, are the more complex realities of young women's struggles with securing social, civil, and political rights. In many ways current times have seen some young women better able to take a place in the public world and participate fully in their communities. Their greater access to education and certain sectors of the labor market are seen as partly responsible for this. At the same time many young women are even more alienated from civic life than before. However, the lived realities of these contradictions are not attended to in broad narratives about girls' success in citizenship and leadership. In this chapter I will explore these key images of young women and also consider how they are sustained by the construction of other kinds of young women as bad citizens.

Changing Meanings of Citizenship

Citizenship itself is a contested notion, but it has been most commonly understood through the theoretical formulation of the noted theorist of citizenship T. H. Marshall, who described it as a cluster of three types of rights. Marshall identified these as social rights (primarily economic security), civil rights (individual entitlements to free thought, choice of faith), and political rights (to vote and stand for elections). Citizenship thus refers to an individual's place in the community, and the relationship he or she has with the state. The state protects the rights of its citizens and in doing so enables them to participate equally and actively in the community. Traditionally, the only reciprocal obligation required by community members to be entitled to citizenship was to relinquish personal self-rule. That is, citizenship rights are bestowed in exchange for individuals abiding by a system of government. More recently this concept has been extended, and citizenship is increasingly constructed in terms of broader obligations of individuals to the state, rather than the state's obligation to provide them with rights to which they are naturally entitled. For some commentators this gets at the heart of the contested notion of citizenship as being primarily about either rights or responsibilities.[1] This contestation has become part of public debate, and Marshall's original emphasis on rights has been recently overtaken by a new discourse of active citizenship, which focuses on duty, responsibility, and individual effort. The issue of rights now tends to be addressed in terms of how these might best be balanced, or drawn into mutual reciprocity, with responsibilities. This dilemma has been reactivated and takes on new meanings in the new economy.

New economic trends have had particular effects on social policy, effects that reflect and shape the nature of citizenship. Marshall's original conception of citizenship was closely associated with a functioning and expanding welfare state, which would ensure that individuals' social rights were met. As a consequence his expectation was that class inequalities would lessen, and all citizens would be better able to participate in civic life. However, deindustrialization, privatization, and rationalization have seen the contraction of the welfare state, and in many instances state provision of social services such as health, housing, and education have been replaced by private, profit-making enterprises that have bought these contracts from governments. In other instances these services have not even been replaced by private companies but simply no longer exist. The process of downsizing and privatization of social services has provoked a concomitant shift in the language of social rights. In a competitive, individualized, marketized world individuals are not supposed to rely on the state for their economic welfare but are obliged above all to participate in paid work as their primary duty of citizenship. When they cannot find or maintain paid work, which is increasingly the case within diminishing labor markets, stringent regulations apply to those seeking benefits. Compulsory training schemes, work-for-the-dole programs, community placements, and other such arrangements that draw on notions of mutual obligation have been introduced. Economic security is no longer an inherent right that individuals can expect the state to protect, but a personal concern that should be handled without external intervention. Further, one's entitlement to citizenship is implicitly dependent on the capacity to secure a livelihood.

Social rights are thus reconstructed as personal responsibilities, which only if successfully discharged entitle the individual to full citizenship status in other respects. A significant shift in the meaning of citizenship has taken place in terms of the expectations placed on individuals themselves to activate their responsibilities rather than merely have their rights protected. This has occurred both in the West and in postcommunist countries making the shift to marketization. In their contribution to *Youth, Citizenship and Social Change in a European Context*, Ulrike Nagel and Claire Wallace suggest that in both scenarios this is because social planning on the part of the state, whether it be welfarist or authoritarian, has been replaced by reliance on the market. They argue that

> the model of participation and identification in market societies is not one of social citizenship, but rather one of "active citizenship" or self help—that is a model whereby the participation of people in society is based upon self-reliance and individual planning.[2]

As they point out, however, markets are inherently unstable, and consequently, individuals face far greater risk and uncertainty in these circumstances than before.

The other key dimension of citizenship that has been transformed is its connection with a fixed notion of community. Ideas of social heritage, participation, and civil society, which are integral to definitions of citizenship, are dependent on some kind of community that is known and shared. Within a risk society, however, communal ties and traditional bonds have become looser and less predictable. Youth researchers Tom Hall, Amanda Coffey, and Howard Williamson argue that

> citizenship is centre stage today because the conditions for the sorts of commonality and belongingness to which it once referred have shifted. Recent economic, social and cultural changes make shared social membership—a status and identity common to all—problematic, no longer something to be taken for granted.[3]

It is not just deindustrialization and marketization, but also globalization, migration, ethnic and civil conflict, and new concerns with human security that have seen a reconfiguring of the meaning of citizenship. In this context the devolution of economic and personal security onto the individual is a way of activating a new conception of the citizen as self-actualizing and responsible in a world that appears unpredictable. Youth scholar Alan France makes an interesting argument about the shift from rights to responsibility in the context of risk and the perceived loss of commonality. He argues that the notion of the active citizen, who would take responsibility for his or her own welfare as well as the family and broader community, has become a way to deal with fears associated with diminished social cohesion in a changing world. This is particularly effective for right-wing policy and rhetoric; as he says of the U.K. experience, "Citizenship was seen as a concept which could help to 'bind' society together yet sit comfortably within the government's ideas of economic individualism."[4] Anxieties about "unbindingness," economic rationalism, and marketization have all been significant socioeconomic forces in the construction of contemporary citizenship around individual responsibility rather than entitlement to rights.

Youth Citizenship in the New Economy

Young people have been particularly affected by these shifting constructions and practices of citizenship. First, the association between secure employment and citizenship entitlements has had a significant impact on them. Youth rights theorist Hartley Dean argues that adult citizenship is no longer conferred by age, but by one's employment and dependency status.[5] Economic independence is the first step toward citizenship, yet, as Gill Jones and Claire Wallace point out, young people are denied the opportunity to achieve this objective by circumstances beyond their control.[6] Rather than making a traditional one-way transition from dependence to independence at the completion of education and the commencement of full-time ongoing work, young people are at the mercy of "transitional economic statuses" caused by balancing prolonged periods of training and insecure work in the highly competitive labor market. However, new definitions of citizenship still rely heavily on older ideas about linear pathways toward adulthood. The steps young people are supposed to follow, which lead them into a smooth transition to adult status, are marked out by moves toward full-time ongoing work. This "pathway" metaphor is unsustainable in the new economy, but youth citizenship discourse is still heavily dependent upon it. Jones and Wallace argue that

> it is only full time paid employment which can bring economic independence and the right to a stake in national civic life. . . . The longer full time paid employment is withheld from young people, the more training schemes they are

expected to enrol on, the longer they are expected to remain dependent on their parents—the more the goal of citizenship, with its obligations as well as rights, seems to be retreating into the distance.[7]

Young people are increasingly dependent on their families and the state for economic support, but many families are less able to provide, and state assistance for young people has been cut back. The persistence of the transitions model of achieving adulthood, combined with the collapse of the full-time youth job market and restrictive age-based frameworks for social policy, make it difficult for young people to activate their social rights. Dean attributes this situation to a political perspective that regards young people's social rights as the responsibility of families.[8] Moreover, according to this agenda, for the state to maintain the social rights of citizenship would be to interfere with the free market and provide a disincentive to youth to become self-disciplined. Where economic independence cannot be secured by young people, the consequence, as Howard Williamson argues, "has been growing levels of social exclusion and . . . the de facto denial of citizenship through both reducing access to the rights of citizenship and decreasing opportunities to engage in the responsibilities of citizenship."[9] This latter point is important, for while social and other rights are harder for youth to achieve, ever more emphasis is placed on their civic responsibilities.

Thus, alongside a concern with economic independence as the key to citizenship status for youth has emerged "a consideration of young people's entry to citizenship in terms of competency, participation and responsibility."[10] Young people have increasingly become the focus for both concerns about social unbindings and the learning of good citizenship, which is based on individual responsibility. It has been well documented that youth are often targeted as scapegoats who are perceived as the cause of broad social changes, civic disintegration, or unrest.[11] This tendency has reemerged in recent times. Alan France argues that since the mid-1980s there has been resurgence of debate about the moral education of youth and the effects of social change on their behavior. Deficiency, deviance, and delinquency have all emerged as key problems associated with young people living in a changing world.[12] Policy solutions have tended to be informed by frameworks of personal responsibility, punishment, surveillance, and reeducation. This includes "get-tough" legislation intended to deter youth from criminal or antisocial behavior (for example, through mandatory sentencing), combined with efforts to teach them how to be good citizens through a renewed attention to strategies such as cadets programs in schools; a reintroduction of civics education; and work-for-the-dole, workfare, or national service for the unemployed schemes. In these ways young people are expected to learn good citizenship and earn participation rights. Young people need to prove their entitlement to participation in their social worlds, and there is thus an emphasis on their social debt and on the importance of establishing responsibilities before rights.

The emerging significance of citizenship education is reflected in the allocation of government funding for school curriculum development, youth policy, and research grants throughout the Western world. Young people are targeted as those who most need to be involved in their communities, participate in volunteer work, and be set on the right path for civic engagement. However, as youth policy analyst Andreas Walther and his colleagues have found in research in nine European countries, current policies based on the transition model do not contribute substantially to young people's active participation.[13] In other words, contemporary youth policy can actually work against possibilities for young people's active citizenship. Alan France makes the argument that young people are in fact highly responsible and engaged, but this participation is often unacknowledged. Finally, Ellen Ehmke, secretary general of the organizing bureau of European Secondary School Student Unions, demonstrates that school-based education for active citizenship is generally overwhelmingly passive; that is, democracy is taught to, rather than exercised by, students. Young people are not taken seriously as active agents in their social worlds but tend instead to be described as desiring citizenship rather than actually having it.[14] Some of these issues will be pursued further in chapter 5.

The new emphasis on responsibility rather than rights for youth is central to the current reconceptualization of citizenship. Young people are expected to take individual responsibility for themselves, their choices, and their economic security and to accept that rights will not be granted to them simply on reaching the age of majority. Youth researchers Sinikka Aapola, Tuula Gordon, and Elina Lahelma note that representations of citizenship in textbooks for students reinforce that adult status must be earned through a series of set experiences and is not conferred automatically. They say,

> This implies having a grown up body does not bring the social rights of an adult citizen; they are linked with heterosexual relationships, family and economic independence, having a job and becoming a parent. Alternative routes to adulthood and citizenship are either not discussed at length, or are presented as problematic.[15]

Youth are also perceived to be those most at risk of disregarding their civic duties and consequently must be guided and educated to understand these. At the same time, somewhat paradoxically, much of this debate constitutes young people as those best able to steer a way through the new, unknown territory of contemporary citizenship—marked by globalization, migration, ethnic conflict, and new alliances—such as the formation of a European citizenry. Young people are often described as a resource who can show the way to those more fixed in old understandings of community and nation.[16] They are perceived as the future in terms of creating global or ethnically blended notions of citizenship. While this is sometimes borne out and celebrated by young people themselves, these are also rather idealized notions that at times tend to deny their own complex experiences of racism in particular. Seeing youth as a resource can also lead to exploitation and tokenism.[17]

The third major way in which young people have been affected by the shift in constructions of citizenship is by the move in emphasis to consumption. As we have seen, the new economy offers far fewer opportunities for economic security and independence in the form of full-time, ongoing employment. Further, ideas about citizenship have become closely linked to the individual's capacity to achieve this economic independence. Young people are still very much subject to this expectation, in spite of greatly reduced possibilities for achieving financial autonomy. However, alongside this older model of citizenship as attained once one is economically independent and therefore a contributor or a producer, is a new model that links civic viability with consumption. Deindustrialization, privatization, economic rationalism, and deregulation have all shifted the relation between the individual and society from citizen-state to consumer-corporation. Individuals are encouraged to exercise their citizenship responsibilities and rights in relation to privatized service providers rather than the state. Public facilities such as utilities, employment services, or government housing have been subcontracted or sold, and those who rely on them are now customers of profit-making businesses. Under these conditions, as Jones and Wallace suggest, "Citizenship no longer means the right to food, shelter and employment, rather it means the right to 'choose' between services. Choice is restricted to those with money."[18] Civic rights are exercised by making these kinds of consumer choices, and civic responsibilities are linked with holding services to "best practice" standards.

Marketization has seen the construction of youth in particular as consumer citizens. The domains of community and the polity, where civic belonging and identity, as well as rights and responsibilities were traditionally enacted, have become fragmented. In their place are individualized relationships to the market as sources for youth agency and expression. Youth researchers Ken Roberts et al. have found that civic life has all but disappeared in postcommunist countries, and that "nowadays it is more realistic for young people to try to take charge of, and to shape, their own lives via their labour market strategies and consumption practices."[19] They attribute young people's shift away from civic engagement and citizenship organized around the state to a strong reaction against the politicization of every aspect of life that was the norm under communism. However, they note that the same trend is found throughout Europe, beyond the post-communist countries, and argue that the shared reasons for this are "the monetarisation, commercialisation, privatisation and individualisation of daily life in general."[20]

As young people are no longer able to define themselves and engage with social institutions in relation to their work, consumer products have become increasingly important to enacting a meaningful identity in the social world. Clothes and lifestyle products can constitute cultural capital in place of work. Young people are "consumer socialized"[21] at a younger age, encouraged toward debt and credit options, and exposed to a global youth culture market that offers an enormous range of styles, cultures, and products with which to identify. Young people are increasingly engaged as effective citizens only when they consume. Generational theorists James E. Côté and Anton L. Allahar cite such examples as *Street Cents*, a Canadian TV show for young consumers that constructs youth as powerful players in the market.[22] However, the freedoms and choices of the market are not a meaningful substitute for an economically secure life trajectory, and consumer power is not the same as citizenship rights for which states are legally and morally accountable. Further, as Steven Miles argues, young people "do not have either the stability or the resources to operate as fully-fledged citizens of a consumer society because that society offers all the temptation without the secure economic and social foundations upon which such stability can be built."[23] New discourses about youth citizenship reconfigure social rights as individual responsibilities, political rights as the opportunity to participate as a resource or symbol of hope in a risky world, and civil rights as freedom to make consumer choices.

Young Women as the New Citizens

If youth citizenship is constructed around responsibilities rather than rights, highly managed forms of participation, and consumption, young women are differently and specifically affected by these new constructions. As we saw in the previous chapter, some young women are seriously marginalized by their inability to secure economic independence, and this in turn prevents them from enacting citizenship. It is more likely to be members of this group who are perceived as a problem for society, who are more at-risk of civic disengagement, and who are depicted as needing guidance and education for social responsibility and participation. Finally, they are least likely to have the resources to enjoy the benefits of market choice and consumer citizenship. For others, the transferral of the responsibility for social rights onto the individual has been reasonably unproblematic, as they are able to be supported in all ways by their family and social milieu. This group is most likely to be depicted as showing the way for future models of citizenship, participating in local communities, and forging harmonious intercultural connections. They are also those most able to exercise consumer rights and freedom of choice in the marketplace. Ideas about the can-dos as well as the at-risks thus also operate in the domain of youth citizenship. For both the most disadvantaged and the most privileged, the intertwining of discourses about youth citizenship and individual responsibility is equally powerful, but it has very different effects.

These discourses, which in turn inform policy, may well be out of step with the reality of young women's lives and the possibilities that actually exist for them to enact citizenship. As suggested by political theorists Jet Bussemaker and Rian Voet, "Policy makers are full of good intentions as they relate to preparing girls for full citizenship, but have scant regard for the concrete details with which these girls are confronted in their everyday life."[24] As with labor market success, all young women are depicted as leading the way forward for youth citizenship: they are forging their nations, becoming responsible self-made citizens, and are expected to either lead a revival in youth participation in the polity or make successes of themselves without state intervention. However, this representation both relies upon and conceals deep divisions between young women. In the remainder of this chapter, I look more closely at these images of young women taking responsibility for social rights, acting as "ambassadresses" and leaders, as the new global citizens, and as those best able to blend consumer choice into citizenship duties. New models of youth citizenship depend upon young women to make real these vastly changed notions of rights, belonging, and participation. However, many young women are excluded from active citizenship at the same time. How can these profoundly different experiences coexist, and what does it mean for the future of young womanhood as the new model for citizenship?

Social Rights and the Self-Made Girl

As we saw in the previous chapter, one of the most significant ways young women are invested in is as symbols of economic independence in insecure times. Young women are constructed as those most able to succeed financially during periods of economic uncertainty and change. This kind of economic independence, which does not rely on the state and is bound up with a narrative of self-discipline and motivation, has become the key to a new kind of transition to citizenship for youth. Ironically, it is only when young people are able to give up their expectation that the state will fulfill their social rights that they are admitted to full citizenship. Along with the view that young women are best able to adapt and succeed in a world without economic certainties and safety nets is the idea that they are taking personal responsibility for their social rights and, in fact, will become self-made. This means that they will take the initiative in establishing themselves as financially autonomous. As political theorist Ruth Lister notes, women have traditionally been excluded from citizenship because they have been denied access to the public sphere and to economic independence. Today, young women are not only encouraged to take their places in the public world of work, but they are also expected to do this through their personal competencies and from a sense of their responsibilities to their social world, rather than through support structures framed around their state-protected rights to financial autonomy. The narrative organizing young women's relationship to citizenship as economic independence is not about social rights to livelihood, but about personal responsibility, self-starting, and not "sponging" off the state or the community. It is this kind of young woman who is held up as the ideal citizen for our times.

Work and the Citizen Mother

This expectation is borne out in a variety of Western governments' policies and position papers that focus on young women. One good example is the Dutch Girls' Memo, described by youth policy analyst Annemieke Van Drenth as the only European policy specifically aimed at enhancing young women's active citizenship. This policy seeks to "advance the development of girls and young women toward independence in a process of participation and integration in society," but it does this primarily by focusing on young women's own employment choices. Participation in society is measured by participation in the workforce at the highest possible level. Citizenship is constructed as personal responsibility for economic independence. The memo attributes any barriers to this kind of citizenship to young women's own internalized beliefs about gender-appropriate education and employment options. As Van Drenth suggests, "They themselves are responsible for having made the choices that diminish their opportunities to get jobs with high wages and good prospects."[25] The focus of the memo is thus on getting young women to make better choices at school and in work: an approach that locates good citizenship with economic success and the personal capacity of the individual to achieve this, rather than any changes that might need to take place in their socioeconomic environment. In Van Drenth's words, this is a "notion of citizenship that stresses one's responsibility to participate in the labour market without positing a social policy that affords girls more opportunities."[26] The social policy she refers to specifically is one that addresses support for families. While young women are encouraged to pursue social rights through individual effort in securing good work, social policies and values have not adapted to accommodate new family arrangements that do not depend on women as primary caregivers and household managers.

Work and personal responsibility for one's social rights are linked here to young women's capacity to make good choices that will maximize their participation. Young women are constituted primarily as workers in this new formulation, and the work/family balance is a matter for personal negotiation. As Van Drenth argues, at the same time that young women are expected to have and care for children at some stage, their key responsibility as citizens is to work. The good citizen mother is one who figures out this dilemma herself, through private means of support and in ways that do not involve the state excessively. We have already seen that motherhood is still a requirement of can-do girls, as long as it is deferred long enough for a good job to be established first. Policies such as the Girls' Memo indicate how citizenship is awarded to young women who will combine work and motherhood in ways that demonstrate a commitment to independent economic standing.

Such policies demonstrate the constitution of what McRobbie describes as

> a population of "good girls" who will do well at school, go on to get good jobs and from then on juggle the demands of home and work alike but with more help from government than has ever been the case in the past.[27]

It is important to note that these "good girls," or what I am describing as "citizen mothers," are entitled to state support in the form of temporary baby bonuses or maternity leave as a reward for appropriate participation in the workforce. Thus it is not the case that motherhood is completely unsupported by the state; rather, it is only women who enact motherhood in the correct ways, that is, juggled with a good job at a later stage in their career, who will be approved of and assisted. As Michelle Fine notes,[28] with U.S. welfare reform, this takes shape in a clever piece of class-inspired ideological reversal: middle-class mothers are told it is important to stay home for the sake of best-practice child rearing, while poor women are required to leave their children with nonexistent day care so they can work menial jobs.

For this reason, it is the young mother who is a bad citizen, in that she threatens to depend on state resources to secure her social rights. On account of her youth, she is unlikely to have established a career for herself prior to having a child, which consequently defies the new citizenship order of things. She can be represented as the exact opposite of the citizen mothers, in spite of considerable evidence that young motherhood increases commitment to education, training, and employment; improves self-esteem and confidence; enhances interest and involvement in civic life; and is better for a woman's and baby's health than a later-life pregnancy.[29] While there are also many difficulties associated with mothering at a young age, most of these are related to poverty.[30] The point is that the values and commitments that are supposedly important in the new citizenship are frequently held by young mothers. The key difference is that the socioeconomic circumstances of many of these young women necessitate government support. This situation does not sit with new efforts to make women responsible for their social rights and for balancing work and family with minimal assistance.

Young mothers problematize the notion that it is necessarily preferable for women to pursue work now and worry about motherhood later. Their presence brings into view the absence of industrial and family policy, as well as appropriate social values, that would enable a real balance between work and parenting. Their difficulties in finding appropriate and satisfying work that can help them fulfill their family responsibilities make apparent that this work may simply not exist. Consequently, young mothers are held up as examples of bad citizens who drain state resources; good girls are those who establish financial independence and become citizen mothers at times and in ways that better suit the state and the economy.

The Girl Entrepreneur

The idea of the self-made young woman is therefore borne out in new constructions of young women as workers and as mothers. Another interesting example of this emphasis on making oneself is the phenomenon of the girl entrepreneur. Social theorist Nikolas Rose argues that the concept of "enterprise" has become a rationale for new structures of citizenship, writing that "individuals are to become, as it were, entrepreneurs of themselves, shaping their own lives through the choices they make among the forms of life available to them."[31] For young women, making oneself is also connected to making money for oneself. Entrepreneurship is not simply a metaphor for the choice biographer, but a practical scheme offered to young women to ensure economic self-sufficiency. The girl entrepreneur is the ultimate self-inventing young woman who represents a fantasy of achievement accomplished by good ideas, hard work, and self-confidence. McRobbie suggests that "the coupling of youthful femininity with money and success" has become common. She notes that in popular media, such as magazines, "A favourite feature is . . . the enormous earning power of a small handful of glamorous young women."[32] This fantasy of young women striking it rich through pluck and determination is supported through the cultivation of entrepreneurship among young women, which in turn contributes to a notion of self-starting citizenship. Susan Hopkins suggests that now, "The empowered female role model is . . . framed in the language of enterprise and opportunism."[33]

There has been an increase in both government-funded and corporate ventures that aim to get young people, and especially young women, educated for economic autonomy and involved in their communities by developing a commercial idea. Such entrepreneur programs and competitions, very popular in the United States, Canada, and Australia and expanding into the United Kingdom and Europe, generally operate by inviting young women to develop a business idea or plan, for which they can receive start-up funding or undergo the training scheme on offer. Programs have catchy titles such as Independent Means, Girls' Biz, Mind Your Own Business, and Mother and Daughter Entrepreneurs in Teams (MADE-IT). The Australis Self-Made Girl competition, one example of these programs, is an initiative of the teen cosmetics brand Australis, but it is sponsored by three separate government bodies, the Young Women's Christian Association, two young women's magazines, a bank, a tampon brand, and a car company. Like most of the other girl entrepreneur contests, this program aims to encourage and reward young women who are self-starters, who want to make something of themselves, and who can be role models for others. This kind of young woman is held up as an example to others of how they can be whoever they want to be and contribute to their communities. Typically, this involves forging a successful business that guarantees economic independence. The Australian newspaper the *Sun-Herald* reports on one of these Australis Self-Made Girls, Emma Leung. She is a

> 16 year old Ashfield schoolgirl [who] shops for her own clothes, owns a mobile phone and laptop computer, has a holiday job and is about to launch her own business. Ms Leung's company, Prezzie Paks, will package gifts aimed at the youth market. . . . For her business acumen, she won more than $20,000 in cash and prizes as the Australis National Business Plan competition champion.[34]

This sixteen-year-old girl is depicted as motivated, economically independent and savvy. It appears she has financed an impressive consumer lifestyle from her seasonal job and her own developing company. This presumably ordinary schoolgirl acts as a role model for others by balancing school, work, leisure, and her own business. She is one of many of these young women who are frequently highlighted in the media and celebrated in public life for combining typical youth activities with a business practice, public "good deeds," and self-motivated capitalist success. The nongovernment United States–based *Girlstart* website, which claims to provide resources to help girls become "smart from the start" with regard to job opportunities, offers a similar list of inspiring young businesswomen who run their own companies and "do it all." Similarly, three "girl entrepreneurs" who have businesses selling everyday products (earrings, handbags, and lipstick) are highlighted on the U.S. Government Department of Health and Human Services *Girl Power!* website. *Girl Power!* is a national public education campaign that promotes policies to "help encourage and motivate 9–13 year-old girls to make the most of their lives," with entrepreneurship falling clearly within this mission. The U.S. government also emphasizes the importance of introducing girls to entrepreneurship through programs in the Office of Women's Business Ownership.

The can-do qualities of being smart, having power, and making the most of one's abilities and opportunities have become folded into economic self-made success. By implication, any young woman can achieve if she is determined enough. In this respect, the DIY ethic is applied to money-making opportunities but underscores notions of the social rights of citizenship as young women's personal responsibility.

A host of organizations, programs, and books now offers entrepreneurship training to young women, promising empowerment, confidence building, and profit making as part of a feminist, civic, and capitalist package. Texts such as *How to Be a Teenage Millionaire* or *The Young Entrepreneur's Edge*, which offer to show young people methods for "using your ambition, independence and youth to launch a successful business," suggest that young people are uniquely placed to become economically independent as a consequence of their age and desire for success.[35] Once they are empowered to believe in themselves, youth can achieve financial success through personal effort. The story of limitless opportunities for young women in particular is told in the book *Girls and Young Women Entrepreneurs: True Stories about Starting and Running a Business Plus How You Can Do It Yourself*, a featured link from the *Girl Power!* website. In its promotional material it claims:

> There are no limits!!! Once you are encouraged to try, you can accomplish anything. This book is designed to help girls build confidence, take responsible risks, and learn new skills. Starting and running their own business has taught the young entrepreneurs in this book to believe in themselves, act independently, make decisions and set and reach goals—all while earning the respect of their customers, parents and peers. Now these girls have the confidence needed to continue exploring, growing, and achieving life skills that they will always profit from.[36]

Entrepreneur camps for young women aged thirteen to nineteen are another popular way to "empower girls to envision themselves as entrepreneurs," in the words of *Entrepreneur* magazine.[37] NGOs such as the Girl Scouts Association, universities, small businesses, professional associations, private foundations, and government-funded programs all run these kinds of camps. They aim to teach young women how to develop business ideas and plans, how to network, and how to promote their businesses to attract capital. The University of North Florida's camp provides young women with an "etiquette luncheon," a "business fashion show," and a "mocktail party." Columbia College in South Carolina gives campgoers the opportunity to "present a business plan to a panel of real lenders." Independent Means Inc., a private company operating in Australia and the United States, offers girls both Camp Startup and Summer $tock in which to conduct business and investment training. These programs are intended to encourage girls to imagine themselves as adult players in the market, to build their confidence to "do it yourself," to learn about economic independence, and to develop leadership skills. In this, we can see notions about good youth citizenship dovetailing with marketization, consumption, and narratives of self-invention.

Thus entrepreneur schemes for young women are not just represented as holiday programs or leisure activities. Embedded within their framework is the construction of young women as makers of their own economic success. Business ventures are no longer the province of the lucky, the well funded, or older men. It is ordinary, determined young women who are the contemporary exemplars of the successful, modern-day entrepreneur. This image is linked back into meanings of youth citizenship both through the implication that social rights are a personal concern and the promotion of young women as those best able to embody the self-starting citizen. Young women are the money makers of the future. It is no surprise that the U.K. civics education curriculum uses the girls' entrepreneur camps as a prime example of youth citizenship for students to discuss. Nor is it unusual to see the San Francisco think tank, the Institute for Global Futures, imagine the ideal future digital entrepreneur, driving digital capitalism for this century, as a young girl.

Leadership

The proliferation of leadership programs for young women also speaks to the importance placed on them as self-made symbols for new forms of citizenship. While many of these programs draw on the language of self-empowerment and confidence also found in entrepreneurship and self-esteem movements, they are focused on developing young women's leadership abilities for the global good. The notion that girls are the world's future leaders is elaborated through campaigns such as the YWCA's "Power to Change: Commitment to Leadership of Women and Girls," a global fund-raising effort to sustain leadership development of young women. Young women are hereby imagined not only as the future, but as the most appropriate future leaders of a global citizenry. The World YWCA president, Jane Lee Wolfe, claims on the organization's website that "women are the last great resource to be developed."[38] Young women in particular are the focus of this $25 million plan, and Wolfe's resource metaphor alludes to a kind of use value of girls that has been previously unrecognized. At the same time, the opportunity to "give women and girls the chance to learn, lead and change the world" must be more attractive to potential investors than the more mundane and yet enduring issues of young women's more basic needs for health, safety, food, and appropriate work.

Similarly, prominent feminist Naomi Wolf's venture, the Woodhull Institute, is an international training institute for the promotion of ethical leadership among young women worldwide. It promises to "provide access to a global, intellectual community with the capacity to affect public policy, adjust corporate agendas and promote community development." Young women who complete the leadership training presumably join this community and can enact citizenship duties through their new influence on government, the private sector, and at the grass roots. The nature of the leadership training that is offered provides some insight into the kind of citizens young women are encouraged to be. The training focuses on leadership in the context of personal and professional achievements. According to the website,

> Women in the early stages of their careers are often held back by a lack of skills and an inability to identify opportunities for advancement. The Woodhull Institute trains young women in the practical steps needed to implement their ideas and transform their ambitions for leadership into reality. Since there is often a gap between a young woman's private aspirations and her accomplishments, the Institute's training is intended to bridge this gap by offering leadership training and providing access to colleagues and mentors who will counsel and encourage these young women throughout their careers. Woodhull offers empowerment courses on financial literacy and basic business skills, public speaking, negotiation and advocacy, writing, ethics in the workplace, and networking and acquiring mentoring relationships.[39]

Leadership here is reduced to the realm of the professional. Becoming a good leader means establishing economic literacy, networking, and discovering one's own power to realize ambitions. Young women are imagined to be constrained by their personal limitations in developing the right skills or taking advantage of opportunities. Once these individual barriers are removed, they will be able to accomplish their aims and become ethical leaders. In this example, *leadership* is fundamentally an equivalent term for *contemporary youth citizenship*. Economic self-sufficiency, self-belief, and role-modeling are all intrinsic to the new ways young women are supposed to position themselves as citizens.

This is just one example of a new emphasis in public policy and youth services for young women that focuses on leadership and confidence. Both governments and NGOs have taken up these themes in recent times as the key to young women's futures as active citizens. As we have already seen, when limitations on young women's success are acknowledged, these are generally depicted as low self-esteem and lack of confidence. Consequently, various programs and strategies exist to encourage them to develop leadership skills and learn about independence. Clubs and community programs for young women sometimes utilize outdoor education, personal empowerment workshops, and "survival camps" to overcome their personal obstacles of low confidence and to encourage them to become leaders in their communities. The significance and purpose of cultivating leadership among young women is linked to their capacity to be good citizens. Young women thus need to be guided into good personal choices, helped to overcome misconceptions about the limits on their options, and taught that they can do anything. In these ways they can then become responsible for their future, lead and integrate their communities, and act as role models for others.

Ambassadress for the Nation

This theme of individual responsibility and leadership is also evident in new discourses of young people's civic duties and commitment to community. It is echoed strongly in the content and structure of civics education in school curricula. Education for citizenship, or civics, has become central to debates about curriculum development in a range of Western countries. Howard Williamson notes that behind this drive, "There appears to be almost a 'holy grail' momentum seeking to discover new mechanisms or frameworks for binding or re-integrating young people into generational, community and social networks, a function implicitly fulfilled historically by the entry into employment."[40] Given the collapse of the youth labor market, citizenship has to be both taught and refigured in new ways. As Williamson points out, this is not just in relation to social rights and the construction of good citizens as those who can fend for themselves economically, but also in regard to identification with civil society. Deindustrialization and globalization have profoundly altered social worlds, and education for citizenship has a renewed importance in connecting youth with their changing communities. The content of such programs, however, tends to reinforce neoliberal notions of self-invention and responsibility, again often with young women at the forefront.

Another version of the self-made girl as ideal citizen is the young woman who overcomes adversity and becomes a success through her own efforts alone. An example of this can be found in the representation and celebration of young migrant and refugee women through national awards, media features, and civics lessons. This is what feminist and critical race theorist Sonia Shah describes as "the celebrated immigrant." One illustration of this phenomenon is the Young Australian of the Year competition, won in 1998 by a young woman named Tan Le. The civics curriculum materials developed by Curriculum Corporation for the Department of Education, Science and Training describe her thus:

> She was so clever and hard working at school that she went to university when she was only 16. Since then, Le has worked very hard to help the Vietnamese

people of Melbourne, Victoria. She became president of a group that works with immigrants and helps them find jobs. . . . She is now working to help people do business with Asian countries.[41]

Accompanying media reports detail her childhood experience of escape from Vietnam and arrival in Australia in a fishing boat. This narrative of triumph highlights how self-invention is possible in the most difficult circumstances. It also allays fears about social disintegration due to migration by demonstrating the power of the self-made (refugee) girl to create harmony and social connections (as well as economic growth). Tan Le is smart and disciplined; she is a helper, assisting other immigrants by integrating them into the workforce, and now encouraging "people" (presumably Anglo Australians) with profit-making pursuits in Asia. Not only does this image of the self-made girl citizen draw on a variety of cultural stereotypes about Vietnamese migrants, it also highlights how responsibilities of the state have been devolved onto individuals. Tan Le is rewarded for taking personal responsibility for the social rights of other citizens, for helping them develop business interests, for assisting migrants, and most importantly, for doing it herself.

Self-made citizenship is thus something that young women are idealized as excelling at, in that they are entrepreneurial, act as role models for others, are involved in their communities, and have been responsible for their own success. Significantly, good citizenship is constructed not just by agents of the state, as in the case of Tan Le, but also by private corporations, as we shall see. Young women are leading examples of DIY citizenship, but they are also invested in as key players in comforting narratives of national continuity in times of change, mass movements of people around the world, and the loosening of traditional social bonds within communities.

Girl Soldiers

One of the more literal ways young women can perform a defense of the nation is through military activity. Military service in the contemporary context is frequently represented as an experience capturing the key elements of the new young citizen: self-sufficiency, leadership, confidence, responsibility, and fun civic engagement. The debate about young women's participation in the armed forces and acceptance at military academies has been framed primarily as a feminist one. Their integration into this last bastion of male separatism is imagined as the final victory for women's liberation. Indeed, it represents the reversal of some women's status from oppressed victim to empowered liberator in a very interesting manner. Military action has frequently been performed and justified in the name of liberation of an oppressed people, often represented by the status of women. For example, the American campaign in Afghanistan in 2002 and

Fig. 3.1 A British Army equipment operator with a command post vehicle on exercise with her unit. She is 17 and has been with the Regiment for four months. Crown Copyright 2000/MOD.

the war in Iraq in 2003 have both been sold in part as missions to liberate people from backward, particularly Muslim, extremism. The most commonly used symbol of this extremism is the burka. With the integration of young women into the armed forces, they are now being invited onto the side of the liberators. It is now their duty to free the women who are still oppressed, who do not have the advantages of personal freedom or the opportunities enjoyed by the can-do girls. In other words, it is the future girls who are best able to liberate those stuck in the past.

Military recruitment drives are revelatory in terms of depicting how defense of the nation is entwined with can-do girlness. Young women, such as the seventeen-year-old gunner equipment operator of the British Army depicted in figure 3.1, are featured prominently on the webpages and print and television advertisements of a number of national defense forces. However, they constitute only a small minority of defense forces' serving members: 15 percent in the United States and 13 percent in Australia.[42] One example of this trend toward girl promotion can be seen in the recruitment campaigns of the Army Reserve in Australia, the United Kingdom, and the United States. These countries are particularly interesting because their governments have been the most aggressive in both the so-called war on terror and the war in Iraq, and they have been highly active in the construction of an extremist, threatening Muslim "other" who must be defended against. The Army Reserve websites of each of these countries highlight young women as typical reservists. They include photos and profiles of young women talking about their roles and responsibilities and the benefits of membership. While each draws on some generic elements of the can-do girl discourses to promote the Army Reserve as a good choice for achievement-oriented young women, local peculiarities also shape the selling of military service to girls.

The U.S. Army slogan is "An army of one," and the Reserve-specific slogan is "Wear a uniform once a month. Be a soldier every day." On the website a head-and-shoulders photo of SPC Sarah Ahrens accompanies this script.[43] She wears a military uniform and gazes out confidently and unsmilingly past the viewer. Her demeanor is at once hopeful, determined, and self-assured. She conveys that she has a job to do and will do it, although her disposition seems fresh and sanguine rather than grim. Her name implies she is not Latina, and her picture suggests that she is not African American, although these populations are overrepresented in the armed forces compared with their percentage in the general population.[44] Beneath this image is the following message:

> When you join the Army Reserve, you're making a commitment not only to your country, but also to yourself. You'll be a stronger person. A better citizen. And the world will see your strength. You'll be an Army of One in the Army Reserve.[45]

This narrative underscores the self-making and self-sufficiency of the can-do girl, as well as appealing to an older American frontier/vigilante discourse. The defense of the nation is at the same time a defense of the individual. Against the common image of the military as an homogenizing and deindividualizing institution, the message here is that the Army Reserve enhances strength of self. Again, we see the devolution onto the individual of responsibility for the public good. By implication, all those who are not reservists are suspect or lesser citizens. The Army Reserve promises to remake the girl self, such that she will "be a soldier every day." In other words she will not be absorbed by the army and thereby lose her identity, but it will become part of her.

The marketing of the Australian Army Reserve takes a slightly different angle on the merging of the ideal military reservist with the can-do girl. Its slogan is "the part time of your life." The website also features photos and stories of successful young female reservists, including Lance Corporal Sharyn Hoekstra, who is quoted as saying, "The Army Reserve teaches you to believe in yourself, it teaches you to have a go, to be confident and know that whatever is put in front of you, you'll have a go at it." Unlike the American narrative, the Australian story is that participation in the Reserve is lifestyle enhancing rather than life shaping. It picks up on the aspects of flexibility, fun, challenges, confidence, and work/play blending inherent in young female citizenship. Its webpage script is as follows:

> Where else can you work part-time in an exciting outdoor environment, train on high-tech equipment, build up personal skills, make great friends, get fit and earn tax free pay? Where else but the Army Reserve? . . . The Army Reserve is a great way to experience new and exciting challenges without re-arranging the rest of your life.[46]

The individual is still central, but the Australian Army Reserve promises to work against deindividualization by emphasizing personal lifestyle choices and fitting into a busy schedule. Its publicity suggests it is closer to a health camp or a vigorous holiday than a military training scheme. This is particularly evident in the print advertisement for the Reserve (figure 3.2), which is an example from the campaign as run in young women's magazines such as *Cleo* and *Cosmo* throughout 2002.[47] Under the image of three armed figures standing on a rocky outcrop and performing some kind of strategic military activity, it reads, "Reach the hill. Identify a landing position. Establish radio contact. Call in air support. Pick up the dry cleaning. Be home in time for 'Friends'." In this commercial, military activities are depicted as consistent with fun times and the enactment of a popular culture and consumer-oriented femininity.

The British Army webpages use a similar pitch. These include not only cadet, reserve, and army careers features, but also a choice of four online war games and a special club for thirteen- to seventeen-year-olds who are "army barmy!" Entitled "Camouflage," this club provides "helpful facts, career advice, free downloads, competitions and special offers . . . diaries, games and quizzes." Members get a starter pack with a "unique passcode," a free magazine, invitations to special events, and "fun, quickfire quizzes." The crossovers with the marketing strategies employed by girls' popular magazines and webpages are striking. Quizzes, diaries, and competitions are the mainstays of female consumer culture, and it is hard to imagine these inducements addressing any other market.

While the military borrows from feminine popular culture, this culture also now borrows from the military. In 2003 the DC Comics superhero Wonder Woman underwent a transformation that included a camouflage bustier and short, spiky hair. Illustrator Jerry Ordway says, "In this series, she has plenty of battles and she looks like a soldier. Here we have someone who is a fighting machine. She's suddenly put in a situation and she can handle herself."[48] Although the lower echelons of the defense forces continue to be made up of young people who are without cultural and economic resources, the makeover of military service means it is now sold as an experience for the successful and glamorous can-do girl who can now also excel as a fighting machine.

Fig. 3.2 Military activity as a lifestyle choice for young women. Australian Army Reserve advertisement. Reprinted with permission.

Multicultural Citizenship

Young women have also emerged recently as symbolic defenses against social change created by globalization, migration, civil conflict, and threats to human security. These conditions have triggered uncertainty about national identities, and, in many cases, xenophobic policies and attitudes have flourished as a consequence. As cultural sociologist Nira Yuval-Davis has argued, young women throughout history have been utilized symbolically as the spirit and honor of nations. A quite concrete example of this was the opening ceremony of the 2000 Olympic Games: a theatrical performance of the history and culture of Australia, led by a white, blonde, thirteen-year-old girl.

In recent times young migrant women have taken on a particular role in calming fears about social disintegration caused by war, poverty, and especially migration by personifying an unthreatening blended citizenship. Both Nira Yuval-Davis and psychologist Oliva Espin among others have discussed the ways in which women come to symbolize appropriate "acculturation"—those migrants who are best able to carry the hopes and traditions of their cultures of origin and blend these unproblematically with the values and lifestyle of their new nations. In her book *The Modern Girl* education sociologist Lesley Johnson notes that during the late 1950s a role emerged of the young migrant woman as "ambassadress" for the nation. She analyzes this phenomenon in terms of the meaning of beauty contests at the time. She argues that a young woman's success in these contests, a sign that she had accomplished the making of an appropriate young feminine self, became bound up in the making of nations. This was especially significant in countries such as Australia, which were seeking to manipulate and manage fears about the meaning of migrant populations in the defining of a new, modern social world. Attractive young women were picked out as "typical" representatives of the broader migrant population. Johnson writes that "images of innocent, youthful femininity (the migrant girl) served to defuse the sense of threat, the sense of the foreign as dangerous,"[49] and she shows how these images were circulated via public events such as debutante balls, beauty contests, and sporting meets. For example, the selection of Russian-Australian Tania Verstak as Miss Australia in 1961 and Miss International Beauty in 1962 served to reassure Australia and other "young" nations that migrants were an unthreatening asset who were keen to please.

Significant parallels can be drawn with the function of the young female migrant in the construction of national identity and citizenship today. This is perhaps particularly so for countries, such as Canada and Australia, that are structured by racism and yet labor under the illusion that they have no clear national identity.[50] In these instances multicultural policies are constructed to unequally manage relations between dominant colonizing populations, global movements of migrants and refugees, and the rights of Indigenous peoples. Multicultural citizenship involves "tolerance" or "acceptance" on the part of the dominant population on the one hand, and aspirations to the dominant lifestyle, adoption of dominant values, and maintenance of the attractive and nonthreatening dimensions of the culture of origin (costume, cuisine, festivals) on the other.

The promotion of certain kinds of young female migrants as ambassadresses captures the construction of good multicultural citizenship in action. The enthusiastic reception of Tania Verstak on the part of the media and social commentators in the early 1960s mirrors the promotion of the Russian-Australian pole vaulter Tatiana Grigorieva during the 2000 Sydney Olympics. In both instances the image of the attractive and charming young migrant woman is considered an excellent embodiment of the nation's values. Both Verstak and Grigorieva symbolized the migrant success story of determination and hard work resulting in internationally recognized achievements. Both were unequivocal about representing their new country, in spite of being first-generation migrants. And significantly, both achieved ambassadorial success through the display of the ideal feminine body, as constructed during each of these eras.

Verstak represented "glamour, poise, a figure correctly proportioned and a charming personality,"[51] and exhibited these qualities through passive display, as a beauty mannequin. Grigorieva, however, personifies contemporary, youthful femininity through active embodiment of a physical self that is not just "to be touched and looked at,"[52] but is powerful, strong, and capable. Cultural studies scholar Susan Bordo notes that this change in ideal from a general, soft slenderness to taut slimness is peculiar to our times. Johanna Wyn suggests that today, "Young women's bodies can also be seen as a form of compulsory performativity," and she notes in particular the importance of the display of a midriff that is toned and therefore controlled.[53] Tattoos and belly-button piercings are popular modes of decorating and highlighting this part of the young female body as a site which has been worked on. Grigorieva represents this shift to an ideal young female body that is toned and trim, with good, but not excessive, muscle definition and very little fat. Her midriff tattoo (a flower), peeking out from the top of her sports briefs, is also a sign of a more assertive female sexuality and is as much an ideal accoutrement for a successful contemporary young woman's body as Verstak's long white gloves were for a previous generation. And just as Verstak's heterosexuality was celebrated with her transformation into Mrs. Peter Young,[54] Grigorieva's is assured by her marriage to a fellow Russian immigrant.

The celebration of Verstak and Grigorieva as embodiments of a blended Australianness and as ideal role models for young Australian women occurred within times of significant unrest and uncertainty about youth, gender, and nation. Both the late 1950s and late 1990s saw rising concern about the place of migrants in a "new" Australia. The construction of the good migrant, who worked hard and did not complain, became conflated with both a good femininity and an appropriate national identity. Through the 1990s and into the twenty-first century, more and more cultural groups were drawn into this picture. This is well illustrated by the treatment of migrants from Southeast and East Asia. As people from these regions, predominantly women, became more visible in their protests against labor exploitation—for example, in outsourced "sweat shops"—a new image of the good Asian girl emerged as a symbol for the nation. This also coincided with rising concern in the form of a moral panic about young Asian gangs, drug dealers and users, criminals, and dole (welfare) cheats. The emerging threat of young people of Southeast Asian origin, either first or second generation, who were not grateful, who did not assimilate, and who were becoming politically organized and active was counteracted by strong messages about "good young Asians." The construction of the quiet and studious Asian girl, which had circulated for some time previously,[55] was combined with the added qualities of civic spirit and entrepreneurship to create this image, as we saw earlier in the case of Tan Le. And in 2001 the young "Asian" girl as the ideal Australian citizen was reinforced by the selection of fifteen-year-old Hayley Eves, a young woman of South Korean origin, to make a keynote address, as the representative of Australian youth, at the centennial commemoration of the opening of the Australian Federation Parliament. Eves was described in the media as "young, gorgeous, feisty and political,"[56] her can-do, girl-power qualities clearly enhanced by her role as civic representative. Le and Eves serve as powerful counterpoints to "troublesome" young Asian migrants.

Equally, the mid- to late 1990s also saw trouble from young Indigenous Australians, who were increasingly organizing around ideas of a treaty and a formal apology to the Stolen Generation,[57] and who were driving a broader movement for reconciliation between Indigenous and non-Indigenous communities. Not coincidentally, 1998 was the same year that the highly successful Aboriginal athlete Catherine Freeman was named Australian of the Year. The civics curriculum materials cited earlier describe her as "a very good runner [who] won a scholarship to boarding school where she was able to have professional coaching." By implication, a good young Aboriginal woman is both athletically and intellectually gifted, but she must leave home and become acculturated (with perhaps an implied slide into tacit approval for the removal of Aboriginal children from their families?) to maximize her opportunities. The reinvention of Catherine Freeman, from Aboriginal activist—when she was censured for carrying the Aboriginal flag at the 1994 Commonwealth Games—to national hero, was complete with her win at the 2000 Olympics, when she became simply "our Cathy." The complicated and painful work of reconciliation was seemingly accomplished in the 49.11 seconds that Black and white Australia cheered her on during her four-hundred-meter run.

Young women have been drawn into the defense of national identity, citizenship, migrant assimilation, and human security at a time when all of these concepts appear to be under threat. The construction of the girl as the ideal citizen, ambassadress, or savior/leader of her nation suggests the ways in which new forms of young womanhood are invested in to counter the perceived threats of globalization and migration. Sport, entertainment, and glamor have become important modes by which young women are drawn into allaying fears about the loss of social bonds and homogeneous national identities. Events as benign as the Eurovision Song Contest are opportunities for the performance of comforting narratives about nation, and this is more and more likely to be achieved through such figures as young Swedish women of African origin or Russian-born Latvians. Global citizenship in the hands of girls is gentle entertainment. The World Association of Girl Guides and Girl Scouts recommends the promotion of world citizenship through slide shows about other countries, barbecues with international cuisine, and singing in another language. New toys for girls position them as global citizens; for example, the action figure dolls the Get Real Girls come with passports, travel stamps, postcards, and a digital video journal to record their international adventures. Fears about immigration, multiculturalism, and the disappearance of strong national and cultural borders are quelled by the images of young women as either the unthreatening face of the "other" who only seeks to be accepted and to entertain, or the ethical and caring future leader of a global citizenry. As we shall see next, another complication is that the construction of these self-made girls and ambassadresses blends national and commercial interests in defining contemporary youth citizenship.

Consumer Citizens

The third way in which young women are configured as the new citizens is by their representation as smart consumers. As outlined earlier, civil rights have been reconstructed as choices, freedoms, and powers of consumption. Côté and Allahar suggest that "young people are encouraged to narrow their thinking and to focus on issues of personal materialism and consumerism, from which big business is the principal beneficiary."[58] Young women are apparently taking up these freedoms with great gusto. The Australian *Sun-Herald* newspaper article "Girls Just Wanna Shop" reports on market research demonstrating "the marketing power of Australia's latest spenders: self-aware, assertive and consumer-savvy teenage girls." The manager of the market research company who conducted the survey of girls' consumer habits connects self-confidence with consumer power. He is quoted as saying, "We have a teaching environment that has created the knowledge that girls can do it, girls should and they will achieve." This kind of girlpower translates into young women's increased capacity to wield power as consumers, to buy what they like, and to spend their discretionary income on carefully selected products that make a statement about who they are.

Interestingly, the market research company director suggests that this new kind of powerful girl consumer is fundamentally different from her mother's generation, and when she grows older

> there won't be that angst, that self-doubt, that wrestling with the sort of issues that their working or at-home mothers are heavily and noticeably debating. It won't even be a factor, it will be "this is my choice, this is what I'm doing."[59]

Although he does not make clear what these issues are, the logical inference is the balance of work and family, with the implication that now that young women have been liberated from lack of confidence, money making and a consumer lifestyle will take precedence. These young women are seen to have effectively solved the problems of their mothers simply by being empowered and decisive, which they have learned about through consumption. Youthful consumption is a way to rehearse the guilt-free making of choices that can then be articulated on a larger scale later in life. Specifically, it helps young women choose to become different kinds of citizens, in fact, the kinds of highly valued citizen mothers discussed earlier.

McRobbie argues that this linking of neoliberal ideologies about individual choice with a distorted kind of feminism serves to reconfigure young women's political agendas "through the seductions of individual success, the lure of female empowerment and the love of money."[60] In short, real capacity to have a voice, to participate, and to make social change is reinvented as the ability to make personal choices about consumer products. Just as entrepreneurship has come to stand in for social rights, so too has consumption become bound up in one's capacity for citizenship in other ways. Hopkins argues that "the new 'power girl' is a role model, a savior and a market niche. Certainly, savvy marketers have recognized and catered to the power of girls and young women as economic agents."[61] The combination of the imagined capacity of young women as economic agents and their desires to be political agents makes for rich marketing material. Making a difference to one's social and political world and making a choice in a shopping mall have become somewhat blurred experiences for young women. The kind of advertising that accompanies products pitched at girls suggests how citizenship power and purchasing have become interchangeable. As journalist Nina Munk has concluded from her analysis of advertising catalogues pitched at young female consumers, "If you want to sell to the girl-power crowd, you have to pretend that they're running things, that they're in charge."[62] Advertisers are thus aware that young women would like to be "running things," and they use the language of political power to sell their products. Munk quotes a U.S. girls' clothing line company which knows that "every 14 year old girl today really believes she can become President" and seeks to tap into this belief through a girlpower message in its advertising.

The purchase of particular products presumes to offer young women the personal qualities to become leaders and creators of social change. Girls' studies scholar Jessica Taft cites an advertisement for Barbie that claims, "You can be a leader, you can be strong, you can be confident. Girls can do it all." Rosalind Gill offers other examples that draw on feminist and girlpower language, such that a gentle, even ironic political act can be accomplished by wearing or using a particular product; for example, a Triumph bras slogan suggests that their product is "the bra for the women's movement." Other campaigns work by associating brands with political positions, so that a young woman must buy something produced by that brand in order to be empowered. Sports sociologist Shelley Lucas analyzes Nike's "If You Let Me Play" commercial, which she argues operates in the mode of a public service announcement so that Nike can stand in for an entire social cause. The advertisement makes the connection between young women playing sports and increased confidence, mental and physical health, and delayed motherhood. It features a number of young women responding to the phrase "if you let me play sports" with a series of statements about good outcomes. However, it is not simply playing sports, but the purchase of Nike merchandise that really gives young women these opportunities. And not surprisingly, given the function of ethnicity in constructing different kinds of young female citizens, in the commercial it is a young Asian-American woman who speaks the line "I will have more self-confidence," a young Black woman who says "I'll be less likely to get pregnant before I want to," and a white girl who says "I'll suffer less depression."[63]

Empowerment and consumption are thus closely linked through the associations made between products for young women and being confident, strong, assertive, a leader, a role model, and in charge. Consumption is a shortcut to power. As Jessica Taft argues, in these ways "girls' power is defined only as a power to buy, rather than a power to create, think and to act. As such, it promotes another barrier to girls' expression of social critique and their political and civic participation." This blending of the political aspects of citizenship with one's ability to consume has particular effects for those young women who are shut out of the consumption process due to lack of money. Being unable to participate in the right kinds of consumption processes means one is "at-risk" of engaging in disordered patterns of consumption, thereby being excluded from occupying powerful social positions. As Chris Griffin argues, "The subject position of the consuming girl is not of equivalent relevance for all girls and young women: it is profoundly shaped by class, ethnicity, sexuality and disability."[64] Power, visibility, and the occupation of public space are achieved through shopping, but shopping depends on disposable income and the cultural capital that enables one to engage successfully in consumer practices. This returns us to the new conditions for social rights: Young women are expected to be responsible for their economic independence in an extremely limited labor market and with no help from the state, and the evidence that they have accomplished this goal is in their consumption patterns. Therefore, those who cannot consume are doubly disengaged from citizenship.

It is interesting to note how the self-made girl, the ambassadress, and the consumer citizen all come together in a construction of ideal youthful femininity bound by discourses of self-invention, entrepreneurship, consumption, and success. Two of the young women cited earlier as examples of ambassadresses have built up considerable financial investments and branched out into products and branding associated with their status as ideal girls. Tatiana Grigorieva's webpage describes her as "conquering the fashion and sport world" and invites viewers to purchase her Teen Girl line of lingerie as well as enter her Teen Girl competition for girls aged thirteen to nineteen "who would love to be a model and [have] the positive qualities embraced by Olympic silver medallist Tatiana Grigorieva." Nikki Webster, the girl of the Sydney Olympics opening ceremony, has become a pop star and also sells a brand of makeup (see figures 3.3 and 3.4). Her webpage explains how she is the "new face" of Jager cosmetics, whose slogan is "Jager, it's a girl thing." Now transformed into a sexualized teen, rather than the child in a pink sundress of the Olympics opening ceremony, Nikki Webster is shown both on the webpage and in her film clips in several outfits with her midriff exposed; that is, displaying the new universal bodily sign of sexy, cute, can-do girl femininity.

It is not simply that good citizenship and success are achieved for these young women by their involvement in marketing consumer products. Rather, they are part of the production of a narrative about young feminine citizenship as a purchasable commodity, as made most real in the act of consumption. Being self-made and motivated, achieving financial success, and representing one's country become bound up in a story about girls' citizenship as product. Makeup, lingerie, sporting goods, fashion, and music are the accessories for citizenship. The "positive qualities" that these role models represent can in fact be purchased. While consumer choice has become an important way for young women to express themselves, it is only a small minority of young women who have the disposable income to become consumer citizens.

Fig. 3.3 Performing Nation: 13-year-old Nikki Webster as "Hero Girl" with Aboriginal dancer Djakapurra Munyarryun at the Opening Ceremony of the Sydney 2000 Olympic Games. Photo courtesy of Getty Images.

Fig. 3.4 From Hero Girl to pop star: Nikki Webster in a publicity shot for her pop song "Strawberry Kisses," released in the year following the Olympic Games. Photography. The Names Agency © 2002 BMG Australia Ltd.

Thus, it is also no real coincidence that the girl ambassadresses and entrepreneurs who are promoted as the ideal self-made citizens tend to have established businesses that sell "girl" products. Cosmetics, handbags, jewelry, cheap giftware, and accessories are the mainstays of the girl entrepreneur industry. This is the kind of merchandise being produced by the young entrepreneurial women who are winning competitions and being promoted in webpages, books, and magazines. Both economic independence and ambassadorial status are best realized in entrepreneurship, and entrepreneurship is best realized in the making and marketing of disposable lifestyle commodities to be purchased by other young women. In this way the new production and consumption dynamic of youth citizenship is being perpetuated by girls. The production aspect is somewhat compromised as a creative process of contribution if it primarily entails the manufacturing of an object for quick consumption and profit. More particularly, if the chief market for these products is other young women, to what extent could it be said that girl entrepreneurs are really breaking into the business world and its markets, and to what extent are they merely being encouraged to exploit their peers? All young women are made complicit in the new citizenship, for even if they lack the abilities to become entrepreneurs, leaders, and ambassadresses, they are still expected to buy. Those who cannot even participate via consumption are deemed at-risk, partly because this reveals their limited hold on social rights, and they are potentially shut out of citizenship altogether.

Conclusion

In this chapter we have seen how social, political, and civil rights have been reconfigured, such that young women are constructed as personally liable for their economic independence, as exemplars of civic responsibility and unthreatening multiculturalism, and most powerfully as consumers in the marketplace. Narratives of personal responsibility, economic success, and "being the best you can be" are drawn into contemporary modes of young citizenship for all youth, but for girls in particular. In these ways young women are imagined and constructed as the ideal new citizens for a changing world. They are representatives of their nations in times of uncertainty, and they lead the way for new modes of civic life that must manage reconfigured interactions between the state, the market, and communities. They are supposed to take personal responsibility for their social rights and manage the work/family nexus without state support in the form of welfare or policy change. Political engagement takes the form of making consumer choices and modeling self-starting leadership. The neoliberal model of youth citizenship thus merges well with a version of can-do girlhood that emphasizes self-invention, personal responsibility, and individual economic empowerment. This new citizenship delegitimizes other forms of enacting rights such as making demands on the state or participating in political protest. Some young women, such as young mothers, "disordered consumers," or antiracist activists, can thereby be split off from the mainstream of good girl citizens. In the next chapter we will see how this process of regulating and separating young women according to their adherence to the principles of new citizenship takes place in specific sites such as schools, workplaces, welfare and justice systems, and shopping malls.

CHAPTER 4

SPACES OF REGULATION
School Halls and Shopping Malls

Young women are imagined as the ideal subjects for the new socioeconomic order. Their success and capacity to prevail are constructed as the mainstream experience, and this success is depicted as a consequence of individual self-invention and good choices. Young women who do not succeed have also attracted attention, but they are perceived as a small minority who face particular personal problems preventing them from joining the mainstream. We have seen many of these narratives about self-making and risk in public policy, programs for youth, the media, research agendas, school curricula, and marketing strategies in relation to young women. As Peter Kelly writes,

> Within transformed practices and spaces of regulation there are moves to normalise youth as rational, choice-making citizens (to-be), who are responsible for their future life chances through the choices they make with regard to school, career, relationships, substance use, etc. At the same time there are increasingly sophisticated attempts to differentiate among youthful populations, via the identification of risky behaviours and dispositions (factors) that place at-risk those practices and capacities of the self which can effect a secure transition to these preferred futures.[1]

In other words, normal, rational youth make good choices to secure their futures, and those who don't make good choices have personal problems that leave them outside the mainstream. The purpose of this chapter is to examine more closely the sites where the production of this split between can-do and at-risk takes place and to begin to understand what implications this has for young women's capacity to tell other stories about their experiences.

I argue here that the scrutiny that girlhood has come under in recent times must be understood in concert with a new regulation of spaces for youth. Specifically, the production of subjectivities organized around success or failure takes place within contexts of surveillance. Young women are expected to occupy differently the new and reconstructed spaces of young people's lives that are made available today. Here I look at several examples, including schools, workplaces, and juvenile justice and welfare systems, as the key spaces where the regulation of the can-do and the at-risk occurs. As Nancy Lesko notes, schools, prisons, and residential treatment centers are the three places youth "may be mandated to attend,"[2] but as I argue, work or the simulacrum of work is fast becoming another such site. I then explore other kinds of spaces traditionally associated with young people's leisure and assembly, such as the street and shopping malls, and consider how these have also become subject to new kinds of regulation and monitoring. The purpose of this investigation is to consider how particular kinds of young womanhood are being contained and produced through these environments, and how young women's expressions of ambivalence, disquiet, and political resistance are made more complicated by the restructuring and appropriation of their spaces.

Youth and Space

The analysis of youth in terms of the spaces they utilize has a long tradition in youth studies. One of the first sociological studies of youth subcultures, William F. Whyte's 1943 *Street Corner Society*, develops an analysis of young male identities and group culture around the meanings of their occupation of this public space. From this time onward, studies of youth subcultures, predominantly male, have focused on the ways the street and other public places are used by youth. During the 1970s ethnographic research became a popular way to understand the meaning of group formations for young men that moved beyond a simplistic assessment of them as delinquent. Ethnographies of youth were devised to examine their own motivations for using public space in ways that were felt to be or constructed as intimidating to the general public. This was accomplished through analyses of various subcultures or "gangs" such as mods and rockers, and skinheads and punks.[3]

More recently, however, the research focus has moved away from these more spectacular groups of young people and toward investigating "everyday" youth and the meanings of public space for them. Researchers have continued to demonstrate, however, that public space is by default adult space, and young people's use of certain places in public is an attempt to mark out some small area they can have for themselves. Adults retain the power to decide where young people can move about and what kinds of activities are appropriate to an environment. As geographers Gill Valentine, Tracey Skelton, and Deborah Chambers argue,

> Studies on teenagers suggest that the space of the street is often the only autonomous space that young people are able to carve out for themselves and that hanging around, and larking about, on the streets, in parks and in shopping malls, is one form of youth resistance (conscious and unconscious) to adult power.[4]

This occupation of public space is contested, however, and young people are frequently subjected to regulation to discourage them from hanging around.

The other major way in which youth studies has been organized around youth spaces is in educational research. Schools are a logical place for youth researchers to go, as they constitute a significant site in the lives of young people. Here, young people are constructed primarily as students, and school culture, curriculum, educational policy, classroom practice, and so on have been the central concerns of much youth research. Some of the most interesting approaches have focused on how subjectivities are produced by schools by way of teaching styles, dress codes, and the enforcement of rules and discipline.[5] These studies show how young people "become somebody," in the words of social psychologist Philip Wexler, as the school environment disciplines them into appropriate gender, cultural, and class positionings. In his book *Learning to Labour* youth scholar Paul Willis demonstrates how these forces shaped the making of working-class "lads" in 1970s Britain. Lesley Johnson explores a process of the making of a modern femininity in the schools of Australia in the 1950s. Similarly, other researchers document the micropolitics of the space of a school in producing young people's subjectivities, through uniforms, playground occupation, classroom conversation, and extracurricular activities.[6] Within this kind of research, schools are understood as both a physical space where young people spend considerable amounts of time, as well as a symbolic space where discourses about how to be a young person can be circulated and taken up.

Apart from the street and the school, the other space where young people have been located and investigated is the home. Curiously, this site has not been the subject of an enormous amount of research, in spite of the time young people actually spend in their homes, but it warrants attention because it has been significant in shifting the research focus from young men to young women. During the 1970s and 1980s feminist researchers mounted a challenge to the male-focused, subcultural model of studies on youth and space by reexamining the private sphere. Angela McRobbie and

Jenny Garber, Mica Nava, and Chris Griffin argued that the home, and in particular the young woman's bedroom, was a much richer source of meaning-making for young feminine subjectivity than the street. Studies of girls' friendships, popular teen magazines, dance, fashion, and music attempted to understand how private spaces operate as sites for the construction of femininity. These studies revealed that while young women were much more restricted to the home than young men, they could use their private spaces to experiment with dominant and alternative ideologies about being a girl. Although they were not as visible in public spaces such as street corners and youth clubs, young women were still negotiating spaces within which they were both regulated and attempting to express themselves.

The street, school, and home remain significant spaces in young people's lives. However, the contemporary meanings of these spaces, the ways in which they are regulated, and the emergence of other youth geographies must be interpreted through the lens of risk society and the new economy. As has been seen in previous chapters, new times are characterized by a sense of danger and uncertainty about the world, and this is expressed in the management of public spaces. At the same time the new economy has required young people to move beyond their designated spaces of the home, street, and school into other sites such as new workplaces, training programs, and new spaces of consumption. In one sense there are now more places where young people are seen. However, while the number of places that young people are able to occupy has expanded, these are also subject to increased regulation.

Contemporary youth policy is largely concerned with placing and accounting for young people in terms of their productivity. As Chris Griffin argues in her book *Representations of Youth*, "The notion that young people's unstructured free time is a breeding ground for 'social problems' and that they need to be taught to use this time in 'constructive' ways lies at the heart of the discourse of education and training."[7] Specifically, they are always expected to be at least "somewhere," that is, if they are not in education they must be in work, and if they are not in work they must be in an unemployment program or training scheme. They are expected to occupy more of these spaces simultaneously than ever before: for example, students in school are part-time workers, and full-time workers are also part-time students. For those who do not find their place in work, study, or training, other new places have developed in which they can be regulated. The defense forces have become invented anew as a respectable place for these youth to be parked. Various punitive and rehabilitative programs, activities, schemes, and facilities for youth have also flourished in recent times. Juvenile justice centers and prisons have expanded rapidly, and specialty schools and programs for "delinquents" or troubled youth have also become acceptable spaces for some young people to be placed.

At the same time that structured spaces for youth appear to be proliferating, albeit sometimes problematically, other less purposeful places are subject to surveillance. The street, recreational areas, and shopping strips and centers have become sites of new kinds of contestation. Formerly free spaces for recreation are increasingly becoming privatized, and youth leisure has become a profitable industry. Spare time is increasingly constructed as a problem, and regimes of classes and programs are implemented in the lives of many youth to keep them occupied with adult-approved activities. With the creation of some new places for youth and the loss of others, new ways of occupying these spaces can also be seen. Not only might young people be under greater surveillance than ever before, but the purpose of this attention is to construct certain kinds of subjects who can be managed into work and training, who are focused on success and productivity in the new economy, and who have little time and no space for unregulated leisure that does not involve consumption. Those who "fail" on this path are also managed into new kinds of regulatory spaces, such as at-risk programs in schools; government workfare, work-for-the-dole, and training schemes; and juvenile detention. In the remainder of this chapter, I examine more closely the spaces of schools, work, detention centers, and leisure to understand how new times have affected the spaces of young people's lives, and young women's lives in particular.

Where the Girls Are

The constructions of femininity around domestic labor, sexual vulnerability, family life, and household management have had direct effects on young women's occupation of space. As McRobbie claims, this has meant that "girls negotiate a different leisure space and different personal spaces from those inhabited by boys."[8] Young women's spaces are primarily located in the home and at school, two places where they are under close supervision from adults. These are the two spheres they are expected to occupy and where they are provided with considerable information about being appropriately gendered, classed, and raced. The presence of young women hanging around on the street has typically signaled sexual availability and invited harassment.[9] "Good girls" have traditionally been confined to the family home until they have established an appropriate heterosexual relationship; only then are they able to make their own homes. Their absence from the youth subcultural research of the 1940s to the 1970s has been attributed to the absence of girls themselves from the public sphere. As Valentine, Skelton, and Chambers explain,

> Girls' leisure was more restricted than that of boys; they were often unable to
> engage in spectacular leisure activities which were dirty, dangerous or hedonis-
> tic, such as motorcycle riding or hanging around the urban streets; girls spent
> more time in the home, supervised by parents.[10]

Young women who were found outside the home tended to be treated as aberrant and deviant. Researchers' attempts to find young women elsewhere, for example in youth clubs, have resulted in frustration. McRobbie reports from her 1977 study of working-class girls in Birmingham, U.K., that they "would have been happy to transform the youth club into a home from home. The main point of tension in the youth club hinged around their unwillingness to participate and the fact that they were expected to do so."[11] Even when researchers found young women in public places or sites more traditionally associated with young men, the girls' reference point for creating a comfortable environment within it remained the family home.

However, as a consequence of the broadly felt impact of feminism combined with the new economy, young women are no longer constrained to the private sphere. Instead, their visibility and sense of entitlement in occupying schools, institutions of higher education, and workplaces have been widely noted, as we saw in chapter 2. Numbers of young women in senior secondary education and in a broader range of professions have increased dramatically since the 1970s. As the explosion of texts about the third wave of feminism suggests, young women expect to be visible in public places.[12] The public presence of young women and the iconography of young womanhood are evident throughout popular culture, as seen in chapter 1. Television shows such as *Sex and the City* reinforce images of young women assertively taking their place in the public "man's world," both as sexual agents and as cultural cartographers of "the city." They are no longer expected to construct their identities exclusively around the home and domestic life. These spheres have themselves become reworked, as more young, professional woman are living alone or in shared households with their peers.[13] Many young women are creating and legitimating new kinds of households around groups of singles and maintaining separate accommodation even when in partnerships.

With the advent of more effective and widely accepted contraception and changes in values about sex and relationships, the presence of young women on the street no longer automatically invites sexual harassment and assumptions of promiscuity. Young women are increasingly likely to spend leisure time in mixed-gender groups, and young people tend to relate to one another as friends rather than purely as potential sexual or romantic partners.[14] Youth leisure and welfare services are today much more attentive to girls' interests beyond the domestic sphere and are expected to deliver non–gender-stereotyped programs which take into account their entitlement to occupy physical space. This is not to suggest, however, that more traditional conceptions of young femininity have disappeared. Rather, a variety of ways of being young and female have become bound up together, such that new spaces can be occupied with old and new meanings attached simultaneously. However, it is young women's cultural and material resources and the differential regulations associated with these that continue to shape their experiences of the occupation of space. Next, I want to examine some of these spaces in order to demonstrate how regulation of success, risk, and failure is a process enacted in specific sites of young women's lives.

School

Schools have always been sites for the production of normative femininity and "appropriate" young women. Some of the first advocates for adolescent girls' more rigorous and institutionalized formal education, such as the founder of adolescent development theory, G. Stanley Hall, developed their cases through the argument that, as girls were by their feminine nature morally weak and sexually corruptible, the need for them to receive guidance was greater. Moreover, such commentators also suggested that girls had an important part to play in the upholding of nations and white races via the good management of families and households. This could be learned most effectively in school. For Indigenous girls the role of school was perhaps most significant, as native promiscuity and immorality were to be overturned by good education, and young Indigenous women were constructed as important facilitators of colonization and assimilation. Historians Kuni Jenkins and Kay Morris Matthews write of the New Zealand/Aotearoa experience: "Curriculum documents and Church manuscripts point to the fact that it was Maori girls, rather than Maori boys who were charged with bringing about the transformation of Maori society."[15] Adoption of white, imperial values was achieved through the learning of a feminine ideal characterized by Christian notions of family, morality, and nation. Nancy Lesko notes that turn-of-the-century schooling of girls in the United States and the United Kingdom focused on the need to "safeguard their purity and docility and prepare them for useful roles as wife and mother."[16] Domestic science became central to the curriculum, and extracurricular programs such as the Girl Guides flourished with the same messages about girls' domestic strengths and responsibilities. These narratives about young women's roles were constructed around notions of being a good, nation-building, and nation-defending citizen.

Consequently, young women's sense of agency and civic efficacy was inherently tied to a feminine, family-focused, heterosexual identity. In *The Modern Girl* Lesley Johnson demonstrates how this process was also enacted in the mid-twentieth century, again through the domestic science focus of the school curriculum. The classroom, as well as the school itself, became a physical space within which femininity could be marked out and literally taught to students. She says,

> Through the rituals and practices of domestic education, the secondary school of the 1950s and 1960s was involved in mapping a particular terrain as the feminine. . . . The secondary school had become a space . . . designed to produce a set of attributes in certain sections of the population as defining and necessary to the feminine.[17]

Once again, the successful female school student was one who learned household and homemaking skills as well as cooking, health, deportment, and self-presentation. The production of normative femininity was concomitant with the production of the good female student as well as that of the modern citizen. The concept of housewifery as a career was widely promulgated, such that schools effectively taught young women that to accomplish this job well was to achieve the heights of success as a modern girl in the modern world.

Since this era the curriculum has of course opened up considerably for girls. Domestic science, needlework, home economics, typing, and deportment, if they still exist, are "scientized" or degendered as generic life skills that are taught alongside accounting, computing, and woodworking to both boys and girls. Girls are now to be found in, and often actively encouraged toward, math, science, technical subjects, and other more diverse academic pathways than ever before. However, the space of schools is still designed to produce and regulate notions of appropriate young womanhood. What is different today is that the terms of this construct have changed. As we have already seen in previous chapters, successful young women are defined by academic and material accomplishment, early planning and commitment to good career outcomes, flexibility, resilience, multiple skills, independence, and self-sufficiency. Schools have a significant part to play as spaces in which this kind of subjectivity is produced, both in a focus on the relentless pursuit of self-made success, and in the splitting off and management of failure and risk as individual weakness to be rehabilitated or punished.

Schools are now one of the primary sites where young women experience regulation and surveillance, no longer simply to produce good wives and mothers, but to set them on a pathway to particular kinds of training and work. Just as at the turn of the twentieth century and again in the 1950s, a new future girl is currently being developed within the site of the contemporary school through narratives and practices of being a success-ful student and young woman, as well as a flexible and individualized adult and citizen. Here I will look at two examples of the ways in which this oc-curs: first, in the differential production of girls' success by elite and other schools, and second, in the management of girls' failure by programs for at-risk youth. In both cases, it is clear that the new presence of large num-bers of young women in the site of the school is not simply a fact to be cel-ebrated, but an opportunity for understanding how the new places of young women's lives, such as the senior classrooms of secondary schools, are disciplinary in nature.

Producing Girls' Success in the Classroom

As the literature on girls' educational achievements suggests, many educa-tional policies and schools themselves now focus to an unprecedented ex-tent on maximizing young women's academic opportunities. This is a key objective for high-tuition schools, especially elite institutions that may cater almost exclusively to the daughters of the wealthy. Education theorist Jane Kenway's research into such a school in Australia demonstrates the mechanisms by which success is produced and demanded within this con-text. She suggests that what is striking from first glimpse at the school ethos is the way in which the domestic sphere and women's domestic labor are derided and how pathways that prioritize family, relationships, and households are considered a terrible waste. In this sense the kind of suc-cessful young woman being crafted by contemporary school environments is almost the opposite of the early-twentieth-century and the 1950s girls. Kenway argues that the students are required to adopt "the individualistic, competitive value system of the world of careers," to work toward nothing but high-status jobs, and to imagine themselves as independent women within this world of work, all of which require a renunciation of the do-mestic sphere. She argues that "high academic achievement, preparation for prestigious tertiary study and a meritorious career combine as one of the main messages from the school. . . . Choice, meritocracy and invest-ment, financial debt and waste are the central motifs in this discourse."[18]

This discourse is practiced within the school system in a variety of ways. Some key mechanisms include career nights and motivational speeches by successful alumnae and other professionals, career counseling away from anything but the most prestigious professions, stigmatization of not grad-uating, constant intelligence testing, and the promotion of the belief that the ability of the student body as a whole is higher than average. Staff, par-ents, and students are all called upon to share in the project of creating suc-cess and casting out failure into a mythical otherness represented by public (government-funded) schools, working-class youth, manual labor, drug use, sexual promiscuity, and wasted lives.[19] Kenway observes that the students' conversations about school expectations of them are peppered with words such as "perfect," "right," "correct," and "successful."

This research was conducted at a time when the academic success of young women was first being prioritized. Since then there has been a redoubling of effort on the part of these prestigious schools to keep young women on the success track. In particular, schools like these now construct excellence as simply taken for granted, and they produce thereby a normative femininity based on outstanding performance that is refigured as unremarkable. As Walkerdine, Lucey, and Melody suggest, "It is difficult to overstate the way in which very high academic performance is routinely understood as ordinary and simply the level that is expected."[20] Intellectual superiority is figured as a base measure, an inherent characteristic of the student body. This has particular implications for the vast majority of young women who do not succeed in these ways; their "inadequate" performance is what is perceived as exceptional and out of the ordinary. The site of the elite school is thus important in the production of a new young womanhood around taken-for-granted excellence and forward planning for brilliant careers.

Success can be borne out in different ways, however, in order to engage nonprivileged young women who are still subject to a can-do story about academic achievement. This is particularly so in the case of good but nonelite schools, such as those exemplified in education theorist Valerie Hey's research on U.K. "beacon schools." Hey notes that the success trajectory is crafted slightly differently for young women in schools that are well regarded but not in the elite category. She differentiates between what she describes as the "star girls" of the elite schools, and the "beacon femininity" that is produced by these less-privileged institutions. She suggests that the latter place an emphasis on effort and striving to do one's best, which positions students as working hard to do well, but not necessarily in the context of innate ability or competition against others. She says,

> The "beacon femininity" . . . is on the surface a more capacious subject position from "star girls" largely because here the competitive individualism is mediated through notions of "effort" which presumably is a moral rather than intellectual quality. This is likely to offer more space for more girls than could be accommodated in a pure "elitist"-class homogenous school. . . . It did not matter what ability one had, the *duty* of the girls was to "do the best you could against your own standard."[21]

Success is still therefore dependent on personal effort, but it is the striving rather than the outcome of this effort that is important. As Hey notes, this enables a modesty and a connection to family and community not possible in the individualistic discourses of competing against others and claiming an inherent cleverness. The young women in her research, many of whom were migrants and working class, were able to relate their own efforts to their parents', and especially their mothers', resilience and hard work in the face of personal and material hardships. In this way striving for success did not involve casting off one's family or moving away from a familiar world. The atomized, competitive individual is a schoolgirl subject position much more readily taken up by white, middle-class young women.[22] For those whose cultural, racial, and class affiliations create more possibilities for community and responsibility to and respect for others, competitive individualism may be a contradictory and painful lesson. Schools such as those in Hey's example may provide more young women with more meaningful narratives of success, but as she notes, "Beacon schoolgirls are well aware that there is winning and winning and whilst all might aim for prizes, A stars are after all A stars."

Mainstream academic success and high achievement are bound up with aspirations for and ideals of a middle-class status that is fundamentally associated with whiteness. Consequently, the performance and recognition of a successful schoolgirl identity for those outside this category involves what Signithia Fordham terms "acting white." Her study of high-achieving African-American young women demonstrates that considerable renunciation of culture, race, and class identity is required for these students to position themselves in the success discourse. Schools researcher Ralph Folds elaborates the role of school in "white culture training" in the context of rural Australian Indigenous communities. He argues that schools provide a fantasy to young women about possibilities for success in urban white Australia without valuing their own skills and resources or properly educating them for an environment that values others. He says, regarding the young Pitjanjatjara women in his research, "Despite their best efforts at school, [they had] their hopes . . . dashed. School had not equipped them with the academic skills to pursue further training and the lifestyle they had been encouraged to embrace was now out of reach."[23] At the same time these young women lost connections to their communities and cultures, as school necessitated a rejection of tradition with the false promise of a ticket to a glamorous white lifestyle.

In the Australian Indigenous context at least, "white culture training" is frequently bound up with inculcation into white, "respectable" feminine heterosexuality and bodily display. Schools are often charged with the implicit responsibility of making Aboriginal young women chaste, feminine, and appropriately engaged with the dominant culture. For example, educationalists Sally Ashton-Hay and Penny McKay discuss the successes of young women from traditional Aboriginal communities in remote far north Australia attending an urban Christian school in this way:

> Many teachers . . . remembered their first arrival. They had been extremely soft-spoken and barely able to make eye contact with anyone. Their heads were hanging down low. This was a very different picture from the two confident young ladies who arrived at their senior formal in a limousine and looked like princesses with coiffed hair, gowns and high-heeled gold sandals.[24]

This debutante-style narrative and the material practices associated with it have been used to regulate young Indigenous women since colonization. For these young Yolgnu women, being a successful schoolgirl is not merely, or even primarily, about academic accomplishment, but about becoming a modern, Western "young lady." Without discounting the obvious pleasures of dressing up and performing glamor for many young people, particular meaning must be made of the role of the school in effecting this kind of transformation on some students more than others. The mission to make Indigenous young women "respectable" through white (feminine) culture training suggests that schools hold up the adoption of white middle-class values as one of their measures of success. For Indigenous young women, success is achieved by becoming respectable rather than by gaining an enriching educational experience.

Finally, success is maintained as white by the construction of many young women as inappropriately aspirational. In her book *Young, Female and Black*, education scholar Heidi Safia Mirza argues that young Afro-Caribbean British women who are positive about education and who have high career and social-class aspirations are seen within the school environment to be overambitious. In the schools she investigated, Mirza found that their opportunities were significantly curtailed by staff who were keen to scale down their expectations in accordance with racial stereotypes. Similar findings have been established in more recent studies, such as sociologist Nancy Lopez's book *Hopeful Girls, Troubled Boys*, about second-generation Caribbean young people in the United States, and education scholar Katherine Schultz's work with young urban women of color in the United States.[25] Lopez sheds more light on the "acting white" phenomenon. Her research suggests that even when students do not themselves fear losing cultural affiliations if they are academically oriented, the school environment often assumes youth of color are not interested in educational success. The myth of the overly aspirational migrant or urban teen operates to reserve high educational and career goals for those for whom these are "appropriate," namely, members of the dominant culture, and to blame individuals and families for unrealistic expectations when educational choices and career plans are not rewarded with labor market opportunities.[26]

Constructing Failure in At-Risk Programs

Schools also operate as sites for the regulation of those who threaten to disrupt the fiction that high performance and career success is ordinary, normal, and equally available to all. New school spaces now exist for the management of inadequate performance, and in particular, for the explanation of this as a consequence of unfortunate personal circumstances or lack of application. Schools have become important places in this process, for, as seen in chapter 2, whereas once young women who were "non-academic" could leave before graduation and find work, today they are obliged to get qualifications in order to compete for jobs. Consequently, they remain part of the student body, disturbing assumptions about new, high-achieving, career-oriented, can-do girls who eschew the domestic and outperform boys.

Such young women are increasingly represented as at-risk and as requiring intervention programs either to get them onto the success track or to manage their failure in ways that do not disturb the notion that most young women can be successful and that they are an exception. As I have already shown in chapter 1, the concept of the at-risk adolescent has been developed as a way of both understanding and constructing youth who may not succeed. As youth researchers Johanna Wyn and Rob White argue,

> Young people (and their families) are seen as "the problem," the solution to which is to remedy the deficiencies in their attainment and performance. The concept of young people "at risk" defines the nature of the social problem of failure in a particular way. Young people who are "at risk" are those who are or will be unable to use the opportunities that school presents.[27]

Thus, schools have now become important places where these at-risk youth can be dealt with through programs to tackle their needs. In their international comparative report *Programs for At-Risk Youth*, educational researchers Graeme Withers and Margaret Batten describe in detail a range of school-based programs, including their objectives, target groups, and strategies. Typically, these define at-risk youth as vulnerable to low literacy, teen parenthood, drug use/abuse, unemployment, and street frequenting. The programs aim to keep such youth in school, and they offer classes, resources, and support to prevent bad outcomes. Some schools create crisis teams for special response, made up of teachers, administrators, nurses, counselors, psychologists, special educators, parents, and so on who are "trained to identify either students at risk or any school situations which are risks to students and capable of immediate interventions with the students who are in risk situations." Others use incentives such as "edibles, trinkets and money" to keep students in programs, or they rely on dramatic measures such as off-campus retreats and signed contracts to prevent "backsliding into risky behaviours."[28] Robert Stevenson and Jeanne Ellsworth describe these as "carrot and stick" strategies that locate the problem of the at-risk student with his or her character deficiencies.[29] The general purpose of the programs is to improve young people's commitment to school by developing certain social and personal "competencies" that should then lead to educational success.

At-risk programs thus attempt to tackle those circumstances of young people that may prevent them from succeeding by focusing primarily on their behaviors, choices, and attitudes. In this respect success is constructed as something that is achieved through the right personal choices and individual effort. As girls' studies scholar Sumru Erkut and colleagues describe, "An assumed correlation between self-regard, motivation and success has informed most theories and interventions around 'at risk' youth."[30] Young at-risk women who achieve "against the odds" are thus rewarded for their commitment and separated out from their cohort by their willingness to simply try harder. In their introduction to *Urban Girls*, editors Bonnie Leadbeater and Niobe Way argue that "the success stories of urban girls are seen as the exceptional struggles of heroic or resilient individuals."[31] Further, the space of the school that includes an at-risk program creates a framework of constant vigilance and intervention, such that youth are seen to require the surveillance of trained adults to keep them on track. Some programs adopt interventionist styles that may exploit young people who are vulnerable; others openly bribe them with gifts, food, and cash. Schools researchers Jennifer Pastor, Jennifer McCormick, and Michelle Fine suggest that in the case of young, poor women in U.S. schools, "help" that is offered in the at-risk context is often felt as surveillance. They say,

> Many of the girls of colour in our discussion groups live ever ready to question and resist such help, which they experience, rightly or not, as prying, overdetermined conclusions that await them at school, silencing or appropriating their narratives to fit what the state has allocated "for" them.[32]

Young women defined as at-risk either prevail and defy the expectation, or they fail because of personal limitations of character. They are monitored and relegated to a separate space within the school for the supposedly aberrant minority who do not follow the "normal" developmental pathways to success.

Work

The workplace is also significant for the creation and regulation of new modes of young womanhood according to success, risk, effort, and responsibility. Just as many more young women are to be found today in schools, so too are they found increasingly in a variety of workplaces. Of course, great numbers of young women have always worked, but it has only been with the vast changes brought about by the new economic order combined with the successes of feminism since the 1970s that paid work has become central to their identity. In the case of middle-class young women, it has also become pivotal to their hold on material comfort and social status. Today, the desire for and performance of particular kinds of work is critical in the constitution of a successful young woman. The trajectory with most social approval is one whereby a young woman commences part-time work while studying at secondary school, continues to balance this with her movement into post-secondary training, and then moves into full-time work in a well-paid career. Young women are now expected to be at work from a very young age in order to gain experience, get the edge on peers, develop skills, and attain some independent income. From unskilled and low-paid work in fast-food chains to volunteer work in the local community, all work engaged in by school-aged youth is seen as an important career step to demonstrate job-readiness and to fill the résumé.[33] Youth who do not have part-time, after-school work are seen as at a serious disadvantage in the labor market.

The Lifestyle Workplace

The purpose of mapping out a career plan from early youth is to attain a prestigious position in the exciting new world of careers for young women. Bound up in this ideal of the successful worker are ideas of autonomy, freedom, "being what you want to be," glamor, and a consumer lifestyle—in short, a promise of independent and materially secure subjectivity achieved.[34] The new careers that young women are invited into are presented as achievable through hard work and talent. As we have seen, they offer not only high status, but enormous spending power. Hence successful young women workers demonstrate that they have made it through displays of material wealth and lifestyle products. Production is meaningful only insofar as it enables consumption. The proliferation of consumer goods and services relating to home décor, entertaining, leisure, food and drink, vacation travel, lifestyle, and self-improvement suggests the styles through which this display ought to be enacted.

Consequently, employers themselves no longer simply offer jobs, they promise to reward or produce a flexible and glamorous subjectivity. The help-wanted pages of newspapers reveal this construction of new work identities. For example, a multinational corporation advertises in an Australian newspaper for an "Accounts Manager—medical solutions" with a photograph of a blonde, white, and beautiful young woman, casually dressed in a trendy T-shirt. She holds a large coffee cup and gazes off to one side, unsmiling, cool, and self-contained. This advertisement, for what is essentially a sales position, calls for candidates who are "results-oriented, flexible and resilient in nature." It suggests the position would suit someone with a background in nursing, a traditionally feminine career, who is seeking to move into a company and an industry that is more innovative and has greater growth potential. The projected successful applicant is therefore a new kind of young woman, eager to move out of a constraining, old-style female work identity and seeking a career that better expresses her contemporary image.

Workplaces for this kind of employee are represented as fresh, fun, young, sexy, and flexible; in short, they are a lifestyle choice and an expression of identity. The Australian newspaper *The Age* reports on a marketing, public relations, and media company run by a thirty-two year-old whose staff are "young, savvy and successful." It is described as having "an ethos that's very different to the traditional corporate approach. There is no dress code or time clock mentality, but . . . staff enjoy their work and often put in long hours."[35] The successful worker is thus autonomous, self-disciplining, and flexible, and is rewarded accordingly. This is the kind of work that young women are supposed to want and strive for.

At the same time, as we have seen earlier, the full-time youth job market no longer exists, and the broader labor market has been radically restructured and delimited. Becoming a successful worker in this context is a difficult task, one that can only be accomplished effectively by those with other resources in place. In spite of this, success is presented as the mainstream experience. Dwyer and Wyn write, "This heavy promotion of success associated with the mainstream serves the purpose of masking continuing inequalities affecting the education and employment outcomes of young people."[36] Geographers Sophie Bowlby, Sally Lloyd Evans, and Robina Mohammad suggest from their research with young Pakistani Muslim women in the United Kingdom that

> the various social networks through which employers and young people build up conceptions of the "ideal employee" and the "ideal job" circulate racialised and gendered representations of workers and paid work which also interact with images of age and stage in the life course.[37]

Those with considerable social capital have valuable networks to smooth their pathways to ideal jobs. However, the perception that these can be equally accessed, and that the work itself, once secured, enables all young women to self-invent and act independently and successfully, does not account for the significance of these social networks. As argued by Linda Hughes-Bond,

> In terms of answering the autonomy needs of young women, the world of work which awaits them may be deficient. . . . Factors such as gender segregation in the schools and in the workplace may continue to limit women's employment choices and necessitate the selection of jobs in clerical and service fields which may be less than challenging and exciting. . . . The lower wage rates assigned to women's work and the growing dependence on part time work make financial

security elusive. . . . It is arguable, then, that the quest of young women for personal autonomy faces serious challenges in the workplace.[38]

In spite of this, the "lifestyle workplace" sell is evident in prestigious schools, the media, and neoliberal discourses that draw on feminism to demonstrate how gendered barriers to equal participation in the best careers have been removed. Young women's career aspirations are correspondingly high, and yet, as was shown in chapter 2, these must be dramatically scaled down once the realities of the limited labor market are confronted.

Training Schemes

Alongside this imagined site of the glamorous workplace, spaces have also emerged to manage young women who are not making it in the new world of work, especially those who are at-risk of never getting started. Youth training schemes and workfare programs provide young women with a place to be occupied in the absence of work. Being unemployed is a status often hidden behind such programs, which fill the space where work should be and redefine unemployed youth as "trainees" and other euphemisms. Feeder courses for training schemes construct holding spaces outside schools where low-achieving students can be siphoned off away from the successful. Heidi Safia Mirza discusses a somewhat ironically titled course, "Looking Forward," which she characterizes as a means of "mopping up the unemployable." She says this "was objectively a way of 'containing' difficult girls who missed their ordinary lessons by being sent off the school site for their practical activities." These activities consisted of visits to department stores to enable students, in the words of the course information materials, "to learn more about work and leisure."[39]

Although training schemes and other similar programs are represented as short-term, effective strategies to reintegrate youth into the working mainstream, their real results are considerably less impressive. As Dwyer and Wyn argue, "A large array of international evidence . . . demonstrates that training programmes do not by themselves create jobs and that improving the 'skill factor' in the unemployed has only a marginal impact on unemployment numbers."[40] This is known on some level by many young people who are obliged to participate in such courses. Youth researcher Jennifer Angwin's Australian study of youth in a job and course preparation program reveals considerable disillusionment among the participants. One young woman, "Lynne," states, "I wanted a job. I thought when I left the [course] that it would be easy. But there 'are no jobs.' That's why I had to do another course."[41] Similarly, in *The Unknown City* Michelle Fine and Lois Weis document the stories of young, impoverished, African-American women who are both committed to acquiring more training and disillusioned about the employment outcomes these courses promise but do not deliver. The young women posit the idea that training schemes are diversionary tactics rather than real solutions, and they express frustration at their increasing debt—generated by student loans—and diminishing job prospects. What these programs do achieve, however, is the construction of a holding space for youth who are marginalized by the labor market, and they contribute to a powerful discourse of personal responsibility for joining the ranks of the successful.

Young people who participate in such schemes are encouraged to take responsibility for their lack of employment and training and to see their opportunities for joining the imagined mainstream of successful young workers as simply a matter of personal choice and commitment. This discourse of personal responsibility has been taken up by young women in particular, who are obliged to come up with some compelling explanation for their lack of success in a girlpowered world that is supposed to benefit them like never before. Education researchers Peter Rudd and Karen Evans's U.K. study finds greater optimism about job prospects among female vocational training course participants, along with a strong belief in the importance of individual effort. They say, "There were strong suggestions that these students generally believed in the idea of a 'meritocracy' and that if you 'failed' . . . then this was probably your own fault and down to a lack of effort and determination."[42]

Ironically, it may be those young women most committed to these ideologies who are most frequently failed by them. Policy analysts Marieka Klawitter, Robert D. Plotnick, and Mark Evan Edwards report from their U.S. study of determinants of entry onto welfare by young women that "contrary to expectation . . . greater commitment to work is associated with increased rates of welfare use."[43] Unfortunately, a "commitment to work" may not be enough to actually gain work in a radically restructured economy. Similarly, youth researcher Pat Allatt refers to a U.K. study of young women on a housing estate "characterised by indicators associated with an alleged underclass and the reproduction of a dependency culture [who] 'saw their preferred futures in work and in steady relationships and not in terms of welfare dependency and lone parenthood.'"[44] This strong preference is encouraged as possible so long as one tries hard enough, in spite of the real structural limitations in place.

Economic rationalist reforms of welfare for the unemployed emphasize personal effort, especially for youth, by requiring hard evidence of a commitment to work. For example, welfare provisions for unemployed youth in Australia are often conditional on the recipient's production of a "dole diary," in which they record their daily job-seeking activities and prove they have fulfilled the quota of approved activities. The intimacy of the diary, in contrast with the public provision of welfare, is used to insert regulation into the personal space of the unemployed, and it forces them to become agents of the state, surveilling themselves. As youth researcher Jan Edwards notes, this ensures the personalization of responsibility and requires individuals to "act on themselves." Welfare has become a payment earned through the display of certain moral and personal characteristics, particularly the proof of effort and acceptance of responsibilty, rather than a system of support to assist the young person in securing satisfactory work.[45]

In the examples of schools and work, two pieces of ideological work go on in relation to young women's success. First, a false image is maintained of a large mainstream of young women who do well in secondary and tertiary education and who go on to find successful professional careers. Second, the sites themselves work on producing a kind of young feminine subjectivity around flexibility, individualization, self-invention, and achievement orientation, such that young women themselves are encouraged to believe that the only barriers to their success would be a lack of self-esteem or effort. Self-regulation and personal responsibility are emphasized in this representation of making it. We have seen already how, sitting alongside excellence-producing classrooms and flexible, high-achievement-oriented workplaces, there are other spaces that operate as catchalls for the excess—those young women who are not successful subjects. Programs for the at-risk and work-for-the-dole or workfare schemes become spaces where large numbers of young women are managed into positions of aberration and exception, where failures are attributed to personal deficiency, and success is maintained as simply a question of application. In these ways, through these sites, the fiction of a successful mainstream can be sustained.

Detention

Within this context another important space for the management of "failed" young women must be addressed, namely, incarceration. The juvenile justice system operates as another significant site for the surveillance and regulation of young women who are at-risk. Young women's incarceration has risen at an alarming rate throughout the deindustrialized world in recent years. Given that the rollback of welfare always has the greatest effect on impoverished women, it is not surprising that young women shut out of opportunities for self-made success are resorting to illegal means of livelihood and recreation. However, increase in arrests and detention does not necessarily reflect an increase in illegal behavior, but it certainly points to a new vigilance in finding, monitoring, and punishing these activities. A report commissioned by the U.S. Office of Juvenile Justice and Delinquency Prevention has found that, in the United States, arrests of female juveniles have increased dramatically in recent times. Young women are also becoming involved with the justice system at an earlier age, and one in five girls incarcerated is now aged fourteen or younger. Girls are twice as likely as boys to be detained for their offenses, and their detention generally lasts five times longer, even though their offenses are less serious.[46] In the United Kingdom, young women are also far more likely than young men to receive a custodial sentence than community service.[47]

There is considerable debate over why this might be. It has long been observed by feminist criminologists that jails, prisons, and detention and treatment centers are sites where behavior and attitudes that do not fit prescribed modes of femininity are punished and modified.[48] The far higher numbers of young women than men charged on status offenses attest to this. However, within the contemporary context of incarceration and detention, young women's offending has also been constructed as a consequence of personal deficiencies and reluctance to take responsibility. As Wyn and White note, juvenile justice models have shifted from welfare to law enforcement, with a focus on the choices and responsibilities of the offender.[49] Prominent examples of this are "three strikes" laws, mandatory sentencing, and zero tolerance legislation. Deviation from traditional feminine behaviors is still punished, but alongside this is the regulation of deviation from contemporary femininity, which is characterized by personal responsibility for good choices. What criminologist Kerry Carrington describes as "individualised intervention schemes" have become common ways to manage the problem of offending young women. She describes these as working through "deficit discourses" which "locate the source of the pathology in a defective individual or dysfunctional family, thus providing the rationale or administrative logic for punitive juvenile justice or child welfare intervention which works through the punishment of the child."[50] The at-risk narrative is taken up here to justify high levels of regulation and intervention in young women's lives, because this will lead to greater responsibility on the part of the individual and family. In this way personal failings can be focused on as the major source of the deviant behavior, and personal effort becomes its solution.

Even while policy has shifted from welfare to justice, some young women are punished more than others. We have already seen that young mothers who are poor, especially if they are not white, are the targets of highly interventionist and punitive mechanisms within criminal justice systems.[51] Criminologist Jody Miller's analysis of probation decision making in relation to "delinquent girls" in the United States reflects the deeply racialized ways in which these constructions of young women are made.

Her research illustrates how paternalistic language is used to discuss white and Latina young women, whereas African-American young women are described much more punitively. She concludes that middle-class African-American young women are more likely to be placed in detention, and poor, white young women more likely to be placed in treatment.[52] In the U.S. juvenile justice system at least, race frequently overrides class as a stratification device, such that unlike white girls, African-American and Latina girls are suspended at almost the same rates as their male counterparts. It is well documented that the number of young women of color in contact with police and juvenile justice, including African-American, Latina, and Indigenous young women, constitutes massive overrepresentation.[53] This contact is far more likely to lead to some form of custody or detention. As criminologist Christine Alder notes,

> Youth institutions have not been places where girls of privilege are frequently found. . . . For privileged girls there have always been alternatives, "finishing schools" in Switzerland, European excursions to get them out of parents' hair, kith and kin who are willing and able to offer alternative accommodation, and in more recent times, private medical establishments in which to place them.[54]

As has been seen in chapter 1, privileged young women who are at-risk are much more likely to be managed privately and outside the punitive gaze of the law. The juvenile justice system serves to keep some young women's experiences, difficulties, and bodies out of view—specifically, the poor and nonwhite. This is not simply an issue of race and class politics, but of economic rationalist logic. Put starkly, the privatization of such public services as the incarceration system has made good economic sense out of increased detention. María Elena Torre and her colleagues demonstrate as much in explaining how their research about women in prison was received by the New York State Legislature at a hearing on criminal justice reform. The legislator hearing their testimony agreed that the objective of incarceration was "to warehouse Black and Brown bodies in State facilities," and added himself,

> In New York State, Downstate's crime is Upstate's economy. With all of the building of prisons in our state, the economy of the Northern part of New York State has been rebuilt on the backs of minor criminal behaviour in the City.[55]

Increasingly, it is poor young women who are providing those "Black and Brown bodies" that generate such attractive profits for the prison industrial complex.[56]

The stepping up of the regulation of "failed" young women must be interpreted against the backdrop of economic restructuring. This is instrumental both in providing a profit motive for detention, and putting the blame for diminished opportunities for livelihood onto young women themselves. Since the 1980s there has been considerable panic over the imagined nexus between youth unemployment, free time, and delinquency.[57] The structural problems of reduced labor market opportunities are refigured as the personal problems of deviant youth. The criminalization of young people who are without work has taken a particular turn in relation to young women, for they are perceived as those most able to prevail in the new economy, and those young women who do not succeed disrupt this perception considerably. The increased interest in managing unruly young women through detention must also be understood as a mode of regulating groups of youth who may turn their disaffection into political action. It is a way of punishing and individualizing some young women for their lack of success in the new economy and—importantly—of keeping them "far from our view."[58] Christine Alder reports that

> both Australian and US research indicates that when young women in the juvenile justice system are asked about their most pressing needs, they will talk about their desperate need to find economic means of independent survival, including jobs, housing and medical services.[59]

And as Dorothy Bottrell argues, it is a simple but powerful truth that labor market marginalization and offending correlate for young women.[60] The widespread struggle of many young women to survive in the new economy where the welfare state has been profoundly scaled back can be concealed through the construction of their circumstances as aberrant and personal, and their responses to these circumstances as criminal and pathological.

Leisure

Traditionally, spaces of youth leisure have been "those sites in which young people . . . are outside adult . . . supervision [and] lie beyond the confines of the schoolroom and the (waged) workplace."[61] Sites of leisure have typically been places where youth can express themselves outside of surveillance. As we have already seen, the classroom and the workplace have become even more significant as places where young women are managed into a new female subjectivity of self-disciplining, individualized success. Training programs and the juvenile justice system also operate alongside these spaces to regulate and individualize failure and to remove the failed from view. Consequently, leisure sites have in some respects become the last line of defense in the preservation of surveillance-free space for youth. However, recently even these have become bound up in both the supervision of young people and the production of disciplined young subjects. The effects of unemployment and reduced welfare provisions are felt and seen in the physical environments of cities and communities. Many of the sites where the scars are most visible are places where youth are also to be found—run-down housing projects, empty streets, closed storefronts covered with graffiti, abandoned playgrounds, and parks vandalized and used for drug deals. Youth themselves come to be perceived as the cause of this social and urban decay.

If it is young people who are constructed as the source of fears and anxieties about these changes, it is also they who must be policed and regulated accordingly. This process has occurred in a variety of ways. First, recent times have seen a shift in public rhetoric as well as public opinion about the safety of the streets. The streets, and particularly young people's apparent occupation of them, have become a target for a range of anxieties and fears about social and economic change. As Wyn and White argue, "The visibility and presence of young people in the public domains of the streets, shopping centers and malls, particularly the more marginalized, non-consuming individuals, has been met by concerted attempts to exclude or regulate them."[62] Youth and their supposed capacity to disrupt social order on the streets have become the focus for debate and policy. As youth researcher Karen Malone suggests, "Adults' fear of youth, constructed through media hype, stereotyping and moral panic, has diverted attention from the source of the unsafe situation and allowed young people to be the easy scapegoat."[63] Thus young people's, especially young women's, apparently increasingly delinquent behavior is seen as one of the main reasons why the streets are no longer safe. Concerns about gangs, drugs, random violence, property offenses, and public disorder have justified punitive measures to control young people's use of public places. Youth curfews have been introduced and taken up with vigor in parts of the United States, Europe, and the United Kingdom.[64] The streets must be kept safe for the community, but this generally excludes youth.

If the streets are being kept safe, this means that young people must be placed elsewhere. As we have already seen, there is now an expectation that youth must go somewhere, and that aimless leisure time is problematic. As sociologist Sara McNamee notes, "Youth culture is now more often taking place in supervised and protected spaces."[66] Regimented activities for young people to participate in after school have become normal and desired, such that their days are both filled and regulated throughout. In some extreme cases video cameras exist in after-school care venues and in both public and private places in schools (such as toilets) so that adult authorities can check up on young people's activities. Cell phones are often issued by parents so that young people, and in particular young women, can be contacted at any time.[66]

A cohort of young people with time on their hands is seen as a problem that must be handled by the appropriate authorities rather than an opportunity for them to creatively do as they please. Ethnomusicologist Kyra D.

Gaunt offers a pertinent example of this in her analysis of the policing in the United States of double-Dutch, a song and rope-skipping activity practiced in the streets primarily by young African-American women. The involvement of the police in moving double-Dutch off the streets and into a formal and rule-bound competition that could be monitored by authorities resulted from a concern with inner-city youth idleness and young women's self-expression and sexuality. Gaunt says,

> The rules of the "Double-Dutch Cops" ended up policing the bodies and movements of girls who once played the game with not only their athletic abilities but accompanied by oral poetry and musical variations. The verbal expressivity of double-Dutch was *arrested* by official rules and adult interests in creating an authentic sport for girls.[67]

A wider range of programs, activities, and centers has emerged to place young people in authentic and adult-approved sites. Much of this has been welcomed, for example, local councils' efforts to create places like drop-in centers, skate parks, dances, and so on. At the same time, however, there are now no excuses for young people to be in public purposelessly. There has thus been a renewed suspicion and monitoring of youth who do not use these approved facilities, who still prefer to skateboard in public, organize and attend raves, or meet up on the street or in shopping malls. In these sites electronic surveillance technology is used to monitor youth activities. Outside of the structured programs, which are still few and underfunded, there are limited opportunities for youth to freely and safely hang out. Environmental psychologist Cindi Katz argues that this is a consequence of "the decay and outright elimination of public environments for outdoor play and recreation," along with an increase in a vigilant public watchfulness of those few sites left.[68] At the same time, indoor places, where the vast majority of young women still spend their time, are subject to even greater surveillance than before.[69]

Within this context of fewer accessible public spaces and a greater emphasis on surveillance and regulation of youth leisure activities within adult-managed programs and environments, a self-disciplining youthful subject is produced. Young people learn in an environment of constant but often unknowable surveillance to self-regulate. As Karen Malone suggests, "Young people, such as Foucault's imaginary inmates of the panopticon, do not know when they are under surveillance; they may or may not be being watched: in response, they police themselves."[70] In doing so, they draw on sophisticated knowledge, or what environmental psychologist Caitlin Cahill describes as "street literacy," which involves taking personal responsibility for knowing the spaces they occupy, combined with a somewhat cynical opinion of representatives of public order. Self-regulation is especially required when young people are both blamed for creating danger and held responsible for avoiding it. They must ensure they are not perceived as causing trouble, and at the same time, they must take measures to keep themselves safe from the threat posed by overly vigilant agents of surveillance as well as realistically assess any dangers in public places.

Commercializing Public Space

It has been well documented that young people are not considered to be citizens within their communities with equal rights to the public domain. However, what is also becoming apparent is that the public domain is itself a contested site, and with privatization much of it has been rezoned as commercial. Consequently, for youth to rightfully enter into these spaces they must demonstrate their viability as consumers. Social policy analysts Phillip Mizen, Angela Bolton, and Christopher Pole argue that

> where there were once municipal recreation grounds, youth clubs, community discos, free or below cost sport and extra-curricular activities, as well as subsidised transport to get there in the first place, there now exist private leisure centres, bowling allies, multi-screen cinema complexes, clubs and theme pubs, accessed by privatised bus companies or taxis. The point to underline is that children's leisure is increasingly constituted according to the dictates of the market, whose only entry requirement is the possession of money.[71]

This is where the presence of young women in public has become central to attempts to construct and manage all youth as new kinds of subjects, and, particularly, new kinds of citizens. Young women are imagined and produced as ideal consumers, as seen in chapter 3, and the enactment of this subject position gives some of them access to leisure spaces that were previously free, public, and open to more equal contestation by youth as well as other parties. With the privatization of the public sphere, including streets, sports facilities, open land, and leisure facilities, young people can only make a claim insofar as they are able to buy or consume in these places. Young women are imagined as well positioned to do this, given their apparent increased disposable income, interest in consumer goods and lifestyles, and desire to stake a claim in the public sphere. However, at a time when young women are finally able to access this sphere for leisure purposes, there is in fact very little public space left. Consequently, the capacity for young women to now be in public space is contingent on taking up a position as a consumer citizen. Thus, a certain kind of female subjectivity is produced through new leisure spaces. Nowhere is this more evident than in the shopping mall.

In the absence of other kinds of public leisure places, and with the replacement of strip shopping and local neighborhood shops with centralized megamarts and the construction of shopping as central to youth identity and leisure, shopping malls have become one of the main places for youth to hang out. Malls actively invite youth to spend time there, as they generally offer multiplex cinemas, youth-oriented brands and products in the shops, entertainment centers (such as video arcades, bowling, and pool/snooker venues), Internet facilities, cafes, and fast-food outlets with youth appeal, and sometimes services such as employment agencies. They are usually open long hours and provide a range of entertainment options and services. Shopping malls, and the stores within them, offer particular leisure possibilities for young women. Cultural theorist Hillevi Ganetz suggests that

> the department store is still a safe as well as an exciting place for women: it is safe because unlike the street it is supervised and guarded, and it is exciting because it remains a public place to which everyone has access and in which unforeseen encounters can occur.[72]

Young women are more likely to gain parental permission to go to a mall than to just hang out, and they tend to feel safer in shopping areas than on the street.[73] They are able to socialize with friends without having a particular activity scheduled, and the environment creates the possibility of meeting new people and expanding their milieu. A good number of young women also actually work in service and retail at these shopping centers.

Clearly, shopping malls function as far more than merely places to buy products. In fact, in research cited by Ganetz and elsewhere, it is commonly found that young women may not actually make purchases when at a mall, or if they do, these tend to be inexpensive. Young people, like the public at large, use shopping centers for reasons beyond consumption. As Steven Miles suggests, "Malls play the role of harbingers of pseudo-communities, providing a means or a focus by which young people are integrated into subsequent life trajectories."[74] Shopping centers thus stand in for public leisure spaces for young people. However, to participate in this space, they must enter into an implicit contract with the center to be a consumer. In this way the civic activities of participating in community life, claiming space in the neighborhood, conducting local business, and socializing are replaced by consumer practices. The only ways that young women can effectively exercise their civic entitlements to leisure and enjoyment of their communities is by shopping.

Shopping centers themselves are owned by large private corporations, and their purpose is to make a profit. Anna Booth, of the Shopping Centre Council of Australia, quotes the U.S. Urban Land Institute as saying, "The shopping centre has been perhaps the most successful land use, real estate and retail business concept of the 20th century. It has become the most powerful and adaptable machine for consumption that the world has ever seen."[75] Unsurprisingly, it is young women who are able to use the shopping center for consumption as well as social purposes who are rewarded for their participation in this public yet private space. Wallace and Kovatcheva note that "it is students, mostly middle class, who emerge as the most leisure-rich consumer group."[76] Thus a particular kind of young woman—a student who works part time and has disposable income—is most rewarded by the shopping center. However, many other young women also seek to use the shopping center in place of the more traditional civic spaces in order to congregate and socialize.

The ambiguity of the space, "having a dual status as privately owned public space,"[77] contributes to confusion about its social role. On the one hand, these are private, profit-making businesses; on the other, as one Australian magistrate has found, "Shopping centres are placed in areas that service large residential suburbs and often are the only places available to young people to shop, meet, be entertained and carry out everyday business."[78] It is the young people who use the centers for these other purposes, and are seen as simply hanging around and not shopping, who are closely policed by the private security within these spaces. It is not uncommon for youth to be banned from a shopping center at the discretion of the management and private security guards. Chris Grant, of New South Wales Legal Aid, Australia, cites banning that has occurred on the dubious grounds of "obstructing traffic flow" and "suspicious behaviour." When the ban is breached, the young person can be charged with trespass—a not-infrequent occurrence. Racist regulation of young women in shopping centers is evident and is arguably even more of a concern than racist policing, as there exists little public accountability for private security services.[79]

The restructuring and regulation of leisure spaces has seen the production of a young female subject who is ideally self-policing and consumption-oriented. Civic rights such as participation, access, and free enjoyment of public space have been reconfigured as consumer rights. Young women avoid surveillance in youth leisure spaces by effectively regulating themselves or only negotiating public spaces where they can be easily integrated as consumers. Those who persist in taking up space are policed and punished, especially those who are not white and middle class.

Conclusion

This chapter has explored some of the most significant spaces in the lives of young women. I have suggested that the spaces where young women are expected to be have changed. Although they occupy more spaces than ever before, these sites are increasingly under regulation. At the same time, free spaces have become more circumscribed. It is commonly understood that they must be somewhere, and that this somewhere is under the surveillance of authorities. Schools, workplaces, detention centers, and leisure facilities are all sites where young people, and young women in particular, are regulated into individualized competitors, responsible choice-makers, flexible and glamorous workers, and consumer citizens. Those who do not measure up to these standards are constructed as personally liable for their failures. These other young women are processed through the welfare and justice systems, warehoused, and denied access to educational, employment, and recreational opportunities that demand material and social privilege for entry. Consequently, as youth scholar Henry Giroux argues, "The only places that appear available [to them] are unskilled work, highly policed public space, or the brute reality of incarceration."[80] The sites of young women's lives are characterized by surveillance and vigilant attention to construct particular kinds of success as normal and possible for all young women, and by management of and punishment for failure as individual inadequacy. In the next chapter I explore how the reworking of the public/private divide has made this kind of regulation possible. Given that this management of place has serious implications for young women's capacity to express and enact alternative and critical subject positions beyond success and failure, I also examine the issue of girls' participation as sociopolitical actors in the public sphere.

CHAPTER 5

BEING SEEN AND BEING HEARD
The Incitement to Discourse

Schools, workplaces, the juvenile justice and welfare systems, and the shopping mall are all environments where success and failure are aligned with personal choices, individual responsibility, and self-regulation. In this chapter I want to take this issue of the government of young women's spaces further by considering the intersection between young women's private selves and the public sphere. Specifically, I address the issue of the current reshaping of the public/private division and its impact on young women. I examine the insertion of regulation into young women's private lives and the incitement to display their interior selves for public scrutiny. I shape this discussion around two themes: first, the regulation of interiority through the culture of display and confession, and second, the new emphasis on youth participation in political life. Both of these trends indicate a preoccupation with encouraging young women to express themselves personally and politically. Both are also part of a broader reworking of the public/private split, in that as the public sphere diminishes, increased regulation occurs in the sphere of interiority. This space becomes a site for the display of young women as successful and responsible citizens. In this chapter I therefore extend the notion of a regulated space to include the space of the interior life—that is, emotions, sexual desire, the private parts of the body, and in particular, the voice of the "true" self.

There is a new understanding that young women ought to make their private selves and "authentic voices" highly visible in public. I begin by exploring the ways young women are encouraged to display their internal world for surveillance by looking at popular culture, mass communications, and the cultural trend toward confessional practices. I then examine how this process is played out in the context of the invitation to political participation as an opportunity to speak one's true self. I argue that at the same time the private world of young women is becoming public, participation is being offered to young people in their private and free spaces, such as leisure sites. Consequently, there are few free or private spaces left for them to keep to themselves; political and civic duties are brought into private space as though this is where they should be enacted, and the realm of the intimate is exposed for public scrutiny. The implications of this refiguring of the public/private split and the incitement to discourse[1] are threefold: First, young women are increasingly exposed to surveillance, and particular models of successful subjectivity are produced and regulated through this scrutiny of young women's interior lives. Second, opportunities for critique are shut down when participation and speaking out are highly managed. Third, the disappearance of a genuine public sphere is concealed when the debate about young women's participation is structured around their personal barriers to civic engagement.

The Regulation of Interiority

As many cultural theorists have noted, image and information have become important ways in which power is deployed in a late modern world.[2] Both time and space are refigured with advances in global communications and information technologies. We are able to know about and connect with far-off places much more quickly, and we are both seeing and being seen by others around the world more frequently. The combination of this new emphasis on the visual and a sense of instant intimacy has made the cultivation of a public image important to young people's identities. This has been borne out in the popularity of interface technologies and the creation of online personas and communities among youth. In particular, the emergence of mass communications, new technologies, and globalized popular cultures has generated an invitation into public visibility for young women. We have already seen how this has translated into new opportunities for traversing physical space, but it carries other meanings that are more about recognition than actual material presence.

Specifically, the attainment of visibility and the ensuing opportunity, as Susan Hopkins suggests, to "live large" is a new measure of success for young women. She says,

> The new hero is a girl in pursuit of media visibility, public recognition and notoriety. She wants to be somebody and "live large." In the postmodern world,

fame has replaced marriage as the imagined means to realising feminine dreams . . . fame is the ultimate girl fantasy.[3]

It is in a world of celebrities, pop stars, supermodels, actresses, and entertainers that young women are encouraged to become somebody. Indeed, it is often these kinds of figures who are supposed to illustrate how young women have made it; they are emblematic of the arrival of the can-do girl in the public world. We have already seen how glamor has been downshifted into everyday life, such that certain kinds of motherhood and work are represented as prestigious lifestyle opportunities. In their book *Choice, Pathways and Transitions Post-16: New Youth, New Economies in the Global City*, education sociologists Stephen J. Ball, Meg Maguire, and Sheila Macrae argue that in the case of work, "Style, fashion and the body are part of ordinary employment and part of a claim to participation in 'cool careers' and fantasies about 'glossy futures.'"[4] "Glossiness" is now a potential element of "ordinariness," such that the regular young person is able to work on him- or herself as a celebrity project and gain some kind of public profile in the process. With determination and effort, visibility and therefore success can be accomplished. Living outside the public gaze is for those who do not try hard enough. Trendy new lifestyle publications and television programs pitched at glossy youth emphasize the importance of working on one's personal image and personal space as though these are always open to view. The interior décor of one's apartment or the food in one's fridge can show how a life worthy of publicity is being achieved.

Visibility and display are both the medium and the message of young women's cultural and leisure products, such as magazines, TV shows, and popular music. The significance of image and packaging has matched and sometimes overtaken the substance of the product in much marketing for girls. Possibilities to also shape oneself into the image of a celebrity are promoted by the various media of the entertainment industries. Reality TV, makeover shows, search programs for supermodels and pop stars and the like indicate how ordinariness can be overcome and a celebrity life attained. The effort that is put into these goals is itself on display through the televised coverage of auditions and the documentation of makeovers. Pop stars such as the Spice Girls and Britney Spears are frequently depicted as "just like other girls," except for their extraordinary determination to succeed. Common features of teen magazines are articles on "how to get that look," which detail the work involved in becoming famous or glamorous, while at the same time suggesting that the steps that must be taken are straightforward and easy.[5] Television and magazine narratives about celebrity, effort, and self-invention make public the processes of transformation from ordinary to superstar. As McRobbie points out, these efforts are no longer to be hidden, but displayed, shared, and enjoyed. She says,

> Everything in magazines like *More!, Sugar, 19,* and *Just Seventeen* has a stagey feel about it. . . . Every individual who appears in the magazine, from the well-known star or celebrity to the unknown reader having a make-over, is, in a more self-conscious way than would have been the case in the past, performing a role, with the act of performance permitting some degree of distance from what it is she or he is doing.[6]

The exposure of the performance suggests that everyone has equal access to these celebrity opportunities and that this work on the self, and not merely its end product, is valued and appropriate for public display. Many social commentators have observed the emergence of a confessional style in popular culture and entertainment, for example in TV talk shows, talk-back radio, and Internet facilities. The personal stories and opinions of ordinary people, especially if they are revelatory, have become entertainment, and at the same time they compete with expert opinion as legitimate sources of information about the world. This confessional style has become a particularly common mode of engaging young women in popular culture, for example, in teen magazines that call for embarrassing stories, in reality TV shows that require deceit and then confession, and in makeovers that invite the display of the original, imperfect self. The culture of confession demands the exposure of interiority, and it transforms intimate details and experiences into material for popular consumption.

"Living large" is made to seem accessible and important to contemporary feminine success for young women, and the heights of feminine achievement are reached in becoming a version of what McRobbie calls the "TV blonde."[7] In other words, wealth, power, and a public life of glamor are blended in the project of inventing oneself through determined, competitive effort. At the same time, however, the notion of a public life is itself being refigured. Specifically, it is the exposure of the private sphere and the private self that is a new feature of the contemporary entertainment and culture industries. Traditionally, there has been entertainment value in exposing the private lives of public figures; today, however, it is the creation of a public life for a private citizen that draws audiences and consumers. TV surveillance and reality shows such as *Big Brother* and its spinoffs, for example *The Bachelor, Temptation Island,* and *The Villa,* open up the private sexual world for public scrutiny, and in the process this kind of programming constructs the ordinary person as a celebrity of sorts. These kinds of shows suggest both that we can all potentially be the stars of TV programs, and that voyeurism is natural, harmless, and acceptable.

However, it is the Internet and the phenomenon of webcams that are perhaps the most controversial examples of how the surveillance of young women's lives is made possible and desirable. Webcams are cameras that record live images or digital still shots that are then displayed on a website. Most personal webcam sites are hosted by young women, and their numbers are growing rapidly.[8] The popularity of websites that offer live streaming video from a young woman's bedroom or entire home is indicative of the immense interest in exposing and observing the private lives of girls. Webcams provide regularly updated images of the space where they are aimed, and "camgirls," those who host such sites, are the protagonists of these home shows, sometimes stripping or performing sexual acts for the camera. The establishment of a webcam is a reasonably lucrative move, in that an income can be drawn from being paid to provide links to pornographic sites, drawing viewer registration fees, selling advertising space, or by inviting viewers to send gifts to the camgirl from a linked wish list. Webcams reinforce the notion that even the ordinary girl can become a celebrity, and that this is a path toward success, independence, and fortune. As Hopkins argues,

> For this rising millennial generation, constant surveillance can be a dream come true—an affirmation of identity. Today, it seems, you're nobody if you're not on camera. . . . Cams make manifest the postmodern desire for omnipresence through communication technologies. If you have a life that is constantly recorded, you are culturally inscribed as important—someone worth watching.[9]

Webcams underscore the rewards for a public display of the private, for exposing one's most personal moments and spaces to an unknown public. In this way omnipresence is only achieved, paradoxically, by being the subject of omnisurveillance.

In less spectacular ways (and for those who lack the technology), the exposure of the young female body can be achieved simply by following fashion trends. As we have already seen, the popularity of clothes such as hip-huggers that reveal the stomach or thongs that show off the buttocks indicates new opportunities to display private parts of the body that have been worked on for public viewing. Even trends in hair removal, for example, the fashion for total or near-total pubic hair waxing, suggest an invitation to young women to expose more and more of the intimate, sexual body.

However, it is not just the body or the private space of the bedroom that is increasingly displayed and regulated by this kind of inversion of public and private spaces. Young women's private thoughts, conversations, and feelings are also cultivated as suitable for public scrutiny. Cell phone culture has had an enormous impact on the traditional public/private division. As social researchers Sheila Henderson, Rebecca Taylor, and Rachel

Thomson write, "The mobile telephone facilitates a reworking of public and private boundaries, as the individual becomes the center of a network of communicative practices, easily accessed and able to access others."[10] Cell phones have increased the public visibility of young women by providing a security device, so that going to unknown areas, associating with new people, and staying out later all become imagined as less dangerous experiences. Young women are the most avid consumers of these phones, and they are generally used to make plans with friends as well as to check in with parents. In the United States, 24 percent of young women own a cell phone, and in the United Kingdom, 71 percent of young women aged fourteen to sixteen have access to one. In Australia, 86 percent of young women aged fourteen to twenty-four own, use, or seriously intend to buy one. The figures from many Nordic and European countries are equally high.[11]

Arguably, young women have won new freedom of movement in exchange for new modes of surveillance. Cell phones construct their users as always available and potentially always overheard by those present when a conversation takes place. Phone conversations are no longer held in the private domain; they can occur anywhere. Although privacy is a key advertising feature of phones with text messaging or SMS (short message service) capability, text messages are often constructed, circulated, and read by a collective, and they are intended and used as public communications for a public audience.[12] Similarly, rather than simply enhancing one's personal space, cell phones can intrude on privacy. Young women report that parents often call or text message several times in a night to check up on them. Social psychologists María Elena Torre and April Burns quote a participant in their cell phone research with young U.S. urban women of color as saying, "What good is your freedom if you have to tell everybody where you are?" Cell phones are experienced as surveillance devices by young women whose parents demand access to them at all times. Cell phones thus ensure that more young women are visible in more places, and that their voices are more frequently heard; at the same time, they are more accessible to those who wish to monitor their movements.

This trend toward a regulation of young women's interiority, whether the private space of their bedrooms, bodies, emotions, or personal conversations, suggests that the normal girl's life is one that is lived large. The normalization of the insertion of the public gaze into the private regulates young women by demanding a constant display of self. Young women become ever-available and ever-monitored. Ironically, this situation is held up as desirable, as the celebrity life is the exemplar of the can-do experience. However, at the same time that all young women are invited into public display, there remains a hierarchy of who is able to be seen where. As the previous chapter indicated, young women are located in different places according to their relationship to social and economic resources.

The public display of the private is aligned with success for can-do girls, but in other ways it is also demanded of those who are categorized as at-risk. Ethnographer Norma Mendoza-Denton discusses the makeover of Latina and African-American "gang girls" on the talk show *Geraldo* as an example of the public display of rectifying "aberrant" young women. Hair-dressers and stylists went to work to replace their big T-shirts, cargo pants, and woolen caps with mini-skirts, high heels, and coiffed curls. Once transformed, they paraded before the audience and the cameras as their new selves. This process served not only to feminize and heterosexualize these young women, but also to mark their original class, gender, and racial performances as problematic yet redeemable. They were required to exhibit their transformation publicly and then to demonstrate ongoing commitment to their new, better selves. Mendoza-Denton writes, "Geraldo bounded up to Linda to ask her whether she would continue to dress like this. 'Um, yeah,' Linda said rather unenthusiastically. 'Maybe.'"[13]

As Walkerdine, Lucey, and Melody suggest, "A huge number of self-help books and television chat shows (from Oprah to Parkinson to Letterman) tell us how to present our selfhood for public scrutiny, mirrored by the work accomplished in the social work office, school, or law court. . . ."[14] That is, alongside information about how to enact a successful, public, celebrity self is institutional regulation of an exposed, failed self. Surveillance of the private sphere is becoming more common as a way of managing young women in the welfare and justice systems. The use of the dole diary already discussed is a particularly pertinent example of this because it demonstrates how the most personal artifact or experience must now be exposed for scrutiny. A diary is typically the documentation of one's most private thoughts and true feelings. The girl culture of lockable diaries and secret journals has a long history. A diary is generally written for the author alone and is not intended to be published or made available to others. The use of devices such as diaries and journals by welfare regimes requires an exposure of the private self to agents of regulation.

Similarly, the use of mechanisms such as tracking devices or offender bracelets for home-based detention is another example of the insertion of the public gaze into the private sphere in the context of criminal justice. Further, confessional culture regulates young offenders by requiring public statements of personal responsibility for their errors and circumstances. For example, a confessional narrative of responsibility and self-blame on the part of young women who are incarcerated or on welfare is increasingly solicited to secure parole, retain custody of children, or gain admission to support programs. María Elena Torre and colleagues describe this as

> a language of redemption, echoing the therapeutic talk characteristic of coun-selling, 12-step programmes, support groups, church and even of discussions about upcoming parole board hearings, wherein narratives of old "bad," "un-worthy," "negative" selves are traded in for narratives of new "positive," "pro-ductive," "good" selves.[15]

Public declarations of responsibility and personal transformation that reveal a deeply intimate working on the self are sought before support is made available. As Jan Edwards argues in the case of economic rationalist, panoptic welfare policy, "It not only observes the subject directly, [and] en-lists others in the observation of the subject, but also requires the subject to examine self and conscience to occupy the preferred subject position." Self-scrutiny and, more importantly, the public performance of self-scrutiny are integral to the personalization of risk and the reinvention of oneself as on the success track.

The interior world of young women is invited out into the public sphere in the service of new kinds of regulation. The culture of display, performance, and confession encourages them to express their private thoughts and de-sires, as well as to exhibit the process of self-improvement. This invitation to expression of the private and the insertion of the public into the interior world takes on another important form in the context of political participa-tion. The private sphere has become an important site for the cultivation of young women for civic and political engagement. A major panic has oc-curred over youth disenchantment with politics, at the same time, ironically, that the public sphere is withering away. Accessing young people's private worlds, especially those of young women, who are particularly targeted in the panic, has become central to regulating youth back into participation. Next, I spend some time exploring the debate about youth participation, especially the notion of youth voice, in order to understand how the reshaping of the private/public division has enabled a regulatory gaze into the undisclosed, and potentially critical, voices of young women. I suggest that it is becoming increasingly difficult for young women to live outside the spotlight and that the debate about participation is in part a way of regulating their critiques into compliant modes of citizenship. The incitement to discourse, which is manifested in an incitement to participate more broadly, demands an expo-sure of interiority that leaves little of young women's lives to themselves.

Youth and Political Voice

The interest in young people's active citizenship that was touched on in chapter 3 will be scrutinized more closely here, as it is at the heart of a struggle over young people's ability to be engaged, to speak out, and to be meaningfully critical in their social worlds. The narrative of endless possibility, combined with the production of narrow notions of success and failure within the key sites of young women's lives, has made other, more complicated discourses more difficult to articulate. Spaces for the expression of complexity and exception are diminishing, while those that do exist are highly managed. At the same time that can-do girls are being celebrated for sassiness and public visibility, what they are able to say is perhaps more limited than ever. In other words, more opportunities for display and expression have resulted in the increased management of young people's participation in the public sphere and in fewer opportunities for their privacy. Their capacity to engage with one another beyond the surveillance of adults has been far reduced. As we saw in the chapter on citizenship, a lively debate about youth civic engagement is underway, and as a result several policy packages and programs have been developed to enhance voice and participation. The purpose of this next section is to locate this debate in the context of the reshaping of the public/private division. The incitement to display and discourse, the invitation to invert the interior, and the insertion of the public regulatory gaze into the private are all features of the participation debate. The effect of these processes is a new regulation of young women's voices and expressions.

The Panic about Youth and Politics

As we began to explore in chapter 3, the issue of young people's apparent lack of civic engagement and political voice has been taken up as a serious problem at the level of government policy and transnational nongovernment programs. These programs reflect dual concerns with young people's lack of interest in formal politics and disconnection from community. Much research suggests a strong perception that young people have turned away from formal participation. This is usually recorded in terms of voter registration, voter turnout, and knowledge about political systems.[16] Young people's interest in current affairs, government policy, and political parties and processes is considered to be at an ebb. The purpose of civics education in schools and a number of other programs and techniques that I will examine shortly is to improve this apparent state of indifference. Of particular concern is the issue of young women's participation, as they have traditionally been perceived as those with the least political confidence.[17] When girls are factored into analyses of young people and politics, which occurs infrequently, they are widely believed to be apolitical and lacking interest in formal procedures, systems, and issues.[18] For example, a recent U.K. survey found young women aged eighteen to thirty-four to be those most likely to declare a lack of interest in politics.[19]

However, disconnection from formal politics is only one of the issues raised by those who worry over diminishing youth participation. Also widespread is a concern that young people are no longer engaged in organized social critique and that in this other significant way, they are failing to speak out in the public sphere. Beginning with the social movements of the twentieth century, it has become evident that youth interest in politics can also be measured by their involvement in social change activism. As a result of the protest era of the 1960s and 1970s, when youth became highly visible in antiwar, civil rights, women's, workers', environmental, and Indigenous rights movements, these activities became legitimate indicators of civic engagement. Accordingly, while a concern remains with young people's relationship to the formal elements of politics—in particular, elections—added to this is a more recently identified issue: Why are young people not engaged more broadly in social critique or change? This issue reflects both the accepted view that youth is naturally a time for questioning values, and also the experience of contemporary commentators, many having been youthful participants in the protest movements of earlier times themselves. From their perspective, more political activities have become recognized as legitimate acts of citizenship and civic engagement; however, young people themselves are under more scrutiny than ever before for apparently not articulating these kinds of recognizable political narratives either.

The Generation X Debate

The phenomenon of the debate over Generation X in the early 1990s illustrates the way in which the issue of youth disengagement has been constructed. During this time a moral panic began to develop about the "slacker" generation born after 1968, a date significant not only as a marker of a cohort, but as a politically charged historical moment representing the highest point of youth civic engagement. Generation X was considered to be directionless, lacking motivation, inarticulate, apathetic, and nihilistic. Problems such as youth unemployment, high crime rates, and substance use and abuse were often perceived as symptoms rather than causes of a generational malaise. White youth became associated with self-destructive despair, while violent, antisocial acts were attributed to youth of color.[20] Youth music cultures became a focus for concern, and musical genres such as grunge, hip-hop, rap, and heavy metal were held responsible for contributing to young people's pessimism and depressive or aggressive attitudes. This perspective on youth as somehow lost and needing direction and guidance back into community values represents the most conservative analyses of Gen X.

For other commentators young people's apparent introspection and lack of interest in participation reflected a problematic internalization of such neoliberal values as focus on the self. Terms such as *the me generation* circulated to describe youth as not so much lost and without values, but as having absorbed a message of greed and personal development over any commitment to community or society. For example, one of the champions of Australian and U.K. 1960s counterculture, Richard Neville, compares his generation with Gen X thus:

> Work was just another four letter word, not the meaning of life. You've managed to turn the world of business into the whole world. . . . Our universities were hotbeds of revolution, not composts for careers. We kicked the arse of the establishment, not licked it.[21]

Naivety, selfishness, and lack of historical memory were all attributed to young people who were seen to have abandoned social causes in favor of self-advancement. This came to be a particular criticism of young women, whose apparent lack of engagement with feminist social movements represented the extent to which young people had lost touch with social critique and collectivist politics.

Young women have been a longstanding problem for political science in terms of their distance from formal politics (although this in itself is a point of contention). However, during the Gen X debate, they also emerged as a problem for those with progressive agendas who were looking to young women to articulate a commitment to social change. This occurred particularly in the context of a generational debate within feminism, sparked by some second-wave feminist concerns that young women had abandoned the cause, and resulting in demands for them to speak out. Specifically, it was assumed that young women were silent on key feminist issues either because they felt they already had everything, or because they were too deeply troubled to find a feminist voice.[22] If they were perceived as articulating feminist principles, they did not express these convictions in appropriate ways, being either too absorbed in risk and victimhood or mistaking feminism for simply reversing sexual objectification and having a laugh.[23] Their strategies and abilities were criticized on the grounds of arrogance and inexperience. For example, prominent feminist Beatrice Faust famously wrote that "many young women are so naïve that if you spit in their face they'll say it's raining."[24] The feminism perceived as the girls' own variety was depicted as hopelessly lacking in politics, theoretical framework, social policy agenda, and strategy. In short, it was not a movement. Popular and academic communities commonly disparaged young women for confusing consumer power with political gains[25] and for not knowing how to speak out.

In this debate about the forecast for feminism, young women became the object of a range of fears about the future of social change and political movements in new times. As Chris Griffin argues,

> "Youth" and "adolescence" are powerful signifiers through which societies construct and consider their/our relationship with the future. Such is the force of these representations of youth that it is never possible to consider the position of any young people without reference to the diverse meanings of "youth" for adult society—in this case for adult feminists and for the relationship between young women and feminism.[26]

The post-1960s generation of young women thus came to demonstrate that youth in general are disconnected from politics, cynical about collective action, and too self-interested to engage in protest. The Gen X debate, and its exemplification in the critique of third-wave feminism, illustrates a widely held belief that young people have ceased to be committed and connected to their communities and have lost their capacity to purposefully and effectively articulate political analysis or act for social change. For the most part youth disengagement is seen as a problem of lack of effective voice. As a consequence many programs and policies are now in place to bring youth into the process of participatory democracy or to encourage them to speak their minds about social injustice.

Being Seen and Heard: Youth Participation

Increasingly, young people are provided with ways to speak out about and participate in politics at the municipal, national, and global levels. The introduction of civics education in schools across a wide range of countries is one such example of the priority placed on youth learning about politics and citizenship. Classrooms have become a site where citizenship is taught, if not actually experienced.[27] Other emerging forms of youth participation include national and international youth councils, committees and forums, parliaments, school councils, and hearings. Some of these are NGO initiatives, whereby young people are supported to form representative organizations or councils in their own countries for the purpose of joining up with high-profile, often international lobby organizations. Chapters within the United Nations, YMCAs and YWCAs, Council of Europe, and so on have been effective locales for representatives of these groups to come together and form transnational lobby agendas.

Other methods are more locally based. For example, one way in which the passive learning of citizenship in school has been counteracted is through the development of youth councils and parliaments within and among schools.[28] Youth rights and concerns can be debated and highlighted in schools and communities, and young people are encouraged to take on the responsibilities and duties of representation. For example, the International Association for the Evaluation of Educational Achievement Civic Education Study has found that schools that model democratic practice are most effective in promoting civic knowledge and engagement.[29] Yet another mode of participation that has emerged is the holding of hearings, tribunals, conferences, and forums for youth issues. Youth organizations as well as individuals in some cases can use these opportunities to generate discussion about youth policy and place on the agenda issues that have not yet come to public or government attention. Young people increasingly participate in these forums, and several have developed high profiles either as speakers and activists on youth issues, or as youth representatives speaking out about public policy or social justice concerns more generally.

To the extent that the problem of youth disengagement has been understood as the lack of opportunity to speak up and be heard, this vast array of points of entry into participation seems to constitute an effective solution. There now seems to be little excuse to be outside of politics, and those who remain disengaged in spite of these measures risk being perceived as truly apathetic and suffering attitudinal problems. Now that young people have been provided with the knowledge and forums for political participation, this has become somewhat of a managed process that at times becomes the performance of engagement rather than engagement itself. Youth researchers Clarissa White, Sara Bruce, and Jane Ritchie, from the U.K.-based Young People's Politics project, suggest that

> a balance needs to be struck between empowering and engaging young people and pressurising them to participate and be interested in politics. Young people seem keen to ensure there are appropriate mechanisms for their involvement but they may feel increasingly burdened if there are too many requests for their participation. . . . Moves towards greater participation may be in danger of resulting in what might be termed "democratic overload."[30]

What emerges in this scenario of encouraging youth participation is the possibility that democracy itself becomes somewhat of a manipulation. Being empowered and engaged is something that is done to young people by authorities: the state, NGOs, schools, governments, political parties. This highlights the enduring problem that young people's capacity to be powerful players in politics, decision making, and social change remains to a considerable extent out of their hands. Youth service and policy analysts Tom Hall, Howard Williamson, and Amanda Coffey suggest that "government intervention to promote civic activism and mutuality sits uneasily with the principle that such mutuality should be voluntary and spontaneous."[31] An ironic example of this was an Australian initiative to give young people an opportunity to experience the parliamentary process, which saw a sample of students brought to the Federal Parliament to conduct their own debate about a bill to lower the voting age to twelve. The education minister was quoted as saying, "The experience would encourage students to become more involved in decision-making at their schools and in their communities."[32] The bill, however, was rejected by all the student sessions of parliament.

With the increase in places and organizations for youth participation, there is very little space left that remains untouched in this project of enhancing democracy. Of course, in many ways it is laudable that so many more places exist for young people to express their views. However, this leaves little space to be apolitical, or for youth to define politics in their own ways. As Henry Giroux suggests, youth are denied real political power while being used symbolically for adult fantasy.[33] This project also tends to remain embedded in a model of enhancing their voices, which may not have any enduring associated actions or outcomes. As youth researcher Roger Holdsworth writes,

> A simple focus on "being heard" can merely serve to make it appear that young people are active participants; this may, in reality, act as a "safety valve" to ease pressure for real changes in decision-making or simply be a way of letting decision-makers feel as if they are "doing the right thing."[34]

With the move toward enhancing youth participation, there has now emerged a preferred way of being politically engaged and expressing social critique. Participating means displaying oneself and speaking out in particular ways in particular places, places that are on view to the authorities who grant this empowerment at virtually all times. Consequently, young people's capacity to engage with one another beyond the surveillance of adults has been far reduced, and other, more complicated discourses about politics and the social world are becoming more difficult to articulate.

Forms of participation based on providing opportunities for the voices of youth to be heard may not be the most useful measures for enhancing meaningful participation in any case. In a Council of Europe paper, Lasse Siurala, then director of youth and sport at the council, acknowledges a number of problems with these practices. He raises important points: for example, the questionable capacity for real debate, the tendency for participation to be theatrical rather than real, the difficulty of involving marginalized youth, the use of top-down management approaches, inadequate representation of diverse populations, tenuous links to the electorate being represented, and the lack of legitimacy these forms have in the eyes of many young people.[35] Youth researchers Pat Thomson and Roger Holdsworth also note that youth leadership forums frequently model mainstream politics, with the accompanying reproduction of inequitable economic and social relations. In particular, the leaders and representatives continue to be selected from the privileged, and they then come to stand for "youth" in general. Youth delegates, councillors, and so on may not in fact represent the real diversity of youth, and they may lack credibility and support from their constituency; nevertheless, they become the acceptable face and preferred voice for consultation. This, in turn, may interfere with their capacity to effect change and with the capacity of other young people to participate meaningfully.

This renewed interest in youth participation has brought about prescriptions for being a properly engaged, good youth citizen, along with an increased regulation of young people's lives. Participation can operate as both activism and discipline, as demonstrated by Thomson and Holdsworth. They illustrate how participatory strategies in schools elicit self-managing behavior on the part of youth. Young people are encouraged to identify, personalize, take responsibility for, and fix problems of health, risk, and law and order, all in the name of active participation. This occurs not only through corralling of youth into newly constructed and managed civic spaces, but also through carefully eliciting youth voice by authorities and putting the onus on youth to display their own self-regulation.

Participation and Girls' Voices

Encouraging young people to be seen and heard through projects of participatory democracy has become the predominant strategy for dealing with the problem of youth disengagement. Within these projects young women are constructed as having their own specific set of hurdles to overcome. Given that, historically, young women have not been perceived as performing well in the political arena, it has become a particular concern to address the barriers to their participation and to enhance their opportunities for active citizenship. One of the most influential ways in which this issue has been framed is through the encouragement of girls' voices. This has been a particular interest for some strands of feminism seeking to help young women who, from this perspective, appear to have lost their ability to express their critical voices. Before young women are able to fully participate and be heard in their communities, they must first overcome the negative psychological processes associated with growing up female and, as a consequence, "find their voices."

This attention to the psychological components of young women's lack of critique comes from a particularly powerful strand of feminist research on girls that argues that female adolescence is marked by "loss of voice, the narrowing of desire and expectations, the capitulation to femininity."[36]

This analysis has been developed by the Harvard Project on Women's Psychology and Girls' Development, also known as the voice-centered relational approach framework, which depicts contemporary female adolescence as a time when girls lose their capacity for boldness, resistance, and confidence. For example, Mary Pipher writes,

> Something dramatic happens to girls in early adolescence. . . . They lose their resiliency and optimism and become less curious and inclined to take risks. They lose their assertive, energetic and "tomboyish" personalities and become more deferential, self-critical and depressed.[37]

According to this perspective, the overarching loss that young women sustain at this time is the loss of their resistant voices. Once silenced by their acculturation into contemporary adult femininity, they no longer have the words to speak their minds. In this process they become vulnerable to low self-esteem, psychological disorders, and developmental crises. The proponents of this framework are at pains to demonstrate inclusiveness, and consequently, these experiences have been represented as universal and non–class- or race-specific elements of contemporary girlhood.

This approach claims to find a solution in encouraging young women to reconnect with their preteen, resilient selves by finding their voices again. Thus it is primarily concerned with eliminating silences on the part of young women, for if the problem is silence, the solution is therefore for young women to speak. Young women first have to reclaim their voices and learn to speak in order to participate and then enact social change. This approach to removing barriers to young women's participation has been adopted in a widespread fashion. It is popular within both the rhetoric and content of government policy and programs and NGO recommendations. This is evidenced by the titles of some of their reports, for example, the Australian *Listening to Girls* or Canada's *We're Here, Listen to Us!: A Survey of Young Women*.[38] Authorities are encouraged to create spaces to hear young women, to focus on their voices and their strengths, to let them talk, and to listen.[39] In brief, the suggestion is that young women face particular difficulties in being heard because of the losses they sustain through adolescence, and as a consequence they need their voices elicited in careful ways.

There are a number of problems with this focus on eliciting girls' voices, problems that connect with a broader concern with the ways youth participation is managed. First, by constructing the problem of girls' loss of voice as one that must be identified and diagnosed by psychologists and then solved through dialogue with them, adults are positioned as the authorities and mediators of young women's voices. This emphasis on speaking and hearing the voices of young women is often merely a lead-up to hearing the voices of the adult women experts who are quick to offer their own stories or discourses as solutions or even as descriptions of the problems of girls. For example, after listening to young women, Mary Pipher concludes that it is in fact adults who must take on the roles of strengthening, supporting, and guiding girls and encouraging emotional toughness and self-protection. Gender researcher Judy Mann frames her remedy for uncomplaining, compliant, and silenced girls in terms of the lessons "we" can teach "our" daughters. Feminist Phyllis Chesler sees the need for older women to speak "strong truths . . . in a loving voice" to younger ones.[40]

Sometimes the speaking and listening get so mixed up that the agenda of helping young women speak out is bypassed in favor of young women inadvertently helping adult women reconnect with their youth. For example, the concern that nobody listens to girls, which prompted the research of psychologists Jill MacLean Taylor, Carol Gilligan, and Amy M. Sullivan, was somewhat lost once the researchers made the discovery that

> girls' voices frequently encouraged women to become more lively and to speak more directly from their experience, in part because they . . . recall a voice and a world of relationships that had become a lost time for women—a time of clarity and courage at the edge of adolescence.[41]

Much of this type of research presents the adults as either the ultimate authority, able to offer advice and guidance to young women, or it sees young women as symbolic of some kind of ahistorical silenced state of girlhood and then uses them to help adults reflect on their own youthful experiences of this same phenomenon. For example, Judy Mann writes,

> When I talked to adult women about this book, many of them described their adolescence with painful recollections that invariably had to do with a sense of lost self, a silencing of their voice, a loss of self-confidence and of identity.[42]

The attempt to take seriously young women's perspectives on social and political issues, that is, to hear the substance of their talk, often takes second place to a celebration of the method of listening in itself. It is perhaps here that class, race, and culture could begin to emerge as issues in young women's experiences of being heard, but the tendency to homogenize and psychologize the problem of silence overrides these possibilities for hearing young women talk about socioeconomic inequities. Similarly, the desire to learn from girls sometimes results in an idealization of their strategies and solutions about injustice, along with an abdication of responsibility on the part of adults with greater social power to elicit their stories as well as generate changes in their circumstances.

This opens up a second problem, namely, the extent to which listening and creating spaces for girls' voices to be heard is a strategy of governmentality. This perspective has provided the impetus and the framework for a wide range of government policies, NGO recommendations and strategies, and philanthropic foundations providing funding and programs. It has spawned a variety of texts full of young women's voices, with promising titles such as *Ophelia Speaks*; *Listen Up: Voices from the Next Feminist Generation*; *Girlpower: Young Women Speak Out*; *Talking Up*; *Raising Their Voices*, and so on.[43] On the one hand, we have rarely heard so much from young women; however, most of these policies, programs, organizations, and texts are facilitated by adults. Just as with the movement for youth voice and visibility more generally, it could be argued that the recent enthusiasm to invoke young women's voices constitutes an incitement to speak, which, according to Michel Foucault is facilitated by "apparatuses everywhere for listening and recording, procedures for observing, questioning and formulating." Private experiences and secrets are thereby "driven out of hiding and constrained to lead a discursive existence."[44]

Young women are encouraged to speak their stories and provide narratives of their experiences to adult experts, but at the same time they risk these narratives being scrutinized, interrogated, appropriated, and depoliticized. In short, it could be argued that the more young women speak, the less power they have. Feminist psychologist Maureen Mahoney argues persuasively that the Harvard project's story of voice and silence "denies girls their own complications, their anger at the powerlessness they experience in the face of experts who want to know their secrets, and their active struggles—both spoken and silent—to resist such an intrusion and authority."[45] Human development theorist Janie Victoria Ward notes that silence has racial contours and that the assumption that it always equals capitulation does not account for the possibilities that "self-silencing . . . may have different motives and consequences for Black adolescent girls."[46] The simple encouragement of girls' voices denies young women assertive, dissenting silence, and it does not acknowledge that expressing oneself in a racist and classist society can be a compromising and risky endeavor. This argument has been borne out in the work of youth researcher Adreanne Ormond. She suggests that young people's absence of critique may be their way of retaining ownership of techniques of resistance.[47] The consequences of the incitement to discourse in this instance are therefore similar to those that Foucault documents in the case of sexuality: regulation, surveillance, appropriation, and control.

The desire to hear the lost voices of young women, to encourage them to speak out in order to draw them into civic participation, and to empower them as actors of social change cannot be easily separated from a desire to regulate youth and to construct appropriate avenues and discourses for sociopolitical engagement. New opportunities for young women to be seen and heard and to live large oblige them to give up their secrets and to display adherence to fixed models of responsibility and leadership and commitment to the established political process. Devolving civic responsibility onto young people can conceal the disappearance of the public sphere even while they are encouraged to participate in it. As we shall see next, the insertion of the civic and the corporate into young people's recreational and cultural spaces and identities is another method by which interiority and the private self can be regulated. It is to the issue of the tangling up of young women's voices with state and corporate interests, particularly in the context of youth leisure spaces, that we now turn.

The "Civic-ization" of Youth Leisure

As we saw in the previous chapter, many places where youth have traditionally congregated for the purposes of hanging out, having fun, and being together have been transformed into spaces of regulation or commerce. Many of these sites are also becoming venues where civics and participation can be taught to youth. Not only are there more places than ever for young people to go to participate in politics, but participation is also coming to them. If youth do not actively involve themselves in councils, parliaments, and hearings, knowledge about being a good citizen can still reach them through their places of leisure. We have already seen that free spaces for youth leisure have diminished, and in their place are many new adult-supervised environments. This corralling of youth leisure into surveilled spaces has a particular meaning in the context of the emphasis on youth citizenship and participation. Hall, Coffey, and Williamson note that

> organised youth leisure settings, especially those which can be grouped under the general auspices of the youth service, have historically had an educative agenda, often linked to the notion of citizenship. This connection continues to be made today. The Commission on Citizenship (1990) recommended that citizenship education should find a place not only in schools, but also in youth work and community work settings. Many high profile youth initiatives . . . espouse citizenship themes. . . .[48]

Organizations and services that provide youth with entertainment, support, information, and leisure have always served a variety of purposes, not least being to teach young people appropriate social and civic roles and community values. In the contemporary context, however, where very little free space remains for young people to occupy and define themselves, and where ethics of civic engagement have taken priority, youth work, clubs, and activities enact a particular function in the service of good youth citizenship. Judith Torney-Purta and her colleagues, authors of *Citizenship and Education in Twenty-Eight Countries*, have discovered in their research that "youth organizations have untapped potential to positively influence the civic preparation of young people."[49] Along with the provision of somewhere to go and something to do, young people are encouraged by these services to participate, often in ways that leave them very little room for understanding leisure more freely, or defining participation for themselves. Hall, Coffey, and Williamson add,

> Adult workers and volunteers in these settings may assist young people in setting their own agendas for community engagement, and empower them to follow these through, but they also shape and supervise this process as knowing guides (and arguably gatekeepers) to community participation and membership.[50]

While this has always been a dimension to youth work, the issue today is that it is very difficult for young people to develop leisure activities and cultures outside of these civic-inclined regulatory frameworks. Consequently, the social control effects of youth services are felt more keenly than before, and the meanings of youth leisure for young people themselves can be lost.

This double-edged dimension to youth service provision is very much at issue in the case of services for young women. Whereas once youth centers and programs offered very little for young women and were notable for their overpopulation by young men, a far greater range of opportunities now exists for girls. Frequently, however, especially in the United States, these services are guided by the girls'-loss-of-voice framework, and have a prior agenda to remedy loss and elicit voice, with all the accompanying problems of this approach to young women's issues. Attempts to empower young women to engage with their communities are first overladen with assumptions about their psychological barriers to participation and the need for mediators or gatekeepers to translate between vulnerable girls and the wider world. Education for speaking out in the context of youth work and services therefore takes on a particular meaning in the case of young women, for they are depicted as in even greater need of intervention and assistance. For example, Jennifer Baumgardner and Amy Richards report that

> helping girls be "visible, valued and heard" is part of the agenda of the Ms. Foundation. Girls Speak Out harbors a "healthy resilience." Girls Inc. wants to keep girls "strong, smart and bold." And *New Moon* magazine is committed to "listening to girls and their dreams."[51]

The capacity for young women to set their own agendas or to choose not to be visible and heard in the context of these services is somewhat limited. Opportunities for leisure, unregulated free time, and activity shared among themselves without an adult gaze are replaced by leadership programs, speak-outs, retreats with older women, and self-esteem projects.

Within youth services young women are increasingly obliged to undergo considerable psychological work in order to become vocal members of their communities. This work is facilitated by adults, who are able to convert the space of leisure into one of eliciting youth voice for them to listen to. The psychologizing of youth issues and the location of their rightful place as within the earshot of adults can, paradoxically, serve to deny them political agency. As Henry Giroux argues,

> Prohibited from speaking as moral and political agents, youth become an empty category inhabited by the desires, fantasies and interests of the adult world. This is not to suggest that youth don't speak; they are simply restricted from speaking in those spheres where public conversation shapes social policy and refused the power to make knowledge consequential with respect to their own individual and collective needs.[52]

In other words, the ways in which adults control the youth agenda, define barriers to youth participation primarily in terms of psychological frailties rather than the limitations of sociopolitical structures, and establish themselves as facilitators of the voices of vulnerable and unconfident minors undermine young people's capacity to demarcate their own interests and to articulate their concerns in political ways. These techniques leave little opportunity for young people, and young women in particular, to retain an interior or private space that is outside surveillance. In the context of the work of youth tribunals, and the broader project of encouraging youth to speak out, Maori and Indigenous education scholar Linda Tuhiwai Smith raises the important question, "Is the listener worthy?"[53] The spread of the civic agenda to a variety of youth culture sites opens up the questions of participation in what, and to what ends? Young women may no longer be denied an opportunity to participate, but they are increasingly denied their privacy and their entitlement to keep their conversations to themselves and one another.

Not only is civic engagement of a particular managed sort required in the domain of youth leisure, but this space is also being emptied out of creativity and free and critical expression on the part of youth by corporate encroachment. For example, the construction and management of young women's leisure activities is being taken out of their hands by the private sector. Torre and Burns have found that leisure time is manipulated by the plans offered by cell phone service providers, which encourage young women to use their phones while minutes are free. Young women therefore tend to shape their activities according to the time management agendas imposed by the products and services they buy. As we saw in chapter 3, the tangling up of citizenship with the market has had particular effects on young people. This is borne out in the contest over youth voice as expressed in leisure activities. As corporate interests take hold in this area, and especially as corporations seek to fulfill their own citizenship duties while manipulating their youth markets, young people's ability to control and utilize recreation for their own cultural expression diminishes.

As media studies scholar Stephen Duncombe argues, it is particularly fringe and "sub-cultural" activities and identities that are attractive to advertisers seeking language and images that tap into the latest youth cultures. He says, "This alternative lifeworld is coveted by advertisers, commercial designers and corporate image consultants as a link to a generation of consumers they fear has passed them by."[54] This desire to make market inroads into youth "lifeworlds" has had particular effects on the possibilities for young people to create and manage their own cultures and to continue to use them for social critique or commentary.

Recent times have seen a shift from public funding to corporate funding for youth activities. This trend has occurred in the areas of music, sports, art, creative writing, fashion, and self-expression through style and Internet activities. In North America community sports facilities or programs are now sponsored by enterprises such as Nike. Young people's websites are hosted by market research companies. Music events, especially those featuring independent bands, tend to receive prominent corporate sponsorship. The images and styles of political music subcultures, such as punk or hip-hop, have been commercialized and mainstreamed.[55] The political dimensions of these cultures have been put aside, while the aesthetic has been appropriated by advertisers to promote their merchandise and services. Journalist and political commentator Naomi Klein suggests that critical voices and resistant practices that have traditionally emerged through these kinds of cultures are increasingly coopted by brands in order to sell products back to young people.[56] Creative, productive, and political discourses and activities are appropriated and reinvented as slogans for accessories and merchandise. Young people's cultures and creative expression constitute the sites and discourses of their own civic engagement and critique, but these are being depoliticized and colonized by the private sector. In the process real opportunities for self-defined participation are lost. As leisure and culture are corporatized, the opportunities they afford for youth citizenship and participation have then to be purchased back by young people from the corporations.

Corporatizing Youth Politics: The Case of Grrrlpower

The perceived corporate takeover of a youth-owned culture of leisure and politics is well illustrated in the case of the grrrlpower (or girlpower) movement. As we saw in chapter 1, this was once a social movement for young feminist women that quickly became targeted as one of those coveted alternative lifeworlds. It is worth revisiting in this context, because the process by which this conversion has taken place illustrates the close connections between calls for youth voice and civic engagement and their absorption into global commercial interests. Its sustained legacy as a youth social movement remains an open question, but here we will look at the ways it was, in the eyes of its membership, coopted and undermined as a youth-based politics.

The grrrlpower movement predated the call by second-wave feminists for the next generation to make themselves visible. This timing is significant, because it indicates that young women's own capacity for political thinking and acting was a vibrant force existing and flourishing outside the gaze of adult authorities. Grrrlpower constituted a loose, global network of predominantly white young women interested in feminism, youth politics, punk and other alternative cultural practices, and a range of left-wing political interests (for example, anarchism, vegetarianism, environmentalism). It has been associated with particular youth scenes (grunge, punk), specific places (Olympia, Wash., in the United States), and styles of self-presentation (contrasting feminine and girlish outfits with accessories such as Doc Marten boots, tattoos, and body graffiti). Its reach, however, was far more extensive than these local or style-based alliances suggest.

Its objectives were to create a network of diverse young women to advocate for their needs and interests, to provide support to one another, and to express their anger about and devise solutions to the enduring oppression and inequities that young women face. In the words of one young woman, grrrlpower emerged because

> there is a generation of young women who are angry, who've grown up with few female role models (thanks to patriarchally obscured history of women), with no sense of ever having been involved in subcultures, only looking in from the outside. These women have been robbed of a strong identity, and they are beginning to take action.[57]

Central to grrrlpower was the need to politicize young women, for them to work together without young men or adults, and to agitate for change on a number of issues such as sexual assault and harassment, homophobia, violence, health, work, education, and status. Grrrlpower was primarily a movement to create a political space for young women's social critique that was antihierarchical and girl-run.

Through the mid- to late 1990s, grrrlpower became a subject of interest to the media and to advertisers. Its members became concerned about increasing commercialization and depoliticization. The slogans and style of grrrlpower were drawn on by advertising campaigns for products pitched at a youth market. Young women themselves despaired at this turn of events: for example, Kylie, a participant in the grrrlpower movement, says,

> I think that the whole girl power thing has been co-opted, so that it's just a watered down slogan that appears on babydoll T shirts, or Spice Girls records or Sportsgirl[58] advertisements. I have a problem with empty sloganeering phrases and clichés, particularly with grrrl power, where as a slogan, it gives no sense of the community or movement it originates from.[59]

This phenomenon, of course, is not without precedent. As American studies scholar Andrew Ross argues, "The youth industries have long learned to market the language of rebellion."[60] The difference in this case is that the process of commercialization has taken place at the same time as young women have been admonished for being insufficiently political. These two forces thus to some extent reinforce one another and give strength to the position that young women believe that shopping and politics are interchangeable, and that as a consequence, they are incapable of forging sociopolitical analyses of their world and that they need adult help to learn about civic engagement. Feminist youth researcher Jessica Taft argues that

> by the late 1990s, the discourse of "Girl Power," particularly as deployed by the mainstream media, actually constructed a version of girlhood that excludes girls' social and political selves. In particular . . . the American ideals of the autonomous individual, meritocracy and consumerism provide the foundations for a range of discursive practices that describe narrow limits to girls' power and define girlhood as a non-political space.[61]

For Taft, the association of girlpower with a nonfeminist, consumerist position denies young women the opportunity to see or utilize the politics of girlpower, while at the same time limiting their agency to merely being able to purchase the right products.

Although the grrrlpower movement has been rightly criticized for its noninclusivity and narrow focus on the concerns of young white women, it is an important example of the problematic positioning of a female youth politics. Its members perceived that civic and corporate encroachment on a youth-defined space made this politics both accountable to adults and saleable to consumers. In both cases power was taken out of the hands of young women themselves. At the same time that they appeared to be answering the call of older feminists and other social activists to speak out, their words became material for commercial interests that sought to restrict young people to the role of apolitical consumers.

This trend is also apparent in the relationship between the media and private interests and the members of emerging global social movements such as the anti–corporate globalization movement and the antiwar protests. For example, journalist Leah Rumack discusses *Glamour* magazine's search for an appropriate Seattle rally protestor to profile thus: "She's political but not too political. She's alternative, but fashionable. You know the kind." She continues, "It's now cool to be a grrrl. Fashionable. Sassy. Very millennium . . . as long as you're cute."[62] Similarly, the youth-led protests against the 2003 war in Iraq were subjected to the same kind of representations. This strong indication that young people are deeply involved in political issues, which flies in the face of common assumptions about their disengagement, was met with disquiet and appropriation. Young people's desire to hold their own marches and rallies was trivialized or made subject to excessive policing and alarm. In Australia schoolchildren as young as ten held mass, rolling protests; in return they were chased by mounted police, hurt in clashes with security, and urged to join "proper" marches instead of enacting their own. The media's most commonly used image from these protests was of three smiling, attractive girls. Journalist Virginia Trioli writes,

> There they were, three schoolgirls, midriffs adrift, shirts tied up, skirts slung low, slogans Texta-ed on their bellies, hair in pigtails, peace signs in hand. After three decades dry of what newspapers love to call "the defining image" of a generation, they turned up on the corner of Protest and Adolescence. . . . The grab value of this image . . . was . . . that school students were protesting . . . and they had made it sexy.[63]

This tendency to control and commercialize youth politics through the sexy, marketable image of the cute, can-do girl protestor has made participation, engagement, and activism a complex process for young women. The need to take politics and social change elsewhere has emerged in light of this.

Conclusion

The regulation of interiority, particularly the private lives of young women, is evidenced in the various examples of incitement to discourse I have explored here. Young women's thoughts, emotions, bodies, voices, and private spaces are all invited into the public arena, and this display is linked to successful living. Eliciting public performance of strategic efforts toward can-do success is integral to the management of the future girl. Living large and speaking out are both new measures of contemporary youthful femininity. The current emphasis on youth voice and visibility is occurring at a time when young people have few opportunities for unmediated, unscrutinized expressions of culture, recreation, critique, and social commentary. It also coincides with the disappearance of a genuine public sphere in which participation typically takes place. However, young people's and especially young women's nonparticipation is represented as a problem of psychology, attitude, or opportunity, all of which can be overcome with the help of agents of authority.

Improving participation and civic engagement has become a project to draw young people into appropriate modes of expression, with very little real shaping of the agenda by youth themselves. Importantly, young people's capacity to engage with one another, as a vital form of participation, is far reduced in a climate of regulation and intervention. Spaces for the articulation of political and social disaffection and for the flourishing of cultural creativity and productivity are diminishing at the same time that youth are being heard more than ever. This youth voice, which tells the market how to sell to young people, is elicited through the same strategy of incitement to discourse that is favored by well-meaning youth workers and researchers. This complication is noted by Giroux, who writes, "What appears as a despairing expression of the postmodern condition to some theorists becomes for others a challenge to invent new market strategies to promote corporate interests."[64] Consequently, the notion of speaking up, and the eliciting of girls' voices in particular, is contested and treated suspiciously by many young women familiar with the ways youth politics are commercialized. At a time when young women are required to publicly perform their can-do efforts or their acceptance of personal responsibility for failure, that is, when surveillance regimes take the form of incitement to speak, it makes sense that they may well attempt to find new places and new techniques for critical expression. It is this move that we will explore in the next chapter.

CHAPTER 6

FUTURE GIRL POLITICS

The central idea that has been developed in this book is that young women have become integral to the social and economic futures of Western societies. A mainstream image of young women who are successful and flexible has been constructed in this process. They are widely imagined to be what has been labeled "can-do girls," and those who find this difficult to live up to have their failure, individualized as if these were the result of badly handled personal risk. Success and failure, as measured by self-invention, self-sufficiency, and consumer capability, are managed through both the physical spaces that young women occupy and the discourses they are encouraged to participate in. Constructions of youth space and youth voice are thus critical to understanding the shaping of this future-girl identity because it is here that new modes of governmentality are played out. However, they are also important because they are sites of struggle over expression, resistance, dissent, and youth organization. This is particularly significant in light of the increased regulation of interiority and the incitement to young women to live large and speak out. Spaces for young women to express complexity, to interrupt hegemonic constructions of young female subjectivity, and to organize together have diminished or been refigured as sites for civic education, adult surveillance, and commercialization. Further, opportunities and modes of expression are increasingly regulated through the nomination of appropriate places, representatives, and audiences for youth voice.

Consequently, the processes by which young women are constructed as the future have an enormous impact on their capacity to act or speak outside of the can-do and at-risk positions. One of the most powerful messages of neoliberal ideology has been that of choice, which has devolved regulation onto individuals themselves through "responsibilization" and served to conceal the socioeconomic structures that shape people's possibilities. For young women, success is defined as a personal project of good choices achieved through effort, and this effort is the subject of public display. How young women create or retain private and public spaces where these assumptions can be questioned and challenged, and where the concept of choice can be debated, is the subject of this chapter. There are a number of ways in which this creation of space occurs. I examine both the more overtly activist practices of young women as well as less political methods. I am interested in mapping out how a range of young women carve out unregulated spaces for themselves at a time when they are so scrutinized.

For some this has meant involvement in the cultural politics of new kinds of social movements that have emerged in response to a restructured public sphere, different methods of social control, and new information and communication technologies. In these new politics these young women can articulate circumstances of difficulty without the language of risk or personal failure. The focus on consumption for youth citizenship is turned around into a flourishing of youth production, and the incitement to discourse is met with an active silence of dissent. The perception of a corporate and civic takeover of youth leisure and culture is met with a youth takeover of corporate space. This new kind of activism engages with a feminist, antiracist, anti–corporate globalization political agenda. For most, however, carving out space involves less spectacular activities of a personal or local nature. This often entails the development of networks, communications, and a street literacy that subvert attempts to control the movements of youth.[1] Young women who are not active resisters are not therefore simply passive dupes of the can-do and at-risk discourses. As one young woman wrote to me in the context of this research, "I don't want to give the impression that all women must be angry, feisty and over the top to be rebelling. This is not the case. . . . [Rebellion is also] thinking for themselves as individuals, quietly."[2]

Here I attend to some of the ways young women negotiate regulatory practices and discourses, and I examine how this might be accomplished in different places, because traditional sites for speaking, recreation, and assembly are under new kinds of scrutiny. Given this, I also consider how young women reshape their spaces and networks to avoid surveillance, to build community, and to convert technologies of regulation into new modes for communication. I do not intend to imply that all young women are involved in an underground activist movement or to make a divisive interpretation of brave resisters versus passive victims. Rather, against the backdrop of increased regulation and scrutiny, I explore some practices and maneuvers on the part of young women that trouble dominant images of girlhood and expectations of young women, while acknowledging that their capacity to make these interventions is dependent on material and social resources. First, I discuss young women's own inversions and sub-versions of the reworked public/private divide. Specifically, I look at the ways networks and communications are developed by young women through new claims on neighborhood and community. Second, I examine evolving cultural politics that utilize emergent technologies and media. My purpose is to demonstrate how new strategies of governmentality that work by surveillance, individualization, and responsibilization also acti-vate new modes of resistance.

Mapping Community

There is a growing body of work on the changing recreational practices of young people that accounts for the diminished nature of public space and the scrutiny of the private.[3] Practices like drug use can be interpreted within this context as attempts to construct an unregulated interiority, an internal space for leisure that cannot be appropriated.[4] Similarly, the emer-gence of some recreational activities such as raves has been understood as a strategy for forming a new kind of public space for community.[5] These kinds of "disordered consumption" may in fact be techniques to reshape both private and public spheres in light of the increased regulation of inte-riority and the disappearance of spaces for public deliberation.

Here I want to examine some less spectacular practices on the part of young women that achieve similar ends, specifically, the establishment of community, neighborhood, and friendship networks. Many young women, and particularly those deemed to be at-risk, are engaged in pro-jects of rebuilding a public sphere, inserting themselves and their critiques into public space on their own terms, and creating their own communities for evading regulatory regimes. Many of these practices are low-level, indi-vidual strategies for recreation or survival, and they are not intended as significant political acts. Without seeking to romanticize them, I argue that they warrant investigation as creative mechanisms of resilience and resis-tance that may ripple out into wider possibilities.

Young women living in neighborhoods and communities designated as "bad," that is, ones that suffer from a lack of infrastructure and high levels of unemployment and crime, are prime candidates for an at-risk appella-tion. These areas are also those most typically monitored by police and security forces through patrols and surveillance technologies.[6] Several studies have indicated how these young women work to map their worlds in order to avoid danger, including the dangers of regulation, and to build community. Dorothy Bottrell's study of young Anglo, Aboriginal, and Pacific Islander women in a working-class Australian community reveals how the creation of a network provides them with more positive ways of defining themselves and their neighborhood than the stereotypes of problems and risk. This network is a group of friends and acquaintances who support one another and provide a place to go when they are excluded from school, family, or leisure practices that require disposable income. She says,

> The network is a place of refuge providing friendship, support and escape from problems. . . . Participation in the network entails certain resistances which prohibit conventional options, but . . . while opting for these resistances and alliances may not fit with conventional (middle class, white) notions of a path to success, these forms of self-empowerment may be indicators of resilience and steps towards success in their own terms.[7]

Networks also create opportunities for young women to feel safe in their neighborhoods and enable them to map their spaces so that communities and resources can be placed and public space can be occupied. Caitlin Cahill's research with young urban women of color in New York and her analysis of young people's street literacy indicates how knowledge of the neighborhood and following implicit rules keep young women safe and allow them to make a claim to public space. Similarly, sociologist Nora Räthzel discusses young migrant and autochthonous German women's "rules of behaviour" that allow them to navigate the streets safely. Citing the example of "Marie," she says, "Rules of behaviour . . . give Marie a security, a way of walking securely through the animosities and violence around her. . . . She knows everybody, and seems to have friendships everywhere and, therefore, she is safe—she feels safe."[8] Keeping safe, in many instances, entails avoidance of the regulatory gaze of security and police forces, who monitor young women's use of public space in particularly racist and sexist ways.[9]

Rules, street literacy, mapping, and "collective secret knowledge"[10] help young women negotiate their neighborhoods and avoid at-risk designations by agents of power. Knowing and marking the physical environment can enhance young people's connection to place and help build their support networks. For example, cultural studies theorist Joe Austin, discussing graffiti artists or "writers" in New York City, says,

> Appropriated spaces formed a kind of network that re-mapped the city for writers, constructing a "writers' city," if you will. This "writers' city" emerged from the cracks found in its existing institutional and social structures, which . . . were often places where writers "hid in the light" of adult surveillance without adults being aware of their purposes.[11]

These kinds of literacies and maps and the networks that share them also enable young women to carve out critical spaces within the physical environment of their communities. This practical knowledge of neighborhoods enables young women to articulate which areas are accessible, which are off limits, and why. With this knowledge the borders between the two can be revealed and negotiated. Specifically, young women can reflect on their exclusions and find ways to integrate themselves and their concerns about public space back into the urban environment. Projects like public art and community gardens are ways this can be accomplished, as they enable a creative reimagining and a reclaiming (if only temporarily) of public space. Geographer Myrna Margulies Breitbart demonstrates this in the examples of youth public art projects in the U.S. cities of Holyoke, Mass., and Detroit. She suggests these projects give youth "an opportunity to insert themselves in a very visible way into the landscape and begin to claim a place in the public life of the neighbourhood."[12] This is particularly important in environments where youth who are in public are constructed exclusively as a dangerous problem.

Young women's public art raises questions about who owns a neighborhood and who is entitled to shape it and make comment on it. Social psychologist Corinne Bertram analyzes the painting over of a young women's antiviolence mural in Brooklyn. She suggests that the artwork caused such a furor because it disrupted the entitlement of homeowners to define the nature and causes of problems in their community. Instead, a group of young local women claimed this right. Bertram says the mural "spoke of agency: their assertion of their citizenship as neighbourhood agents, players, people with a voice and a politics."[13] Although public artworks and similar projects are rarely enduring, they serve to engage young people in public spaces as entitled citizens. For inner-city or urban young women, in particular, they can offer new and more positive ways for them to position themselves and to be seen.

At the same time the surveillance of such women may be the impetus for the construction of closed-off, private spaces. Education scholar Jennifer McCormick describes how young women in urban U.S. public high schools spend their days in an environment of high regulation. Metal detectors, x-ray machines, scanners, security guards, and police are all features of daily life in many of these schools. The young women in McCormick's research created an internal space through the writing of poetry, a "sanctuary," to express themselves freely. From this emerged an opening up of a public space of sorts, for other women to come together and participate in shared creative writing activities. Even so, community building and resource sharing may be activities young women prefer to keep hidden. We have already seen that many kinds of participation in public deliberation are regarded with suspicion by youth because they can be perceived as tokenistic and making little difference. As a consequence new kinds of public spheres or, at least, low-level communities are being constructed by young people. Ironically, these are often forged with the same technologies typically used to monitor young people's movements.

For example, cell phones have become an incredibly popular way for young women to keep in touch with friends, make plans, and negotiate parental intervention in their social lives. While I have already explored how this technology is frequently experienced as little more than a tracking device, many young women also use their access to communications technology to extend their social networks, win freedoms from their families, and speak with one another in an uncensored fashion. Sheila Henderson, Rebecca Taylor, and Rachel Thomson have found in their U.K. research that text messaging is used by young women to communicate with their partners and, in particular, as a safe way to articulate sexual desire when landline phone calls or face-to-face conversations might be overheard. The development of ever-changing and increasingly sophisticated text-messaging terminology and symbols serves to deny adults access to young people's conversations. Folklorist Eija-Liisa Kasesniemi writes that in Finland, "Instead of passively adopting the communication culture imposed upon them by device manufacturers, operators and advertising, teenagers have created a rich and varied culture for expressing themselves particularly in text messaging."[14] Youth also undermine the commercial interests of the phone companies by developing codes of "ghost calls," whereby they can communicate messages to one another by calling and hanging up before being charged.

Similarly, the establishment of online communities that are only accessible to those in the know, and are not available to the voyeur, is an important mode of information dispersal and friendship building for many young people who have access to this resource. As young women are so often confined to the home, the Internet has become an important virtual public forum for connecting with others. Developing a virtual identity can create a psychological freedom for young women whose bodies are closely regulated. Even whimsical and personal uses of the Internet can be meaningful in this context. The construction or use of a weblog, online diary, discussion group, or webpage for self-expression can create virtual freedoms for those under surveillance. These often provide a safer place for the articulation of personal feelings and thoughts than a physical journal, which can be more easily discovered by household members. As we shall see a little later, the use of the Internet as a site for global community building has also become central to young women's developing politics.

These kinds of subversions of refigured public/private spheres are important methods by which young women find room to move, to communicate with one another, and to reposition themselves outside of dominant images of success and failure. Although they are not necessarily politically motivated, young women carve out spaces for themselves in ways that have political effects. They can range from the most private, like the "aesthetic safety zones" of poetry, to the more public, for example, African-American young women's street-performances of double-Dutch as discussed in chapter 4.[15] As Michelle Fine and Lois Weis suggest,

> Young women and men, in their constant confrontation with harsh public rep-
> resentations of *their* race, ethnicity, class, gender and sexuality, use these spaces
> to break down these public images for scrutiny, and invent new ones. It is into
> these newly constructed "free spaces," as Boyte and Evans (1992) would argue,
> that young women and men are able to exit from sites of historic pain and
> struggle and enter into new identities, create new alliances.[16]

These new identities and alliances may also have the potential to generate a more explicit politics. For some young women, free spaces are used more deliberately as sites where discourses and practices of future girlhood can be interrogated and undermined. It is to this kind of activity that I turn next.

New Politics and Border Spaces

Modes of resistance among youth have long been the subject of debate and sometimes despair. As discussed in chapter 5, young women have been the recipients of particular kinds of attention within the Generation X (and Y) debates, especially from feminist commentators grappling with a cohort whose political voices seem inarticulate and unfamiliar. The increased regulation of young women has created problems for their capacity to express social critique and enact subjective positions that are outside the can-do or at-risk categories. However, it would be inaccurate to conclude that they have become compliant or that they are unquestioningly adopting models of selfhood that simply fall in with the requirements of the new economy. Instead, many young women may have developed new forms of expression, and found new spaces for these, as a consequence of the scrutiny that girlhood has come under in recent times. New expressions and new spaces are central to a broader move in youth politics toward a different kind of activism.

There exists a considerable amount of literature on new politics and the place of young people in forging activism for the twenty-first century.[17] It has sought to explain the ways that young people are redefining participation and resistance in light of new, dispersed systems of power, the absence of a public sphere, and the absorption of left politics into the mainstream. As social theorist Alberto Melucci suggests, power is increasingly wielded through the control of information systems and symbols rather than material resources as such.[18] Consequently, new politics increasingly works at the level of culture, representation, and narrative, as well as dramatic direct action and public performance. Alternative media are central to these politics. Further, given the ways in which activism has been mainstreamed and regulated, it has also become important for new politics to develop tactics of evasion. These techniques have included the decentralization of movements, a shift away from hierarchy and formal organization, leaderlessness, and fluid alignments of issue-based activism rather than fixed associations and membership. New politics emphasizes the value of local and loose organization that grows organically.[19]

These features are found in new movements and activism where young people are involved. This includes organizing around anti–corporate globalization; reproductive rights; unionization; outlawing of sweatshops; prison activism; gay, lesbian, bi-, and transgender rights; anti–sex trafficking; disability rights; environmentalism; animal welfare; and peace. Melucci distinguishes between what he describes as the "manifest" and "latent" levels of activism. In other words, activism can operate through both new kinds of public actions—like bold demonstrations, interventions, and performances—and other new, less visible political techniques in its networks of communication and the everyday negotiation that occurs among interested parties. It is primarily this latent level that I want to examine more closely in relation to young women's strategies and spaces for resisting and refiguring constructions of the future girl.

Activism has traditionally occurred in those places reserved for public debate and expression. However, these new politics are being enacted in other kinds of sites that sit between the public and the private. This is a direct response to the incitement to visibility and public discourse along with the disintegration of the old-style public sphere. Many young women are electing to work through new networks and new media, forming marginal, creative, and virtual spaces to express themselves and to engage with one another away from scrutiny, while at the same time reframing strategies, meanings, and effects of social change. This is border work because it moves between public and private, building collective secret knowledge and then using this carefully to create manifest activism. Irena Guidikova and Lasse Siurala, Council of Europe commentators on youth issues, suggest that this kind of "youth culture 'politics' is purposefully set apart from adult society's channels of political expression since young people are aware that their participation is commonly misused and their authentic feelings manipulated to serve the establishment's vested interests."[20] Thus young women's border work is not a simple failure of either access to or possibilities within the public realm but an active choice on the part of some who question the incitement to narrowly defined participation while seeking fresh modes for political intervention. Henry Giroux suggests that "when youth do speak, the current generation in particular, their voices generally emerge on the margins of society—in underground magazines, alternative music spheres, computer hacker clubs and other subcultural sites."[21] These constitute some of the new border spaces for critique. Many young women are using these other spaces and other strategies to engage with their peers outside the adult gaze and to develop critiques of homogenized constructions of their experiences. Young women themselves are reflective, critical agents in their moves against the dominant images of can-do or at-risk, consumer or loser. The development of networks, coalitions, and what Giroux describes as "fugitive cultures"[22] among young women may be ways in which they can organize together away from regulation.

In this next section I use examples from the work of young women involved in these new politics, broadly defined, to explore this idea of border spaces for social critique. By this I mean those who are using art, technology, and creative work to express opinions and generate activism about issues they identify as important to themselves and their peers. They use self-publishing, alternative media, the Internet, art, music, and performance to articulate their views and engage with other youth. The material I look at here is produced by young women from a variety of circumstances in a number of Western countries. Their creative modes of communication and dynamic notions of locale disrupt a sense of singular belonging for these young women, which thereby builds transversal alliances. They come from a diverse range of experiences, family backgrounds, and cultures. They speak as isolated rural youth, urban dwellers, middle-class girls rejecting middle-class values, those who live in poverty, and critical race theorists of all colors, cultures, and ethnicities. In their manifestos, websites, zines, artistic productions, and political actions they address and undermine many of the forces by which young womanhood is constructed, homogenized, and regulated.

The Media of Future-Girl Politics

Zines

Part of the reason for doing the zine for me is that . . . you have ways of taking your life into your own hands and ways of expressing yourself, making yourself heard, [that] don't have to be the ways in which the powers-that-be have given you.
—Michelle, producer of the zine *A Show of Hands*

You communicate your opinions without the threat of being censored or heavily edited because you are the boss of your own publication and what you say goes. [The role of zines] is to spread alternative thoughts and ways of thinking and subvert classist/mainstream attitudes that society is so brainwashed with.
—Flea, producer of the zine *Thunderpussy*

The underground magazines that Giroux speaks of—that is, print and on-line newsletters made by and circulated among a community of mainly young, "anti-establishment" individuals—first developed as a marginal space for youth expression during the 1980s. These newsletters are known as *zines*, short for *fanzine*, itself a version of the word *magazine*. As a kind of personalized newsletter and forum for rants originating in punk and anarchist circles, they are alternative media for the voice of the ordinary person. They are a communicative medium emerging from radical rather than neoliberal DIY philosophies, with an emphasis on individuals as producers rather than consumers. The broader culture of zine makers is one interested in dissent and critique, especially of capitalism, neoliberal democracy, and consumerism. Stephen Duncombe argues that

> zines . . . are the variegated voices of a subterranean world staking out its identity through the cracks of capitalism and in the shadows of the mass media. . . . What distinguishes zinesters . . . is their political self-consciousness. Zinesters consider what they do as an alternative to and strike against commercial culture and consumer capitalism.[23]

By the early 1990s a separate category of zines appeared that were produced and consumed by young women who called themselves grrrls instead of girls, in order to articulate their anger and their desire to politicize the category of "girl."[24] When *zine* was combined with the newly coined *grrrl*, it denoted productions by, for, and about young women interested in underground and alternative, feminist and punk politics. Grrrlzines, as opposed to punk fanzines, debate and organize around issues affecting young women including violence, sexual harassment, self-esteem, unemployment, health, sexuality, and the law. Often these take the form of comics, artworks, and poetry. While they still follow the traditional zine mission to provide a place for ordinary people to express their individual gripes, grrrlzines also adopt and expand the punk philosophy of individual responsibility for the creation of social change. They have quickly become a place where young women can communicate with one another and plan to come together at conferences, concerts, and in city-based chapters or organizations in order to politicize other young women and agitate for change.

This culture continues to constitute a global network of young women who self-publish newsletters, magazines, and websites for and about young women. For these young women zines operate as a site for a new kind of politics and a place for debating and refiguring young women's place, but they work as such only insofar as they can operate outside the scrutiny of new regulatory regimes. This is particularly important to their producers in light of their disenchantment with the perceived cooption of the word and concept of *girlpower*, which was once integral to the grrrlzine culture.

Zines are intended to provide spaces for creativity and productivity that is self-generated and self-controlled in a time when youth leisure and critique have been largely commodified.

The Internet

> DIY culture allows one to connect, research and network by using technology in ways which are unprecedented for feminists and women. The ability to move in and out as your own person or feel and utilise the support of a group, are all possibilities many women are exploring. Certainly, young women . . . can create their own space and agenda, and affiliate when they feel they need to and back off when they don't.
>
> —Rosie Cross, producer of the website *Geekgirl*

By the mid-1990s electronic zines and webpages made by young women began to appear on the Internet. These young women often became known as *gURLs*, a play on the word *girl* combined with the cyberterm *URL* (uniform resource locator, or web address). Since this time, young women's occupation and utilization of the Internet have expanded rapidly. E-zines, online diaries, weblogs, listservs, discussion groups, and personal homepages make up just some of the online spaces constructed by young women. This use of the Internet and the proliferation of girl webpages is further evidence of a creative use of border or liminal space for self-expression and political and cultural engagement. As computer culture theorists Pamela Takayoshi, Emily Huot, and Meghan Huot indicate in the title of their article, the Internet can operate as a kind of "clubhouse for girls,"[25] although, at the same time, as musicologist Marion Leonard points out, "A Web page is a public space where women can talk without having to disclose their home address or even use their real name."[26] The clubhouse is thus, even in its intimacy, also highly public and accessible.

This state of simultaneous presence and absence, existing between the public and the private, works well for young women seeking to combine a desire to organize and communicate with others with a need to avoid surveillance and appropriation of their cultures and politics. The Internet is an in-between space that allows them to negotiate this contradiction with greater capacity for political efficacy than is achieved in a purely private space, but with less risk than is afforded by more traditional and regulated public sites. Speaking of the possibilities of the Internet as a safe space for young women who, in the case of her research, are same-sex attracted, Lynne Hillier writes, "The internet is not a geographical space and it has until now been free of the surveillance that in the real world creates invisibility, hostility and frustration for this group."[27] Therefore, some young women use the Internet as a new kind of space for public deliberation, to communicate with one another, as well as to express themselves in places where they feel less watched than either in the physical domain or in their own homes.

Self-taught technical and navigational skills allow young women to construct cyber-networks that can be found only by those who know where and how to look. One filtering method is the use of codewords like *grrrls* or *gurls*. As Chrystal of the e-zine *Pop Tart* says, "[We] use these code-words in the titles of our site to make clear that we're not naked and waiting for a hot chat with you!"[28] For example, a site for AsiangURLs, which uses a particular configuration of the words *Asian* and *girls* to deter surfers seeking pornography, proclaims that it is a "website and community for all women of Asian heritage," and adds, "If you came here looking for Suzie Wong, naked Asian girls, XXX etc. . . . Get Out!"[29] Takayoshi, Huot, and Huot write that

> when one uses the search term *grrl*, one locates a list of sites not only alternate but also antithetical to the *girl* sites; *grrl* avoids belittling representations of what it means to be female in this culture and finds sites that identify themselves as empowering to girls.[30]

Rosie Cross, a founder of gURL culture, believes that for young women, "The complexity of DIY and the social relationships that are evolving and developing via on-line contacts/networks cannot be underestimated."[31] A key dimension of these new social relationships being forged by young women on the web is that they are virtual, marginal, and partially out of sight. The border space within which this process works is significant in transforming young women's spheres into productive places of activity instead of passive consumption, and in providing some room for overregulated young women to be in the world without leaving their homes.[32] New technologies have been central to the engagement of many marginalized young women in organization and critique.[33]

The Internet allows young women to actively manipulate the borders between public and private, inside and outside, to attempt to manage expression without exploitation, and resistance without appropriation. Eva Farrell, who writes as a researcher and a "girl user" of the Internet, describes cyberspace as

> a reality of constantly shifting virtual truths: identity, language, talk, programs, even a deadly virus or two, circling through these invisible pathways of the information jungle out there. It is a book forever being written, rewritten, revised and erased; a world inside one dimension of text on a screen, and yet does not exist in physical space.[34]

The web is simultaneously there and not there. This capacity to be present and absent, public and private, reflects the position of young women today as both too visible and not visible enough.

What Border Spaces Allow

These productions and networks of zines, websites, and alternative media exist, for the most part, outside of commercial youth culture. They function in a countercapitalist economy and use a system of production and distribution outside, but alongside, mainstream media and consumer capitalism. They thus constitute in-between spaces and, as a result, are potentially ideal locales for the creation of narratives that disrupt hegemonic discourses about young womanhood. They are not a formally recognized site for youth voice, and their producers are not readily identified stakeholders in debates about young people, but their very placelessness may enable them to better evade regulation and constraints. This is particularly relevant for young women, for as we have seen, the places they can occupy as speaking subjects are both limited and highly regulated. Ethnic studies scholar George Lipsitz argues that "at a time when oppressive social hierarchies preserve parochial interests by controlling access to discursive and physical space, young people who don't 'know their place' might be the very people most suited to letting us know what time it is."[35] The existence of other discursive spaces, created by young women who question the places they are allocated within their social worlds, makes possible the articulation of stories that disrupt common narratives of their experiences.

These spaces also create opportunities for communication and connection across a range of borders. As young Aboriginal Canadian feminist Melanie Ferris writes, "Because of . . . decentralization, girls do not have a common gathering space, and . . . zines create a space and open up communications across state boundaries."[36] The Internet is clearly the most powerful example of a global network that can be utilized and accessed throughout the world. Alternative media and zines are also part of a widespread production and distribution network. The two producers of the Welsh zine *Hair Pie* describe its readership as girls who are "isolated by geography but not attitude."[37] Art, comics, and music also move across other kinds of borders by creating alternative points of engagement for young people. Melissa, Tamara, and Jade, young Australian women who have created a comic whose hero is Re:Vulva Girl and her catchword *revulvalution*, say,

> The political role that grrl comics provide is a non-academic and non-threatening way of expression. It is accessible to more people and affordable. It is easier for young women to produce, an excellent medium for expression/artistic work. Comics are easy to relate to and do not alienate the illiterate and appeal to many different age groups.[38]

These modes of communication and expression maximize young women's ability to connect up with one another across a range of contexts, maintaining local specificity along with more broadly felt concerns. In this respect these spaces are not imagined as eternally cut off from a public sphere or from the issues that shape contemporary youth politics more generally, but as part of the reworking of appropriate spaces for participation, communication, and activism.

For young women to create and foster these alternative discursive spaces is particularly significant. Historically, young women have been both excluded from physical spaces demarcated for youth, and have been delegitimized as speaking subjects. Girlhood itself is almost invariably located within analytical frameworks of private and domestic worlds.[39] More recently, since young women have taken center stage as the new ideal subject, narratives of girlhood have become public material. However, along with this has come an incitement to particular forms of discourse and a denial of others. Young women's own, more complicated stories, particularly those that they might tell one another, thus fall under Foucault's concept of "subjugated knowledges"; they are part of "a whole set of knowledges that have been disqualified as inadequate to their task or insufficiently elaborated: naive knowledges, located down on the hierarchy, beneath the required level of cognition or scientificity."[40] However, they are well placed to offer critique and to disturb the legitimacy of recognized knowledges. As the young Australian zine producer Michelle says, "There's always spaces in society for men's voices, particularly white men's voices, and so for women to make a forum for themselves in which to speak is really, I think, a political act."[41]

Young women's construction of alternative discursive spaces makes room for the expression of this private, local knowledge, but more than this, it redefines this knowledge as political. Grrrl politics analysts Joanne Gottlieb and Gayle Wald suggest that these spaces

> foster girls' public self-expression, often understood as the ability to tell private stories (secrets) which are otherwise prohibited or repressed by the dominant culture. . . . Thus publicized, such narratives often become the stuff of political commitment and an affirmation of girls' legitimacy within the realm of the political.[42]

Border spaces allow a reconfiguring of what constitutes critique and where it should be articulated. They challenge the notion that young women are politically disengaged by questioning meanings, places, and modes of engagement. In particular, they expose the assumptions inherent in the notion of participation that delegitimize young people's active involvement in their own self-formed communities.

These spaces and cultures enable young women to have a space to themselves in a time when their public and private worlds are either limited or overmanaged. They provide an alternative to the artificial or external creation of a physical place for young people to get together where they can in fact be watched and monitored. However, such are the perceived capacities of both the state and the private sector to appropriate and depoliticize the cultures that young people make themselves that there is considerable effort put into keeping these new sites outside regulation. Young women may feel they are constantly evading attempts to take over their spaces in the interests of incorporating them into active citizenship or that they are eluding the efforts of advertisers to coopt their cultures. They are thus trying to preserve these spaces that allow them to be speaking subjects on their own terms and at the same time forge new communities for participation and activism. There is thus a constant to-and-fro between trying to open up their sites to other young women and attempting to keep them safe from surveillance.

These border spaces have a particular role in undermining, questioning, and playing with the dominant paradigms by which young women's lives are so commonly represented and shaped in current times. As I have argued, this is partly made possible by their location of liminality, in which girls' voices can appear and disappear at their own behest and their expressions can be directed toward other young women with some confidence that surveillance will be avoided. Next, I consider how some young women use these spaces to resist and refigure images of girlhood and the place of young women in contemporary societies. What they actually have to say within these spaces (and many of them operate across some or all of them) illuminates the critical reflection in which they are engaged on the subject of the future girl. I explore four main issues that are addressed in these sites: discourses of success and self-invention versus risk and failure; girls as passive consumer citizens; girls as compliant ambassadresses; and voice and participation.

Troubling the Can-Do and At-Risk Girl

As has been documented throughout the book, ideas about girlpower, success, self-invention, and meritocracy have pervaded interpretations of young women's status and capacity today. Many young women working in border spaces problematize this image and seek to trouble the notion that young women are now free of concerns and ready to embark on exciting lives of prosperity and opportunity. A zine produced by a self-styled "ordinary" young woman living in an impoverished area of an Australian city is ironically entitled *My Life as a Mega-Rich Bombshell,* which parodies this image of glamor and wealth apparently now available to all young women. The youth services and activism she is involved in focus on how underresourced young women can develop alternative ways to be successful through community projects and knowledge sharing.

While seeking to highlight those enduring and emerging issues in their lives that are hidden by the homogenized image of success, these young women are also critical of interventionist regimes that seek to define their problems and provide adult protection. Figure 6.1 depicts artwork in an issue of the zine *Cavity*. This is a collage with a piece of text at the center that reads, "I am sure you are delighted to be here, entering into what is likely to be one of the most exciting and interesting times of your life." Newspaper clippings about AIDs, rape, pregnancy, police numbers, voting requirements, and other instructions for young people surround the text. The pixilated image on which all of these cuttings are presented is a young woman with her middle finger raised. The juxtaposition of the central message ("delighted to be here") with the clippings suggests that these times are not so much "exciting and interesting" as deeply troubling. Attention is drawn to the many issues facing young women in an era characterized by both risk and regulation.

This method of juxtaposition and contrast in images and text is a popular way of communicating the conflicting narratives and double standards to which young women feel subject. Kylie of *Purrzine* says, "Every issue I have a page called 'Girls in Trouble' which is a cut and paste collage of 'beautiful' women from media, as well as text clippings of horrors inflicted on the not so glamorous women in our society."[43] Young women working in border spaces also address the perceived inability of the cultures within which they live to acknowledge their diversity, or to move away from the mainstreaming of success as defined through beauty, glamor, self-confidence, and money. Nomy Lamm's zine *I'm So Fucking Beautiful* targets these ideals head-on; it has spun out into lecture series, workshops, a rock opera, and books and articles explicating queer, fat, disability pride. The website *Ms Mediocre* includes a "download me, print me, cut me out" generic, Barbie-like, plastic doll figure with the quizzical-looking head of a real young woman superimposed. Webpages, zines, art, music, culture jams, and the like are full of other stories of young women who refuse homogenization and insist upon their diversity and their struggles in a world in which they have supposedly all made it. The countermedia they produce insert circuit breakers into the constant stream of mediated images of homogenized successful girlness.

Thus a central issue that is tackled in these spaces is the notion that girls are content to purchase a can-do image, primarily constructed around neoliberal narratives of choice, self-invention, and consumption. Young women often parody representations of girls either having or consuming everything. As Kylie says, "In the mainstream, young women are seen almost exclusively as consumers. They work, shop, and tend to any family needs. Or they work, shop and are 'independent.'"[44] The popular images that are used to sell these stories of successful young womanhood as being about working, shopping, and being independent—sexy, sassy young

Fig. 6.1 "I'm sure you are delighted to be here." A collage from the zine *Cavity*. Reprinted with permission.

women hanging out with their girlfriends, or girls at the threshold of a thrilling, almost-adult life full of unique opportunities—are the ones most savagely critiqued.

Young women also challenge the shadow image of girls as risky subjects or as "losers," identifying regimes of youth regulation that construct and control young women as at-risk. The very existence of cultures of production undermines the image of "unsuccessful" young women as disengaged and passive recipients of state support. The output of these cultures is itself the result of creative and articulate individuals and groups. One website plays on this contradiction through its tongue-in-cheek title *Losergrrl*, ironically belying its name by providing resources, information, links, artwork, creative writing, and reviews by and for activist young women. The young women involved in these cultures complicate the neat borders created between useful and useless, productive and unproductive youth. Many are recipients of unemployment benefits and other forms of welfare, and they use these resources to create their work. Further, they argue that if they are disenfranchised and marginalized, this is a consequence of social and economic conditions rather than personal sociopathic or criminal tendencies. Helen, writing in *Grot Grrrl*, describes her government's idea of "Golden Youth" as "pasteurised, homogenised and depoliticised, recessionally-acclimatised and fully compromised."[45] Another issue of *Grot Grrrl* contains a caricature of a police statement entitled "A Message from Your Local Thug Station." It reads in part:

> All you skaters, party-goers, fans of unapproved music, underage alcohol consumers, punks, hippies, protestors, and especially all you violators of stereotypes that we can't classify: you are social scum! You are criminals that we will punish when we find you. If it weren't for us, there'd be endless crime and violence from you shits. You dipshit civilians live in a democratic society, and don't you forget that. If you don't like it here you can go somewhere else that they don't have freedom and our easy going lifestyle.[46]

Doubts are raised here about the truly democratic and liberal nature of societies that criminalize young people for their cultural, personal, and political expressions. An "easy going lifestyle" is an experience enjoyed by some at the expense of others. If a dominant narrative about youth continues to represent them as "social scum" who are in need of guidance, regulation, and often punishment, (and if this is constructed as their legitimate "civilian" status), then young people will have some fun with these stereotypes through parody and irony. Popular targets for a critique of the construction of at-risk girls are work-for-the-dole and workfare programs. These are seen as characterizing young women who have time on their hands as a dangerous risk that must be managed. The website *Grrrowl* advocates "creative unemployment," saying, "To be creatively unemployed means to spend yr time and energy on (developing) yr interests, community and yr skills." It recommends that young women who are unemployed remain confident and take the opportunity to become active in their communities and develop themselves as creative producers and learners:

> do-it-yourself everything! . . . Yr educating yrself/learning new things on *your* terms and according to what you consider to be important (which can be heaps different to what mainstream society considers important). This goes towards giving you back some sort of control in a society where much has been decided for us.[47]

Unemployment is refigured as an opportunity for creativity and productivity on one's own terms. Not only does this view seek to shift the image of young women without work as losers, but it questions the meaning of work and programs to get youth into work. The concept of social control is introduced into debates about youth unemployment, causing basic assumptions about the value of doing work for work's sake to be challenged. These ideas are disseminated through grassroots organizing as well, for example, through the holding of workshops, skill sharing, and youth-led services for the marginalized and unemployed. There is widespread cynicism about the management and essential productivity of working lives in the context of privatization and deregulation. As the Australian website *catpounce* elaborates,

> During the 80s the 38 hour [working] week became the national standard. . . . As you can see, we have been given these rights, but as privatisation is all the rage, and the private sector is more powerful than ever (more powerful than the government these days), the rights are being eroded. . . . We are being rorted [tricked].

In light of these developments, young women engaged in border work also link up with those who are increasingly involved in the regeneration of unions and labor organizing, especially in homebased-pieceworking, sweatshops, casual and off-the-books employment, and sex work.[49] Their networking and activism around corporate globalization specifically address the gendered labor exploitation inherent in the new economy.[50]

The images of teen mothers and welfare-dependent urban girls are also targeted by young women involved in new politics. The Fed Up Honeys, a collective of young women in New York City, have developed a research project, newsletter, webpage, and sticker campaign to counteract these stereotypes. Their objectives are to understand and interrupt the ways these clichéd images are absorbed by young women and to address the lack of resources within their communities that contributes to their perpetuation. The website operates as a place for resources, information, self-expression through creative writing, and the sharing of strategies and stories. Figure 6.2 depicts their sticker campaign, "Makes Me Mad: Stereotypes of Young Urban Womyn of Color." This is a clever and visible mode of intervention into the at-risk designation. The stickers enumerate a list of stereotypes, all starting with the sentence "Young Urban Womyn of Color are . . . ," and elaborating with statements like "lazy and on welfare," "[a] burden to society," and "promiscuous." They feature the half-seen shape of a young woman's body, hand on hip, in a posture of challenge. The stickers are a small and transportable political message: they can be produced cheaply and stuck anywhere; they can appear all over the city and are easy to replace.

These kinds of creative strategies of future-girl politics spread out messages that disrupt assumptions linking at-risk experiences, attitudes, and behaviors to particular populations based on class, race, and community. Other sites and collectives work to undermine the linking of risk experiences with the personal pathologies of individuals or the assumptions that one bad choice can ruin a young woman's future. The *girlmom* website is a resource designed by and for young mothers to counter the myth of the crisis of irresponsible teen motherhood, proclaiming instead that "teenage girls can be, are, and always have been, both sexual and maternal beings." It states, "Degrading, vilifying, marginalizing and rejecting teen mothers (as is customary in our society) is counterproductive and illogical."[51] While not promoting young motherhood, this website and its associated programs and resources seek to support young mothers and counter images of them as failures.

Noting the ways in which class and race are used to construct and divide girls into can-do versus at-risk, Tammy Rae Carland writes in her zine *I Love Amy Carter* of the conflation of welfare recipients with urban African Americans, which she describes as both racist and an invisibilizing of white poverty. She writes of young, poor, white women being depicted as "sexy and stupid," and of her own struggle to live out the complexity of an experience that does not fit these stereotypes. She says,

> When I was a senior in high school I was (academically) third in my class, and in the Fall, when people were being prodded and guided into looking at colleges, I was being ignored. . . . Basically, I was expected to drop out, and when I didn't, they were at a loss as to what to do with me.[52]

Her personal ability to overcome her circumstances and achieve mainstream success sits uneasily with her, because it is typically only made sense of within an individualizing and apolitical discourse of self-belief and personal resilience. She says, "I truly don't want to think I've 'made it,' or that I'm any better, smarter, or safer than I was when I was fifteen.

Young Urban Womyn of Color are...

Likely to Become Teen Moms

Stereotype #1
www.fed-up-honeys.org

Young Urban Womyn of Color are...

Lazy and on Welfare

Stereotype #2
www.fed-up-honeys.org

Young Urban Womyn of Color are...

In Abusive Relationships

Stereotype #3
www.fed-up-honeys.org

Young Urban Womyn of Color are a ...

Burden To Society

Stereotype #4
www.fed-up-honeys.org

Young Urban Womyn of Color are...

Promiscuous

Stereotype #5
www.fed-up-honeys.org

Young Urban Womyn of Color are...

Uneducated

Stereotype #6
www.fed-up-honeys.org

Fig. 6.2 "Young Urban Womyn of Color are . . ." Sticker campaign © 2003 by the Fed–Up–Honeys: www.fed-up-honeys.org. Reprinted with permission.

Because I'm not." The desire to reintroduce systemic explanations for success and failure can be perceived in the sharing of knowledge through diverse clusters and collectives that make efforts to cross race and class boundaries. These alliances are frequently forged through the new media.[53]

Critiquing Consumption

The second way in which young women working in border spaces open up critique of contemporary constructions of young femininity is by questioning consumption. According to many, locations of citizenship and leisure for youth have been reconstructed as sites of passive consumption. The website *catpounce* rails against materialism and credit culture as they absorb young women into consumption-defined happiness:

> Do you have the right runners, haircut and schoolbag? Fantastic! You will be validated, and given the privilege of making your way through schooldays with ZERO ridicule! Have you purchased the most hip CDs and video games? You know you are supposed to be as sexxxxxy as Britney, and if you are not, you will never get a bonk. Though of course you will always yearn for the romantic, cool, funky love you see on the video clips. It doesn't exist, but the concept will keep you buying. Have you co-opted your individuality for a scabby job with "potential?" Just go buy another Tommy Girl and things might improve.[54]

The development of consumer identities for young women has often taken the form of an appropriation of local cultures or styles from youth, which are then adapted, cleaned up, and sold back to them. Very often, the politics of an image or cultural style integral to an oppressed group is emptied out in order to be marketed to others. The *Blackgrrrlrevolution* webpage speaks of "the mass media objectifying and mythisizing of the bodies and images of black grrrls," and concludes that "co-opting and exploitation of the ways, cultural habits, attitude, and mannerism unique to black grrrls is considered fashionable and commodifiable for everyone but black grrrls."[55] Young women are urged to reappropriate or continually remake their styles and to become involved in the active production of their cultures, identities, and communities rather than merely consuming the lifestyle accoutrements that are marketed to them. In this way they expose the myth of self-invention while advocating a real kind of DIY ethic.

Given that so many youth spaces have been filled up with advertising, another important strategy is the attempt to take over corporate space in response. Sometimes known as "culture jamming" or "ad busting," these methods involve converting slogans and images of brands into parodies of themselves, so that their message is exposed and undermined. This sometimes involves using the instantly recognizable font and layout of brands and changing the words of their slogans, or retaining the text but altering the image to which it refers. This kind of practice occurs in public sites, such as billboards and the Internet, and also in more personal spaces, through the wearing of homemade T-shirts and the creation of artworks. At a time when youth voice itself has become a marketing tool, these methods have become important ways to get into the space of advertisers who are perceived to have appropriated the spaces of youth cultures. Naomi

Klein discusses a young female culture jammer who suggests that "the process of making her own media, adopting the voice of the promoter and hacking into the surface of the ad culture began to weaken advertising's effect on her."[56] While these methods or claims may not constitute a substantial disruption to corporatization, they indicate the creativity of young women with very little room to move and the desire to act productively in spite of the pull of cultures of consumption.

Sometimes in advocating DIY, young women are specifically rejecting the commodification and depoliticization of girl culture and, in particular, the reinvention of girlpower as, in the words of Nicola, a comic book artist, "an exploitative marketing ploy aimed at young girls." She continues:

> It is a clever way of capturing the pre-teen dollar, designed by corporate marketing guys. The way that huge corporations think that people can be bought and sold and the way they identify trends and exploit them for their own gains really disgusts me.[57]

This opinion is reflected in the online discussions among many young women globally who feel that their politics has been discovered by advertisers and is now reshaped into little more than a sales pitch to encourage young women to buy profit-making merchandise. For example, Kylie says girlpower

> is used to give across a certain feeling of danger and independence. But it only uses these feelings in a marketing sense: your independence is gained via certain products, and the danger comes from making the choice of that particular product over any other. . . . Things like the Sportsgirl ads that say "Sportsgirl. The power to be yourself.". . . Anything is possible, dependent upon your purchasing of a particular product.[58]

Similarly, the producer of the zine *Her Heroes Aren't Gone*, writes,

> Now I see Spice Girls and supermodels and sparkly slogan shirts—their version of lame "girl power" is so far away from our original vision of "grrrl power;" co-opted, watered down, marketable, profitable—all style and not a fuck of a lot of content. I walk through the mall and I see a chain store clothes shop is selling me some "girl power" in the form of furry winter jackets.[59]

And Rosie of *Geekgirl* says, if "the revolution, girl-style is now in the hands of Sony or Nike,"[60] other ways need to be found for reflective, political young women to conceive of girls as something other than consumer citizens.

Gill Jones and Claire Wallace note the paradox that "as state support is withdrawn and young people are forced to become more dependent on their parents, the market process has served to construct them as independent consumer citizens."[61] Consequently, there is a refiguring of citizenship on the part of young women around the idea of youth as producers rather than consumers. As Kylie says, "To be able to produce something was very exciting. . . . I felt electrified. It is a statement against apathy, and a statement of positive struggle."[62] Participating in their own cultures is an active engagement rather than simply making another consumer choice. These young women break down barriers between consumption and production, and they exemplify the creative possibilities of a network of communication and activism in which anyone can participate. As Nicola says, "Even if you don't have a record deal or a million bucks or a company, you can put out a magazine, make a record, put up a poster, make a difference."[63]

Duncombe suggests that this emphasis on one's own capacity for production seems straightforward enough, "but in a society where consuming what others have produced for you—whether it be culture or politics—is the norm, the implications are far-reaching and radical, for doing it yourself is the first premise of participatory democracy."[64] For many young women, this is particularly significant in the context of the circulation of narratives about girlhood that are not owned, claimed, or generated by young women themselves. Riikka, a young Finnish woman who has a distribution service, band, and zine, says,

> We need to create our own, new forms of media that really speak to us. I am so fucking sick of the heterosexist, sexist, anorexic, racist, propagandist mainstream media. I want to support and encourage all women to be active participants in the dialogues happening in our society. I want you to be an active participant with this distro, not just a passive consumer![65]

Ambassadresses Answer Back

The third example of young women challenging discourses about young femininity is through the critique of the image of girls as compliant ambassadresses. In chapter 3 we saw how potential threats to comforting notions of nation, cultural homogeneity, and social continuity have been addressed through the construction of young women as the new face of blended multiculturalism. This move has also been effective in attempting to counteract the emerging political activism of young women involved in antiracist, anticolonial, proimmigration, and refugee activities. This use of young women, and young women of particular ethnic groups, to depoliticize their agendas and to renew cultural stereotypes in the service of the status quo has been confronted with considerable vigor by young women in new politics. Sociologist Carmela Murdocca argues that intersections of colonialism, racism, and heterosexism are challenged differently by young women's online spaces, in that these offer "places/spaces of resource in as much as they are places of departure from the realm of more traditional academic feminist theorizing on postcoloniality."[66] The Internet is a space where information and activism can be shared, but it also opens up theorizing to be driven from the collective, interactive, ground-up work of what Mimi Nguyen describes on her website *exoticize this!* as the "cyborg diaspora."[67]

The Internet is a site where young women's antiracist activism and debate flourish. A key issue is how to maneuver around such stereotypes as the "celebrated immigrant" or "overreacting troublemaker." The website *Messtiza* describes this dichotomy of the "good colored" versus the "angry woman" thus:

> Being classified as an angry woman, one is regarded as "over reactive," "race-centric" and in extreme cases, "reverse racist." However, one's work can act as an outlet for other women of color to see their own anger envisioned, written, expelled. (Of course, there is the problematic issue of being labeled "angry" by beneficiaries of dominant culture. . . . How is the historical dichotomy of the "good colored" vs. the "disobedient colored" linked to the roles we assume/are prescribed/inhabit as women of color actively questioning and determining our lives? How are these roles incorporated into how we are seen by others?)[68]

Marginal spaces are important sites where personal stories and consciousness raising can sit alongside collective activism and information sharing. The complexities of expressing anger, its strategic uses as well as limitations, can be debated in a context that is safe. The dichotomizing construction of women of color as either good or disobedient is central to the discussion; that is, the issue is not just how to tackle the ambassadress image, but how to usefully take up anger in ways that are not trivialized or dismissed.

As we have seen in chapter 3, there has been a particular trade in the image of young Asian women as compliant, passive, and eager to please, which has served a number of purposes in the framing of migration, refugee, and multicultural debates. Websites, comics, and zines like *Angry Little Asian Girl* and *Bamboo Girl* disrupt these stereotypes and return politics to the discussions of young women's place in multicultural and globalized societies. For example, Kristina Sheryl Wong, creator of the website *Big Bad Chinese Mama*, seeks to undermine images of "demure lotus blossoms" and "geishas." She takes a proactive and confrontationalist approach by deliberately leading surfers into the "number one mock mail order bride/Asian porn spoof site in the world!" The site lures unsuspecting men looking for "Asian girls" with its keywords and, having drawn them in, proceeds to "deconstruct (their) colonialist patriarchal attitudes."[69]

Similarly, the webpage *exoticize this!* challenges the fetishization of young Asian women and provides a good example of how many young women are resisting racially stereotyped images of girls in popular culture. The site opens with images of a young Asian woman in fighting postures, including punching and kicking, with the text "just try it. go ahead. exoticize my fist." The stated purpose of the site is "to create a 'virtual' community for asian american feminists—as well as act as a coalition-building tool to create networks with asian feminists abroad."[70] The site is a mixture of resources, personal reflections, links to organizations, and information about arts and activism. Sabrina Margarita Alcantara-Tan also does such work in her zine *Bamboo Girl*; in her title she plays with stereotyped images of young Asian women. She says,

> The coolest thing is that I have met so many girls like me who are also ethnic mutts who have felt silenced, who feel like they have a place to air their issues in a really direct "don't fuck with me" kinda way. And also . . . to break the racial/ethnic/homophobic stereotypes. . . .[71]

Her zine and website speak to, and in the process have created, a loosely bound global community of activist "ethnic mutts" and their allies.

In a similar vein, Lela Lee's online cartoon *Angry Little Asian Girl*, which has since expanded into *Angry Little Girls*, "a bittersweet weekly comic strip about young ethnic girls growing up in an imperfect world," plays with one-dimensional cultural images. The comic-strip characters are all parodies of U.S. girl stereotypes, including Kim (the Angry Little Asian Girl), Wanda (the Fresh Little Soul Sistah), and Maria (the Crazy Little Latina).[72] The challenge to find a place to air views, to speak out, is complicated by the use of young women of particular ethnicities as ambassadresses, celebrated immigrants, or model minorities. Websites and zines offer other places for ironic and humorous challenges to these images, as well as sites for debate and resources. They spill out into manifest activism through workshops, meetings, protests and sit-ins, campaigns, and performances. For example, the Canadian network Young Women Connect generates activism around "living at the crossroads of race and gender." Its starting point is new media and DIY culture. It advocates "young women taking space, creating their own media to have voice and share their issues and ideas, creating their own channels to connect to each other." From these spaces, media, and channels, it fans out into publicly visible practices.[73]

Apart from these engagements with stereotypes and the creation of networks, the emerging narratives around national pride, cultural cohesion, and patriotism are also problematized by young women who remain deeply suspicious of these moves as whitewashing of racism. Kylie and Katherine, of the Australian zine *Personality Liberation Front* denounce nationalism as being linked to specific political agendas, and they draw particular attention to what this means in Australia, where racism and colonial ideology and practices continue to undermine the image of a modern and multicultural nation. They say,

> Nationalism, pride of your country, of your flag, of the state. Proud of the country that still can't formally say sorry to its torchered [*sic*] raped native population? It's the biggest form of propaganda the state uses. Nationalism is support for the government.[74]

Collectives like the Australian "yGals," who are non-Aboriginal young women working on reconciliation, or those involved in grassroots projects such as the Redfern Aboriginal Corporation schemes for young Koorie[75] women, take up these debates and articulate them into direct action. The need to actively engage with narratives of nationalism and racism, rather than just reflect on them, is taken up by Mary, in the zine *Wrecking Ball,* who states in her list of "things I'm gonna to stop doing with my white privilege,"

> I'm gonna stop thinking all I can do about my undeserved and unearned privi-leges is THINK ABOUT how shitty capitalistic patriarchal society is. Wallow-ing in my own self-pity is lame cuz I know at the same time I could be using the energy to be actively confronting myself and other white people on our racism.[76]

The e-zine *Messtiza* discusses the political implications of only recently revoked California regulations that required school students to sing the national anthem, and many zines and websites are places for ongoing de-bates about attacks on schoolgirls wearing the hijab in secular countries and requirements for women to wear the burka in orthodox Muslim states. The intersections of nationalism and cultural homogenization as they de-lineate preferred images of youth and gender are interrogated by young women who refuse to participate in this shaping of citizenship and state. Many webpages take up the work of translating reflection into activism by creating networks, community movements, and resources against racism and nationalism. These operate both locally and globally and are trans-formed into manifest activity through events such as youth-led action against the war in Iraq, or performance protest such as designated days for widespread wearing of the hijab by non-Muslim women.

Voice and Participation

The final example of the use of border spaces by young women to critique their place in contemporary societies is the issue of voice and participa-tion. Many raise concerns about the framework of youth voice and its rela-tionship to both commodification and the construction of compliant subjects. As Michelle says, "For young women in particular, I think with mainstream culture people are happy for young women's voices to be heard only if they're basically saying what people want to hear."[77] Conse-quently, the where and how of articulation of voice is an issue carefully contemplated by those involved in border spaces.

A distinguishing feature of their perspective is that it is socioeconomic circumstances rather than personal pathologies that position young women as politically disengaged or disenfranchised. However, as we saw in chapter 5, while many commentators argue that the solution to this prob-lem is that young people need to be included and must be encouraged to exercise their participation rights by having their voices heard, a strong message from some young women is that they are not always interested in having their voices elicited or simply being heard by those in power. This is because they want to talk to one another and make their own networks, as what is variously identified as adults, authority, dominant culture, the cor-porate world, and the state are not to be trusted. Helen uses her website *Astrogrrrl* to advocate for her Cynical Youth Coalition, itself a parody in its depiction of cynical youth as active members of a coalition. She says,

> The kids are the only ones with anything useful to say. The kids, well some of the kids, are the people who have resisted, I guess, psychic death. We haven't been indoctrinated for as long as the adults (who think they are smart) thus we are still vibrant alive perceptive, alleged little shits. Thems oldies don't under-stand/review or even like us. Live/create/love on yr own terms. PIMPLE POWER![78]

In this example adults are represented as the ones who are apathetic and disengaged, or indoctrinated and antagonistic toward young people. Be-cause of this, young people need to band together and talk to one another. Helen suggests that the places created for youth are not those best utilized for this purpose. She says, "We, the cynical youth coalition, reserve the right to . . . spurn state-sanctioned youth activities . . . and to expose them as such." Border spaces create opportunities for assembly and debate to occur in other places. Michelle claims that

> Zines can be used as a call to arms . . . but for the revolution, grrrl style, it prob-ably has to stay underground, the process of creating unity and solidarity has to be done through our own channels. It's really important with any kind of revolution for people to be in a space where they are separate from dominant culture.[79]

Creating and then protecting this space is of utmost importance. Simi-larly, Brigette says,

> *Blackgrrrlrevolution* has to be nurtured and protected legally, from imperialism and colonialism and thievery. One thing that people do let us know through all the resistance is that they think it is a damn good brand, and I always say if *Blackgrrrlrevolution* was a T shirt company then people would be perfectly happy: Black girls for T shirts! But no, it's a real movement with a real agenda.[80]

Young women involved in these cultures reject many mainstream forms of participation and inclusion because they are highly suspicious of the privatized, marketized, and nonrepresentative nature of the neoliberal state and of the interests of those who may be eager to elicit their voices. Their ability to protect their spaces comes from a desire to own their own voices, which in turn may require silence in some contexts if the listener is not deemed worthy.[81] Consequently, it is important to take up the challenge of women's studies scholar Magda Lewis, that is, to fuse "an examination of that silence which cannot be spoken with an understanding of that silence which offers the possibility of a transformative politics—silence born of dissent."[82] As we saw in chapter 5, many of the sites for youth voice and participation have been managed to such a degree that a form of silence seems an appropriate alternative to speaking out.

Enduring Political Effects

There is a widespread assumption that inclusion and participation are good for young women. Many youth researchers have tended to rely on the story of the lost voice of girls to empower young women and create opportunities for them to articulate their views. However, as Giroux states, while

> young people need to be given the opportunity to narrate themselves . . . this suggests more than letting kids have the opportunity to voice their concerns, it means providing the conditions—institutional, economic, spiritual and cultural—that allow them to re-conceptualize themselves as citizens.[83]

Young women involved in border spaces are attempting to do this work of reconceptualizing themselves as new kinds of citizens. As we have already seen, this is partly by attempting to shift citizenship from consumption to production, but also sometimes by trying to articulate new modes of political engagement that break with traditional frameworks. Kylie claims that "the normal political arenas are not at all welcoming for young women—it's pretty male dominated in there. What other avenues does society offer us? [But] there is strength in numbers. We have other plans."[84] One of the ways young people can reconceptualize themselves as citizens is by creating other plans for new forums and techniques for public deliberation. Another is by flagging new practices of agitation and resistance. As *Re:Vulva* girls Tamara, Jade, and Melissa say, "Perhaps our political motivations cannot be categorized or defined by frameworks of older theories circa 1960. [The revolution] is coming—you will smell the fire!"[85]

While the enduring political efficacy of these claims is difficult to ascertain, the desire to speak, act, and agitate elsewhere, outside the normal political arenas or frameworks of older theories, suggests a strong need to take seriously new spaces for engagement and expression for young women. These provide not only sites for young women to gather, debate, and critique meanings of young womanhood in late modernity, but also potential new modes of networking and organizing. As Naomi Klein writes, this practice can be successful by responding "to corporate concentration with a maze of fragmentation, to globalisation with its own kind of localisation, to power consolidation with radical power dispersal."[86] For example, VNS Matrix, a collective of young female cyberartists and technicians, describe the development of their interactive CD and web-based game BAD CODE, which "moves the player through a labyrinthine hive of subcultural tribes, assisting the viral intelligence 'Gen' on her mission to sabotage the data banks of Big Daddy Mainframe, thus activating the germ of the new world disorder."[87] The cultures of young women that exist in labyrinthine hives are felt by many to carry powerful viruses that can both infect other young women and interrupt the production and use of young womanhood.

It remains, however, that the specificities of the political work accomplished by these spaces is not always easy to establish. While the symbolic value of claiming a new kind of revolution should not be discounted, how this sits in relation to traditional political activism is a question frequently posed. Michelle Fine and Lois Weis wonder about the political potential of free spaces because of their very marginality. They say,

> If "free spaces" are disconnected from a prospering economy, a government committed to democratic participation, and to progressive social movements, do they have the capacity to interrupt social injustice and transform social arrangements? Or will they function instead as intermittently as steam valves on old radiators?[88]

What then is the political power of these spaces, if they are unsupported by the traditional structures and conditions for participatory democracy? For some participants in free spaces, it is this very lack of support that grants them their potential. As we have seen, the regulation of good citizenship and participation has become a strategy of surveillance and deradicalization. First, then, if we understand these spaces as providing transient places to take time out and try on new identities and alliances, to network and share ideas and information with other youth away from regulation, they can be imagined as a kind of pre- or even newly figured participatory politics. At the least they can be acknowledged for their ongoing use as rest stops, fissures, places for momentary reflection, and connection.[89]

However, more than this, I would suggest it is possible to see how the more personal work of claiming community, networks and city space connects up with the new politics of border spaces, and how both can suggest directions forward for social change and political protest. Free spaces have more than the potential to link up with progressive social movements; they work to reshape their very terms of reference. The border work of new media and information and communication technologies (ICTs) and the insistence of young women on their entitlement to self-made civic space open up new places for politics, citizenship, participation, and community building. These serve to insert and spread strategies for change and resistance from the bottom up, rather than simply pitching challenges from the top down. As environmental studies scholars Kimberley Fry and Cheryl Lousley argue, many young women activists today do not

> wait for electoral gains or progressive international summits and agreements. Instead they strive to craft multiple spaces of democratic participation and cultural resistance in their daily lives. Ever conscious of the risk of co-optation, their politics have become more playful, more performative and more directly aimed at the culture industry.[90]

These possibilities have been generated by circumstances of surveillance and regulation, along with a lattice of regulatory powers in place of a centralized base of government.

Here I have focused on these less-acknowledged modes of resistance, but this does not mean that more traditional styles of young women's politics have been erased. I have shown new ways in which young women have been creating dissent around images and uses of girls in society today. These strategies have been developed as politics for new times in which power is operationalized in a dispersed and fragmented fashion. They have emerged in response to regulation through incitement to discourse and the dismantling of a traditional public sphere. However, these techniques also feed into manifest activism around exploitative labor practices, corporate globalization, the so-called war on terror and war in Iraq, sex tourism and trafficking, reproductive rights, queer issues, disability rights, and anti-racism. Much of this activism continues to be enacted through traditional means in public places: for example, rallies, education campaigns, letter writing, media exposure, sit-ins, pressuring politicians, and lobbying powerful groups and individuals. This work has been enduring and effective, and I do not wish to suggest it has been eliminated or overtaken. Rather, there has been a recognition among many young women that change can happen and, under conditions of surveillance may best happen, in multiple and connected ways. New media, ICTs, and DIY culture generate networks, spaces, and channels for linking up new and older modes of critique and activism. Therefore a notion of a diffuse and complementary series of spaces and strategies may capture the emerging politics of young women, rather than the simple erasure of the old and the ushering in of an indistinct and unformed new.

Conclusion

This chapter has explored young women's negotiations of public and private spaces in border networks, cultures, and politics and their critical engagement with narratives of young female subjectivity. I have considered the ways some young women create networks and safe spaces for themselves within their homes, cities, and communities, either as sites of critique or simply as breathing spaces. I have suggested that border spaces, including those that flourish around writing, alternative media, artwork, and the Internet, are important sites for many young women because their traditional spaces of leisure, assembly, and critique have been caught up in a process of regulation and production of either can-do or at-risk girlhood. Through this, free spaces have diminished, and youth voice has been increasingly managed through civic-ization and corporate cooptation.

Border spaces, although sometimes idealized as more politically effective or more underground than they could ever really be, do offer room, networks, and strategies for critical engagement with these new social forces, and they build a capacity for connections and information sharing among young women globally. Young women involved in them interrogate the barriers between public and private and open up new spaces for participation and activism. These spaces refigure popular narratives about girlhood, power, risk, and success, and they offer up new analytical frameworks and a range of strategies to better understand how young women are both positioned within and are able to problematize the late modern world. It has not been my argument to suggest that a worked-up, uniform political program is evident here, or that a majority of young women are involved in these activities.[91] At most, I would concur with Irena Guidikova and Lasse Siurala when they say, "Ill-adapted structural conditions of youth transitions . . . unlock peer dynamics and (sub)culture environments which generate new types of relationships, outlooks and life expectations, as well as impetus for social action taking 'strange,' unfamiliar ways."[92] For while the broader-ranging outcomes of these forms of cultural and political activity cannot be entirely foreseen, border spaces at least offer strategies and foundations for new local and global networks within which young women can debate and challenge the construction of the future girl.

CONCLUSION

This book has been about representations of young womanhood, the material conditions young women experience, and the new politics they enact. I have suggested that the needs of global capital shape constructions of the future girl. I have demonstrated how feminist and neoliberal narratives of self-invention have framed policy, advertising, programs, and media about girls' welfare, justice, education, employment, sexuality, parenting, and citizenship. This language of—and some young women's capacity for—opportunities, freedoms, choices, and responsibilities facilitates the coalescence of global economic motives with girls' individual life decisions. Narratives of responsibilization, strategic effort, and choice enlist young women into the service of the new economy. However, it is because these discourses are so pervasive, and because of the new regimes of regulation that manage young women by making them freer subjects than ever before, that new politics have emerged. Different modes of resistance have developed in response to these new strategies of governmentality. I have deemed this *future-girl politics*, and suggest it works by creating alternative spaces and global networks for public deliberation and that it evades surveillance and appropriation by what social movement theorist Abby Peterson describes as "tunneling in" rather than tackling political systems head-on. In short, new times both regulate and constrain young women in unprecedented ways, which unleashes unforeseen techniques of critique and resistance by them.

I have sought to trouble the taken-for-granted notion that girlpower and new socioeconomic opportunities have simply created brilliant prospects for all young women. Major changes in the societies and economies of Western nations have had a significant impact on young people, for whom education, employment, citizenship, family life, and transitions to adulthood have all been rapidly rethought. Flexibility, resilience, and self-invention have become central to securing a livelihood, developing an identity, and ensuring success. "Making it" in the new economy and prevailing as a successful subject have largely become understood as a question of personal resolve and self-invention.

Social expectations of women have also undergone transformation in recent times. The impact of feminism can be seen in the laws, policies, and mores of a large number of Western countries. Young women are widely held to be the beneficiaries of these changes. As I have suggested in this book, the gains of feminism and the needs of contemporary capital have made an unlikely alliance. Young women are imagined and invested in as those most able to prevail and flourish in these new times because, courtesy of feminism, they are the ones who are supposed to be most sold on the message of self-invention. At the same time their bodies and labor power have become integral to the new economy, and they provide comforting images of continuity and cohesion in times that feel risky and uncertain. I have suggested that the construction of young women as the ideal citizens of the future both sustains and renders less frightening the rapid social and economic shifts we are experiencing.

The investment in young women as those most able to succeed involves an enormous amount of regulation and work in order for a mainstream image of young female success to be perpetuated, and the large numbers of those young women who do not succeed to be corralled into positions of bad choices and personal limitations. While success and failure continue to be structured by the enduring inequities generated through the race/class system, making it is widely represented as a matter of strategic effort, personal desire, hard work, and good choices. I have argued that the management of young women into categories of can-do versus at-risk is one of the most significant strategies by which success is reserved for the fictional mainstream of those who strive hard. This management is conducted through the construction and regulation of the spaces of young women's lives, including school, work, juvenile justice and welfare systems, the street, and recreation sites. Increasingly, young women's private and interior spaces are also subject to a monitoring gaze. In these places certain kinds of citizenship, work, consumption, and mothering are linked to successful girlhood, while others are split off and vilified.

One deeply troubling consequence of this regulation has been the diminishing of free spaces in which young women can position themselves differently and express alternative narratives to can-do or at-risk. This has been a very interesting development, for it has occurred in the context of an apparent expansion of places for girls' voices, participation, and self-expression. While women and girls have never had much space to themselves, the proliferation of sites for young women today has not necessarily granted them more freedom. The creation of space and opportunities for young women has also signaled a new interest in observing, monitoring, and regulating them into preferred subject positions. Young women are seen and heard more than ever before, but much of this public presence is stage-managed and leaves them little opportunity to be out of the spotlight. I have used Foucault's notion of the incitement to discourse to demonstrate how an interest in getting girls to speak out, to be seen and heard, can operate as a strategy of governmentality.[1] I have suggested that in light of this, some of the most interesting critiques of and maneuvers around the contemporary positionings of young women have come from those involved in what I have described as border spaces. This includes not only those who might perceive themselves as politically active, but also those who simply attempt to slip under the radar, who remap their communities and develop opportunities for self-crafted expression even while under conditions of surveillance. In documenting these maneuvers, I hope to have shown how some young women refuse new kinds of individualization,[2] develop new strategies for activism, and at the least create some breathing space for themselves, without suggesting that those who do not use these techniques are somehow less capable or insightful.

In chapter 1 I showed how and why young women have emerged as the central subjects of discourses about how to prevail today, utilizing the motifs of can-do and at-risk. I explained how young women are encouraged to become self-disciplining in the production of success and take personal responsibility for failure. The fields of professional ambition, consumption, and motherhood are the most significant for contemporary young women's identity work, and so I discussed the manufacturing of success and failure in these contexts. In chapter 2 I explored this further in relation to education, employment, and the notion of youth transitions to adulthood within the new economy. The requirements on young women to be successful through flexibility and self-invention are felt most deeply here. However, the idea of limitless opportunities in work is undercut by the divisive ways in which young women are actually located in the labor market. This stratification is essential to the functioning of globalized and deregulated capitalist economies, but its fundamental inequities are covered over through narratives of personal effort or lack thereof. In chapter 3 I explained how citizenship for young women has also been significantly refigured, focusing particularly on economic independence, civic representation, social cohesion, and consumption. I argued that the civic qualities that are attributed to young women dovetail with requirements of self-invention, responsibilization, and individual economic empowerment.

My concern in the first part of the book was to explain how young women have been produced as ideal subjects of late modernity through a blending of a kind of individualized feminism with neoliberalism. In the second part I have been interested in the physical and symbolic spaces where this occurs and what this means for young women's own capacity to articulate positions of greater complexity and dissent. In the last three chapters of the book, I have shifted the focus toward the themes of spaces and voices for participation and critique. Young people's lives are managed much more than ever before. Public recreation has diminished, and school participation has increased. Although there are fewer secure jobs available to youth, there are more requirements on them to be responsible citizens. New youth welfare and justice regimes demand personal responsibility and effort from their clients. Surveillance and policing services monitor young people's physical environments. There are fewer ways and places for young women to develop critical narratives grounded in socioeconomic analysis of their circumstances. The spaces young women have managed to wedge open amidst this regulation are important sites for critique to be articulated.

Chapter 4 explored the changing public spaces that young women occupy and attended particularly to the ways success and failure are produced within them. Here, I focused on the question of which bodies are seen where, by looking at sites such as school, work, the street, the mall, and juvenile justice and welfare regimes. I argued that the contraction of some spaces and the expansion of others serve to regulate young women into environments where they can be observed and produced as responsibilized, individualized subjects. Chapter 5 turned to the move toward increasing participation and the encouragement of youth voice and personal expression within this broader analytical framework of regulation. I suggested here that within the context of surveillance of interior spaces and evocation of authentic voices, attempts to corral young women into appropriate sites for speaking out must be examined critically. Chapter 6 was an exploration of the places and ways young women carve out spaces for themselves, within and outside surveillance. I argued that these demonstrate considerable critical engagement with narratives of future-girl subjectivity, and that they offer ways forward for new methods and movements for social justice that account for the changed nature of power structures themselves.

I have sought to make some claims about how enduring or politically effective these strategies of engagement and critique might be (although some are not intended to be political activism as such and should not be judged thus). I am in agreement with many theorists who argue that social movements and political change have taken on radically different forms, and that marginal cultures and local engagements, and their strategies of power dispersal, irony, performance, and so on, are significant elements in this shift. Young people's new modes of activism, and some of the techniques employed by the young women I discuss, can be interpreted through these frameworks. I have attempted to show that diverse groups of young women across a wide range of Western countries are engaged in the work of negotiating and questioning contemporary meanings of girlhood, although it takes place in spaces and through voices that are not necessarily intended to reach an adult/authority audience.

This development suggests that there are positive signs of a nascent next wave of feminism, driven by diasporic and diverse collectives of young women. Over recent years there has been considerable criticism of young women's relationship, or rather nonrelationship, to feminism. The most common concern has been that feminism has sunk beneath the weight of neoliberal reinterpretations and has become simply a superficial gender gloss on an essentially conservative ideology of DIY responsibilization and self-invention. Indeed, much of the debate about the efficacy of so-called third-wave feminism is shaped by the assumption that young women are too easily mistaking neoliberal self-making for real gains.[3] What is evidenced here, however, is a strong push against any narratives of individualization that are in the service of contemporary power structures, which inevitably includes a kind of feminism that is grounded in what cultural studies theorist Rita Felski calls "the humanist project of knowing and achieving the self."[4] These young women are wary of projects of self-making, and they enact other kinds of resistance and struggle that allow them to evade and refuse subjectification.

I believe that the kind of border work that young women are engaged in, as I have illustrated here, indicates a new direction for feminist political activism. This is the beginning of a politics that, in its modes of organization and communication and in its mechanisms for activism, accounts for the absence of a centralized state, the disappearance of the public sphere, the challenges of globalization, and the trend toward appropriation and absorption of dissent by the mainstream. It offers strategies for political community building among youth that may bring new strength to future social movements. Ethnic studies scholar Julia Sudbury notes that "as the new millennium ushers in an era of unchecked capital accumulation and massive and widening divides between information-rich elites and disenfranchised majorities, feminists and anti-racists need to respond by infusing our praxis with the new politics."[5] It is young feminist and antiracist women who are starting to build the foundations and networks of these new politics.

The discussion of appropriate sites for political expression has implications for the future of research and policy regarding youth in general, and young women in particular. As I have demonstrated throughout the book, the "unbindings" generated by late modernity have led to new agendas for youth that focus on citizenship and participation. Engaging youth, hearing from them, and placing them where they can be seen and heard are all strategies through which these agendas are enacted. For social justice youth researchers and activists, these moves seem vital and empowering. However, in the current climate of responsibilization and regulation, they may be perceived warily by young people themselves. I have attempted to explain why participation, speaking out, and acting in the public sphere have become problematic for many young women, bound up as these acts have become in the regulation and production of compliant subjects. Instead, the borders between public and private are being reworked in a way that enables new modes of community, activism, and participation to be crafted. It seems that an issue urgently requiring our attention is how to simultaneously respect a silence of dissent and to ensure that young people are able to position themselves as sociopolitical actors, speaking subjects, on their own terms. The move toward participatory action research as a preferred mode of conducting youth research is surely a welcome step in this direction. Remaining vigilant about the regulatory potential of the incitement to discourse is another. The issue of youth voice—who it belongs to, where it is expressed, who is listening, what is said in its name, and so on—is highly complex. So too is silence.[6] An acknowledgment of this complexity must become part of our conversations about how to construct research projects and policy for, with, and by youth.

Public policy and youth research have also become somewhat fixated on transitions and pathways through education, training, and employment in new times. This move also warrants our critical attention. These emerging concerns about skills training and credentialing continue to be shaped by traditional ideas about the path from youth to adulthood as a series of sequential and linear developmental stages. Policy and research concerns persist in holding on to a modern conception of becoming an adult and a citizen, and they attempt to impose this on the experience of growing up in a late modern world. The inevitable mismatch between framework and experience results in young people being obliged to take responsibility for creating their own successful pathways, traditionally defined, in spite of new and real structural constraints in place that limit their opportunities. I have tried to show how public interest in young women that is centered around their study, work, recreation, and consumption, is often in the service of constructing a new subject who regulates herself onto a success trajectory.

This success trajectory, characterized by a good career, a family, and responsible citizenship, is in essence no different from the appropriate transition to adulthood expected of youth in modern times. What is different is, first, that it is now expected of young women, and second, that current socioeconomic conditions do not tend to support these possibilities. Instead, youth are required to do it themselves while being told that this is the normal and mainstream experience. We are well overdue for a relevant framework of growing up for young people in new times. As Dwyer and Wyn argue, "Because the predictability of the old-style linear model of transition is questionable it is now more important than ever to devise ways of uncovering the complexity and ambiguity of transition in post-industrial society."[7] Research and policy need to develop more nuanced interpretations of transitions, and this means exploring young people's own meanings around adulthood, successful pathways, and desired futures.

In spite of my acknowledgment that the youth research agenda of education, work, and citizenship requires rethinking, I have spent a considerable portion of this book discussing these very issues. Hopefully, my analysis has not just reproduced the old problems embedded in the traditional transitions framework. Its purpose has been to offer some insights into the tensions caused by the clash between old models and new times and how this serves to responsibilize young women. However, in emphasizing these themes, I have left out many other important issues that deserve whole chapters, and books, in themselves. I am particularly aware of paying little attention to issues of young women's sexualities, bodily pleasures, and body image. New practices of body beautification and modification—indeed, an emerging body politics—and new opportunities for sexual agency and expression are surely other important ways to theorize changing sites of power and politics.

Similarly, young women's changing leisure patterns and lifestyle choices, including new spiritual and political affiliations that exist beyond the rather predictable consumption choices offered to them, should be investigated. There is emerging evidence that many young women are rejecting the can-do appellation outright and placing greater value on friendships, relationships, family, leisure, and personal growth than on professional success and acquiring the props for a glamorous lifestyle.[8] Others again may respond to the requirements of responsibilization and self-invention through immersion in ascetic traditions and practices, for example, by recalling traditionalist religious identities. These moves could be interpreted as coping strategies wielded sensibly in an uncertain environment where the old, taken-for-granted processes of youth transition and acquiring material security are no longer in place. However, they could also be understood as an unspectacular but very effective reclaiming of one's life in the face of considerable pressure and regulation to follow particular pathways for success. The extent and effects of these choices remain to be seen and are worth watching closely.

In deciding what to include and what to leave out, I also chose to exclude a discussion of the many and varied programs for young women that seek to support them in developing a critical consciousness and life-management strategies in relation to limited notions of success. I am thinking particularly of support groups, clubs, after-school programs, and the like that are devised and facilitated by adults in the service of young women. I have, however, discussed some of their one-time projects, like public art. This was a difficult decision, for much of the excellent work on safe spaces has been done by analyzing these kinds of programs.[9] And, of course, much of the work of providing options for young women beyond can-do and at-risk happens in these spaces. I have chosen instead, perhaps provocatively, to question the assumptions behind some of these programs, where, as Weis and Fine put it, young people "toil sometimes under the caring eyes of organizers, teachers, parents or peers."[10] It is because these "caring eyes" can also act as a monitoring gaze that I have focused instead on places that young women have to themselves. These have sometimes developed in the face of, and even in defiance of, these other, more formal locales. I felt it important to discuss some of the lesser-known spaces and to take them seriously as sites of critique and political possibility. I sought to emphasize spaces where young women were able to create their own agendas and talk to one another without an adult mediator. This is not to suggest that un-adult-erated spaces are necessarily better or freer, more that they are simply legitimate in themselves. Moreover, the lines between them sometimes become blurry, and the potential for the two to connect in positive ways is considerable.[11]

I am also aware of having presented a somewhat gloomy picture of young women's circumstances, and this is in spite of the evidence of what Dwyer and Wyn describe as a "perplexing optimism" among young people themselves. They suggest that there is a mismatch between researchers' old agendas of work and citizenship and young people's own interest in culture, leisure, and sexuality. Young people's enthusiasm for the aspects of life that bring joy, creativity, and connectedness can seem incongruous against the backdrop of high unemployment, the disappearance of the welfare safety net, expanded police surveillance, and the building of prisons. It can also seem like admirable resilience. I remain deeply concerned about the socioeconomic structures of late modernity that demand so much from young women and provide so little support to them in return. At the same time it is important to honor young women's own capacities to make positive meaning in their lives, to enjoy the agency they have, and to respect their strategies for doing the best they can.

APPENDIX
Who Is a Girl?

Any book that focuses on an age- and gender-based category as its subject of inquiry immediately runs into the problem of implying a natural, fixed state of being for that category. That is, the diversity and fluidity of its membership tends to be flattened out by an assumption of shared basic characteristics. Feminist youth studies has been particularly cognizant of this issue, as both gender and age are frequently used in traditional theoretical and empirical work to create and naturalize artificial categories for study. The construction of "girls" as a universal category has a long and problematic history, and many researchers have investigated how, when, and why the concepts of girls and girlhood have been invented.[1] This idea of inventing young women is illustrated in the problem that researchers and others have in figuring out "how old is a girl?" which demonstrates that girlhood is not a fixed period of time but is subject to historical and social specificities.

Currently, it seems that membership in the girl category is extending out at both ends: female children are becoming aware of a feminine identity at a younger age (hence the "tweenie" phenomenon), and women into their thirties and forties cheerfully describe themselves and their peers as girls. This suggests that the category of girl is constantly shifting and cannot be linked to a fixed age or developmental stage in life. However, there are some parameters to our shared understandings of the period of contemporary Western young womanhood. Earlier onset of puberty, the responsibilities and opportunities of work and consumption, and sexual relationships being available at a younger age mark an entrée to young womanhood in the late preteen years. At the other end, girlhood is not perceived to be entirely completed until the mid- to late twenties, owing to the extension of education, the end of the job for life, and the trend toward later-life motherhood and deferral of long-term relationships.

Although there is tremendous fluidity in the application of the title "girl," normative ideas about appropriate female adolescence that serve a wider social purpose have been simultaneously imposed on young women in an homogenizing fashion. Characteristics of specific groups of girls have often become definitive of the assumed qualities and experiences of all young women. The unseen markers of privilege have frequently come into play in girls' studies, such that the girlhoods of white, middle-class young women have been generalized out into assumptions about all girlhoods.[2] Consequently, the young women who have usually been tested against this measure, being the underresourced and those most prone to regulation, have been found wanting.

I want to expose this very notion of a normal girlhood by drawing attention to some of the contemporary ways that an imagined common experience of girlhood is constructed. I look at the strategies by which particular versions of young female identity are made to seem normal, universal, and equally available to all. I also examine the ways that the specific and unequal locations of young women are rendered as minor personal issues in the greater scheme of a uniform girlhood. At the same time, while I want to make central the diversity evident in the socioeconomic and cultural contexts of young women's lives, I do not want to abandon the idea that we can make some general statements about young women as a group. This is not because they share enduring, inherent characteristics, but because we continue to make meaning, and symbolic and material use, of girls as a category. Cultural studies scholar Catherine Driscoll claims that it is today especially that girls have emerged so clearly as sites for the production of a new kind of self. Accordingly, the study of young women need not be abandoned as a consequence of its false premise of demographic uniformity, but rather, as she argues, "It is thus not only possible but imperative to recognize the significance of girls around us, and the folding of major public discourses into the highly visible formation of late modern girls."[3]

I use a wide range of data to make some claims about both a global creation of the future girl and the specific and local meanings of this process.[4] I have made an effort to include material from a number of different Western countries, including the United States, Canada, the United Kingdom, Australia, New Zealand/Aotearoa, and Northern and Western Europe. I also include pertinent examples from postcommunist Europe where Westernization and marketization are in process. As noted youth studies researchers Peter Dwyer and Johanna Wyn write in their book *Youth, Education and Risk,*

> If . . . the imagery of globalisation and its acknowledged impact on the life-chances, lifestyles and education of the young are to be analysed seriously, some attempt must be made to break through . . . localised research preserves and make connections between the developing strands in each.[5]

Many local studies share similar issues, frameworks, and findings, but they are not always brought into conversation with one another. This is often the case in research about young women, for important information about their experiences can be hidden beneath broader categories of inquiry such as youth or women. However, care must always be taken in drawing together materials from distinct moments in history and from different places to avoid implying that they can be read interchangeably or simply be layered onto one another as though they constitute an easy fit. Such illustrative material must be interrogated for its specificity even while it sits within an argument about globalization and homogenization.

Drawing together materials from a range of places and times is therefore a project embarked on with caution. I do not intend my analysis to be comparative or universalizing. I am not trying to build up a picture of an all-purpose, global girl. At the same time, it is also problematic to define the experiences of categories of young women by simply using national classifications. For example, as soon as I write "German girls," we need to know about their class, culture, locality, and so on before we can understand who we are really talking about. Because of this, I have tried to be very specific about the young women I describe. I examine their lives contextually to illustrate the specific, local experiences of differently positioned young women, but at the same time I make some claims about transnational trends. In other words, in this book the experiences of middle-class, city-dwelling, Afro-Caribbean British girls will bump up against the experiences of poor, rural, white Canadian girls so I can show how global forces are modified by context specificities.

NOTES

Introduction

1. See the appendix for a discussion of the category of "young women" and an explanation of how the term is used in this book.
2. Review of *Gutsy Girls*, 2001:176.
3. Lesko, 2001:5–6.
4. Lesko, 2001:50.
5. Furlong and Cartmel, 1997:6.
6. See Ball, Maguire, and Macrae, 2000.
7. Miles, 2000:68.
8. Kelly, 2001:23. The quoted phrase is from Giddens, 1991.
9. See Johnson, 2002.
10. Blackmore, 2001:125.
11. Beck, 1992:135.
12. Kelly, 2001:30. See also Du Bois-Reymond, 1998.
13. Foucault, 1980a.

Chapter 1

1. Deegan, 1997.
2. Katz, 1997.
3. McRobbie, 2001. The concept of *governmentality* comes from Foucault, 1982:221. He uses *government* to refer both to formal political structures and the modes of action that direct appropriate conduct on the part of individuals. He says, "To govern, in this sense, is to structure the possible field of action of others."
4. Lesko, 2001:134.
5. See Hall, 1979; Bessant, 1993; Pilkington, 1996; Griffin, 1997; Wyn and White, 1997.
6. Springhall, 1986.
7. See Frith, 1984.
8. See Aapola, 1997; Harris, 1999a.
9. See Phoenix, 1991; Carrington, 1993; Griffin, 1993; Lesko, 2001.
10. See Johnson, 1993.
11. Aotearoa is the Maori (Indigenous) name for New Zealand. See Austin, 1991, and Palmer and Collard, 1998, for a discussion of young Australian Aboriginal workers in the nineteenth and early twentieth century.

12. McRobbie, 2000 (chapter 9 "Sweet Smell of Success? New Ways of Being Young Women"):200–1.
13. See Walkerdine, Lucey, and Melody, 2001. As Hopkins, 1999:98, says, "Ambition is in fashion for youthful femininity."
14. See Harris, 1999b.
15. Hopkins, 1999:95.
16. Schneider and Stevenson, 1999:250.
17. McRobbie, 2001.
18. Quoted in Baumgardner and Richards, 2001:180, italics in original.
19. Baumgardner and Richards, 2001:183.
20. Hopkins, 2002a:88, italics in original.
21. Nielsen, 1999:160, italics in original.
22. McRobbie, 2001.
23. Adkins, 2002:65.
24. See Johnson, 1993.
25. Quoted in Nikas, 1998:20.
26. See Barwick, 2001, and Brown, 2000, for U.K. figures; Nikas, 1998, for Australia; and Cuneo, 2002, for the United States.
27. Nikas, 1998:20.
28. Blackmore, 2001:128.
29. See Nikas, 1998; Cox, 2000.
30. McRobbie, 2001; Luker, 1996.
31. Walkerdine, Lucey, and Melody, 2001:194. See also Kenway, 1990.
32. Fordham, 1996:131.
33. Dwyer and Wyn, 2001:146.
34. Furstenburg et al., 1999:216.
35. Dwyer and Wyn, 2001:145.
36. Kelly, 2001:30.
37. Schneider and Stevenson, 1999:85, 86.
38. Schneider and Stevenson, 1999:94.
39. Furstenburg et al., 1999:226.
40. "Female Offenders," 2001:1.
41. Bottrell, 2001.
42. Griffin, 1997:16.
43. See Wilkinson and Mulgan, 1995.
44. See Laflin, 1996; Luker, 1996; Valdez, 1997; Wearing and Wearing, 2000.
45. Greer, 1999:310.
46. Mickelburough, 1999:1.
47. Cooper, 1998.
48. Warnock, 1998.
49. Martin, 1998.
50. See Alder, 1998; Kuo, 1998; Holsinger, 2000.
51. Griffin, 1997.
52. Lesko, 2001:137.
53. Luker, 1996; Lesko, 2001:135.
54. Males, 1996:91.
55. See Walkerdine, Lucey, and Melody, 2001:190.
56. Lanctot and Smith, 2001.
57. Phoenix, 1991.
58. McRobbie, 2001.
59. Phoenix, 1991.
60. McRobbie, 2001.
61. Blake, 1995–1996.
62. Kuo, 1998.
63. Reich, 1999.
64. See Alder, 1998.
65. See Kenway and Willis, 1990; Holmes and Silverman, 1992; Milligan, Thomson, Ashenden, and Associates, 1992; Marshall and Yazdani, 1999.

66. Carol Gilligan had laid the groundwork for this approach to young women's development almost a decade before in her research on gender differences in moral thinking.
67. Baumgardner and Richards, 2001:178.
68. See Ward, 2000.
69. Baumgardner and Richards, 2001:191.
70. Walkerdine, Lucey, and Melody, 2001:185.
71. Griffin, 1997.
72. McRobbie, 2001.
73. Griffin, 1997:17.
74. "Female Offenders," 2001:4.
75. Males, 1996:12.
76. See Bottrell, 2001.
77. Dwyer and Wyn, 2001:65.

Chapter 2

1. Walkerdine, Lucey, and Melody, 2001:3.
2. See for example Miles, 2000.
3. Furlong and Cartmel, 1997:16–17.
4. Wallace and Kovatcheva, 1998:88.
5. See Dwyer and Wyn, 2001.
6. European Group for Integrated Social Research, 2001:105.
7. Walkerdine, Lucey, and Melody, 2001:2.
8. Probert and Macdonald, 1999:22.
9. See Heath, 1999a.
10. See Lagree, 1995; Furlong and Cartmel, 1997; Järvinen and Vanttaja, 2001.
11. Rattansi and Phoenix, 1997:139.
12. Chisholm, 1997:111.
13. See for example Zinneker, quoted in Wallace, 1994:48, and Lahteenmaa, 1995.
14. Dwyer and Wyn, 2001:128–29.
15. Krüger, 1990:132.
16. See Galland, 1995; Jones, 1995; Wilkinson and Mulgan, 1995; Helve, 1997; Rudd and Evans, 1998; Miles, 2000:156.
17. See Basit, 1996; Schneider and Stevenson, 1999:49.
18. Bulbeck, 2001. See also U.S. National Longitudinal Surveys quoted in Hakim, 1991.
19. Looker and Magee, 2000; Wicks and Mishra, 1998:93.
20. Hughes-Bond, 1998:289.
21. Basit, 1996:231.
22. Walkerdine, Lucey, and Melody, 2001:78.
23. Basit, 1996; Wicks and Mishra, 1998.
24. Warner-Smith and Lee, 2001.
25. Johnson, 2002:33.
26. McRobbie, 2000 (chapter 9 "Sweet Smell of Success? New Ways of Being Young Women"):201.
27. See also Yates, 2000.
28. Fordham, 1996:56.
29. Walkerdine, Lucey, and Melody, 2001:112.
30. Roker, 1993.
31. Proweller, 1998:172.
32. Lahteenmaa, 1995:235.
33. Roker, 1993:135.
34. Kenway, 1990; Yates, 2000:157–58.
35. See Fine and Burns, forthcoming.
36. Frønes, 2001:220.
37. Saltau and Ryan, 2000.
38. Walkerdine, Lucey, and Melody, 2001:180.
39. Schneider and Stevenson, 1999:247.
40. Herrmann, 1998:229.

41. McLeod, 2001:508.
42. Wyn, 2000:65–66. See also Proweller, 1998.
43. Schneider and Stevenson, 1999:157.
44. Walkerdine, Lucey, and Melody, 2001:185.
45. McRobbie, 2001.
46. See Manne, 2002.
47. Wicks and Mishra, 1998:95.
48. Walkerdine, Lucey, and Melody, 2001:54.
49. Dwyer and Wyn, 2001:132.
50. See Archer and Hutchings, 2000.
51. Wallace and Kovatcheva, 1998:120.
52. See also Krüger, 1990; Gregory, 1993; Wallace, 1994; Basit, 1996; Dwyer and Wyn, 2001: 131.
53. See Fine and Weis, 1998.
54. Dwyer and Wyn, 2001:62.
55. Hughes-Bond, 1998:288.
56. Chisholm, 1997:112.
57. Furlong and Cartmel, 1997:35.
58. Wicks and Mishra, 1998:98.
59. Wicks and Mishra, 1998:93.
60. Basit, 1996:229–30, 235.
61. Dwyer and Wyn, 2001:17.
62. Jones, 1991:170.
63. Hughes-Bond, 1998:290.
64. Walkerdine, Lucey, and Melody, 2001:212.
65. Chisholm, 1997:111.
66. Dwyer and Wyn, 2001:51.
67. Stevenson and Ellsworth, 1993:259.
68. Wyn, 1998:116.
69. See Furlong and Cartmel, 1997:32.
70. Wallace, 1994:46. See also Mirza, 1992; Heinz, 1995.
71. Jones and Wallace, 1992:42.
72. Gregory, 1993:26.
73. Bates, 1993:23, 25.
74. Walkerdine, Lucey, and Melody, 2001:67.
75. See also Wyn and White, 1997:109; Wooden, 1998.
76. Hughes-Bond, 1998:282.
77. Furlong and Cartmel, 1997:30.
78. See Gregory, 1993.
79. See for example White, Aumair, Harris, and McDonnell, 1997.
80. Looker and Dwyer, 1998:8.
81. Nutter, 1997:206.
82. See McDonald, 1999:191.
83. Ige, 1998:46. Ige states that 85 percent of such farm workers are migrants.
84. Williamson, 2001:36.
85. See Sweet, 1998:7.
86. McClelland, MacDonald, and Macdonald, 1998:108. They suggest that this does not necessarily mean that more young women are homeless, however, but if they are in these circumstances, they may be more knowledgeable about other assistance available to them.
87. Prostitution has become a burgeoning "career" for young women without prospects since the economic restructuring and marketization of postcommunist countries. See Bridger and Kay, 1996.
88. See Spierings, 1999; Wooden and VanDenHeuvel, 1999.
89. Hillier et al., 1998. See also Pilkington, 1996:8, regarding this issue in postcommunist countries, and Dahlström, 1996, for a Norwegian perspective. In spite of the economic necessity of doing so, fulfilling this plan is not easy. Dwyer and Wyn (2001:71) note that throughout virtually the entire Western world, rural participation in postsecondary educa-

tion is well below that of urban, and city youth have greater access to jobs (see also Grace, 1994).

90. Probert and Macdonald, 1999:22–3.
91. Walkerdine, Lucey, and Melody, 2001:7–8.
92. See Bridger and Kay, 1996; Wallace and Kovatcheva, 1998:120.
93. See Penn, 2000.
94. Ule and Rener, 2001:278.
95. Wyn, 2000:70.
96. Holmes and Silverman, 1992; Brown, Ball, and Powers, 1998.
97. Probert and Macdonald, 1999:135.
98. Penn, 2000:7.

Chapter 3

1. See for example Lister, 1997.
2. Nagel and Wallace, 1997:52–53.
3. Hall, Coffey, and Williamson, 1999:512.
4. France, 1998:99.
5. Dean, 1997:59.
6. Jones and Wallace, 1992:25.
7. Jones and Wallace, 1992:22.
8. Dean, 1997:69.
9. Williamson, 1997:203.
10. Hall, Coffey, and Williamson, 1999:502.
11. See for example Cohen, 1972; Hall et al., 1979; Griffin, 1993.
12. See Griffin, 1997.
13. Walther, 2001.
14. Ehmke, 2001. See also Aapola, Gordon, and Lahelma, 2002.
15. Aapola, Gordon, and Lahelma, 2002:13–14.
16. De Almeida, 2001; Lauritzen, 2001.
17. See Riepl and Wintersberger, 1999.
18. Jones and Wallace, 1992:123.
19. Roberts et al., 2001:2.
20. Roberts et al., 2001:16.
21. Miles, 2000:113.
22. Côté and Allahar, 1996:148.
23. Miles, 2000:125.
24. Bussemaker and Voet, 1998:8.
25. Van Drenth, 1998:82.
26. Van Drenth, 1998:88.
27. McRobbie, 2001.
28. Fine, personal communication, 2003.
29. See Fine and Weis, 1998; Probert and Macdonald, 1999; Proweller, 2000.
30. See Phoenix, 1991.
31. Rose, 1990:226.
32. McRobbie, 2000 (chapter 9 "Sweet Smell of Success? New Ways of Being Young Women"):211, 213.
33. Hopkins, 2002a:94.
34. Cox, 2000.
35. Beroff and Adams, 2000; Kushell, 1999.
36. www.girlpower.gov/girlarea/books/entrepreneurs.htm (Accessed May 2003).
37. Cynthia Griffin, 2001.
38. www.worldywca.org/campaign/en/overview (Accessed May 2003).
39. www.woodhull.org/about/index.html (Accessed May 2003).
40. Williamson, 1997:205.
41. Australian Commonwealth Government Department of Education, Science and Training www.curriculum.edu.au/democracy/biographies/tanle.htm (Accessed May 2003).

42. Defense Manpower Data Center, 2002:7; Australian Defence Force, 1999:5.
43. Following the end of the war in Iraq, this image was replaced by one of (a smiling) SPC Jessica Smothers.
44. For example, 39 percent of the U.S. defense forces is made up of minority ethnicities; see Defense Manpower Data Center, 2002.
45. www.goarmyreserve.com/index02.htm (Accessed May 2003).
46. www.defencejobs.gov.au/CAMPAIGN/Army/Reserves/Jump/ARMYRESJump.htm (Accessed May 2003).
47. I am grateful to Alison van den Eynde for supplying me with a copy of this advertisement.
48. Quoted in Griffin, 2003.
49. Johnson, 1993:143.
50. See Gonick, 2000.
51. Johnson, 1993:137–8.
52. Gilbert and Taylor, 1991:13.
53. Wyn, 2001.
54. Johnson, 1993:141.
55. Kelly, 1986; Matthews, 2002.
56. Schubert, 2001.
57. "The Stolen Generation" is the term for Aboriginal and Torres Strait Islander peoples forcibly removed from their families and relocated in institutions, missions, and white homes. This was a key platform of Australian governments' Aboriginal affairs policy up until the third quarter of the twentieth century.
58. Côté and Allahar, 1996:134.
59. Cox, 2000.
60. McRobbie, 2000:21.
61. Hopkins, 2002a:23.
62. Munk, 1997:134.
63. Lucas, 2000:154.
64. Christine Griffin, 2001a.

Chapter 4

1. Kelly, 2001:30.
2. Lesko, 2001:177.
3. Cohen, 1972; Hall and Jefferson, 1976.
4. Valentine, Skelton, and Chambers, 1998:7.
5. See for example Epstein and Johnson, 1998.
6. Johnson, 1993; Willis, 1979; Folds, 1987; Lesko, 1988; Walker, 1988; Davies, 1993; Jenkins and Matthews, 1995; Fordham, 1997; Gonick, 2003.
7. Griffin, 1993:134.
8. McRobbie, 2000:24.
9. See for example Lees, 1986.
10. Valentine, Skelton, and Chambers, 1998:17.
11. McRobbie, 2000:61.
12. See Trioli, 1996.
13. See Heath, 1999b.
14. Kasesniemi, 2001.
15. Jenkins and Matthews, 1995:16.
16. Lesko, 2001:97.
17. Johnson, 1993:81.
18. Kenway, 1990:138, 133.
19. These themes are also found in Amira Proweller's (1998) analysis of an elite girls' school in the United States.
20. Walkerdine, Lucey, and Melody, 2001:179.
21. Hey, 2001:   .
22. See Wyn, 1990; Jones, 1991.
23. Folds, 1987:83. I am grateful to Dorothy Bottrell for drawing my attention to this work.

24. Ashton-Hay and McKay, 1997:9. A formal is a school dinner-dance event similar to a prom.
25. Sociologist Sarah Susannah Willie also provides a fascinating insight into the complexity of racial performance in the context of education in her book *Acting Black* (2003).
26. See Basit, 1996; Schultz, 1999; Matthews, 2002.
27. Wyn and White, 1997:56–57.
28. Withers and Batten, 1995:54, 67, 68.
29. Stevenson and Ellsworth, 1993:262.
30. Erkut et al., 1996:55.
31. Leadbeater and Way, 1996:5.
32. Pastor, McCormick, and Fine, 1996:25–26.
33. See Mizen, Bolton, and Pole, 1999; Dwyer and Wyn, 2001:124.
34. See Willis, 1998.
35. Ryan, 2002.
36. Dwyer and Wyn, 2001:63.
37. Bowlby, Lloyd Evans, and Mohammad, 1998:244.
38. Hughes-Bond, 1998:293.
39. Mirza, 1992:95.
40. Dwyer and Wyn, 2001:68.
41. Angwin, 2000:102.
42. Rudd and Evans, 1998:51.
43. Klawitter, Plotnick, and Edwards, 2000:541.
44. Allatt, 1997:94.
45. Edwards, 2001.
46. "Female Offenders," 2001.
47. McIvor, 2000.
48. See Carrington, 1993; Baines and Alder, 1996.
49. Wyn and White, 1997:135.
50. Carrington, 1996:10.
51. See Carney, 2001.
52. Miller, 1996:233.
53. See Beikoff, 1996.
54. Alder, 1998:94.
55. Torre et al., 2001:164.
56. See also Sudbury, 2002.
57. See Griffin, 1993.
58. Cook and Davies, 1999:5; Sudbury, 2002.
59. Alder, 1998:93.
60. Bottrell, 2001.
61. Griffin, 1993:132.
62. Wyn and White, 1997:139.
63. Malone, 2000:145.
64. White, 1998; Males, 1999; O'Neil, 2002.
65. McNamee, 1998:195.
66. See Kelly, 2000; Torre and Burns, 2001.
67. Gaunt, 1998:281, italics in original.
68. Katz, 1998:135.
69. See McNamee, 1998; Malone, 2000.
70. Malone, 2000:145.
71. Mizen, Bolton, and Pole, 1999:433.
72. Ganetz, 1995:84.
73. See Girls in Space Consortia, 1997; Panelli, Nairn, Atwool, and McCormack, 2002.
74. Miles, 2000:118.
75. Booth, 2001.
76. Wallace and Kovatcheva, 1998:161.
77. Grant, 2001:55.
78. Quoted in Grant, 2001:61.
79. See White et al., 1997.
80. Giroux, 1998:31.

Chapter 5

1. The term *incitement to discourse* comes from social theorist Michel Foucault. In his *History of Sexuality* he suggests that from the seventeenth century on, sexuality was invented as a public issue and thereby regulated through mechanisms such as population research, sex education for youth, and the expansion of confession. These mechanisms required people to speak the "truth" about sex, and for educators, judges, priests, and doctors to hear, document, and analyze their articulations. He says (1980a:24) that through these procedures, sex became a thing to be "managed, inserted into systems of utility, regulated for the greater good of all, made to function according to an optimum." In other words these methods encouraged people to speak the truth about themselves for the purposes of governmentality. I draw on these ideas to make an argument about the ways young women's speech can be elicited for purposes of scrutiny, management, and depoliticization.
2. See Melucci, 1996.
3. Hopkins, 2002a:4.
4. Ball, Maguire, and Macrae, 2000:151.
5. See Taft, 2001.
6. McRobbie, 1997:198.
7. McRobbie, 2000.
8. Hopkins, 2002b.
9. Hopkins, 2002b.
10. Henderson, Taylor, and Thomson, 2002:508.
11. Torre and Burns, 2001; Lowe, 2003.
12. Kasesniemi, 2001.
13. Mendoza-Denton, 1996:48.
14. Walkerdine, Lucey, and Melody, 2001:8.
15. Torre et al., 2001:158–59.
16. See Craig and Bennett, 1997; Furlong and Cartmel, 1997; Rimmerman, 1997; Lagos and Rose, 1999; Buckingham, 2000.
17. See Hahn, 1998.
18. See Jacobi, 1995; Helve, 2002.
19. Wilkinson and Mulgan, 1995:102.
20. See Giroux, 1996.
21. Quoted in Davis, 1999:271.
22. See Summers, 1994, for the "girls have everything" perspective, and Pipher, 1994, for the "girls in crisis" viewpoint.
23. These views are expounded by Garner, 1995, contra Greer, 1999.
24. Faust, 1996.
25. See Driscoll, 1999 for a critique.
26. Christine Griffin, 2001b:184.
27. See Ehmke, 2001.
28. See Holdsworth, 2000.
29. Torney-Purta et al., 2001:8.
30. White, Bruce and Ritchie, 2000, as summarized on the Joseph Rowntree Foundation website. See www.jrf.org.uk/knowledge/findings/socialpolicy/520.asp (Accessed May 2003).
31. Hall, Williamson and Coffey, 2000:465.
32. "Students," 2002.
33. Giroux, 1998:25.
34. Holdsworth, 2000:357.
35. Siurala, 2000. See also Smith et al., 2002.
36. Brown, 1998:vii.
37. Pipher, 1994:19.
38. Milligan, Thomson, Ashenden, and Associates, 1992; Holmes and Silverman, 1992.
39. See Taylor, Gilligan, and Sullivan, 1995:191.
40. Chesler, 1997:1.
41. Taylor, Gilligan, and Sullivan, 1995:11.
42. Mann, 1994:191.

43. Shandler, 1999; Findlen, 1995; Carlip, 1995; Else-Mitchell and Flutter, 1998; Brown, 1998.
44. Foucault, 1980a:32.
45. Mahoney, 1996:621.
46. Ward, 2000:53.
47. Ormond, 2001.
48. Hall, Coffey, and Williamson, 1999:505.
49. Torney-Purta et al., 2001:10.
50. Hall, Coffey, and Williamson, 1999:510.
51. Baumgardner and Richards, 2000:178.
52. Giroux, 1998:24.
53. Smith, 2001:181.
54. Duncombe, 1998:135.
55. Huq, 2001.
56. Klein, 2001.
57. Vis:25.
58. Sportsgirl is an Australian line of teen girl fashions.
59. Personal interview 2001.
60. Ross, 1994:12.
61. Taft, 2001.
62. Rumack, 2001:97–98.
63. Trioli, 2003.
64. Giroux, 1996:47.

Chapter 6

1. See Cahill, 2000.
2. Personal interview, Kylie. Quotations such as these come from a series of interviews and surveys I conducted with young women involved in zines, the Internet, and new politics. This data was collected from 1998 to 2001 in Australia and the United States.
3. See for example Skelton and Valentine, 1998.
4. Wyn, 2002.
5. Redhead, 1997.
6. Young women in these communities are those least likely to have their own private spaces, often having to share small living and sleeping quarters with family or other householders, and are thereby doubly surveilled. See Bloustien, 2000.
7. Bottrell, 2000.
8. Räthzel, 2000:135.
9. See Human Rights and Equal Opportunity Commission, 1991.
10. This term is used by Adreanne Ormond, 2001 (following Patricia Hill Collins, 1998), to describe young people's bank of shared critical knowledge which can be explored together in private. Ormond suggests that young people sometimes appear to be acquiescent and silent as a strategic device to protect this knowledge.
11. Austin, 1998:250.
12. Breitbart, 1998:322. See also Mitchell, 2001, on feminist and lesbian graffiti.
13. Bertram, 2001:129.
14. Kasesniemi, 2001:177.
15. McCormick, 2000; Gaunt, 1998.
16. Fine and Weis, 1998:253.
17. See for example Maffesoli, 1996; Hetherington, 1998; Siurala, 2000; Klein, 2001.
18. Melucci, 1996:100.
19. See for example Highfold, quoted in Hunter, Fagan, and Wilkes, 1998, on the efforts to build an Aboriginal Youth Action Committee in South Australia.
20. Guidikova and Siurala, 2001:10.
21. Giroux, 1998:24.
22. Giroux, 1996.
23. Duncombe, 1998:2–3.
24. See Harris, 1999b.

25. Takayoshi, Huot, and Huot, 1999; Leonard, 1998:113.
26. Leonard, 1998:113.
27. Hillier, 2001:126.
28. Quoted in Leonard, 1998:111.
29. Quote from www.AsiangURLs.com (Accessed July 2003).
30. Takayoshi, Huot, and Huot, 1999:97–98. Italics in original.
31. Cross, 1996:85.
32. See also Leonard, 1998.
33. Some anecdotal evidence suggests that young women with physical disabilities, who are often not accommodated within more mainstream modes for youth organizing, have been at the forefront of the development of information and communication technologies (ICTs) for activism. The isolation of young women who cannot easily leave their homes, whose physical possibilities are different from the nondisabled, and who may be highly managed and surveilled by caregivers, can be counteracted through the use of ICTs. However, while acknowledging these emergent forms of community and political identity building, we also need to remain mindful of information inequality and resist assumptions that all young people can access and skillfully use new technologies. See, for example, Facer and Furlong, 2001.
34. Kaplan and Farrell, 1994.
35. Lipsitz, 1994:27.
36. Ferris, 2001:52.
37. Quoted in Leonard, 1997:239.
38. Personal interview, Melissa, Tamara and Jade.
39. See Hey, 1997.
40. Foucault, 1980b:82.
41. Personal interview, Michelle.
42. Gottlieb and Wald, 1994:264.
43. Personal interview, Kylie.
44. Personal interview, Kylie.
45. Quote from Helen, *Grot Grrrl*, issue 2, no year, no page number.
46. Quote from Anonymous, *Grot Grrrl*, issue 1, no year, page 1.
47. Quote from http://pandora.nla.gov.au/nph-arch/2000/z2000-Feb-21/http://digitarts.va.com.au/grrowl3/verena/index.html (Accessed July 2003).
48. Quote from www.octapod.org/catpounce/catpounce.html (Accessed July 2003).
49. See for example Banks, 2001.
50. See Devaney, 2001, for young women's activism against corporate criminals.
51. Quote from www.girlmom.com (Accessed July 2003).
52. Carland, 1997:193.
53. Future Exchange Forum, 1999.
54. Quote from www.octapod.org/catpounce/catpounce.html (Accessed July 2003).
55. Quote from www.blackgirlrevolution.org (Accessed July 2001). No longer available—this webpage is now a pornography site.
56. Klein, 2001:290.
57. Personal interview, Nicola.
58. Personal interview, Kylie.
59. Quote from *Her Heroes Aren't Gone*, part 1, no year, page 5.
60. Personal interview, Rosie.
61. Jones and Wallace, 1992:139.
62. Personal interview, Kylie.
63. Personal interview, Nicola.
64. Duncombe, 1998:129.
65. Quote from http://grrrlzines.net/interviews/ladybomb.htm (Accessed July, 2003).
66. Murdocca, 2001:218.
67. Quote from http://members.aol.com/critchicks/index.html (Accessed July 2003).
68. Quote from www.messtiza.com/ (Accessed July 2003).
69. Quote from www.bigadchinesemama.com (Accessed July 2003).
70. Quote from http://members.aol.com/critchicks/index.html (Accessed July 2003).
71. Alcantara-Tan, 1997:98.

72. Quote from www.angrylittlegirls.com/ (Accessed July 2003).
73. Young Women Connect, 2001. See also Cummings, 2001, on intergenerational antiracism activism and "new and radical ways of working."
74. Quote from Kylie and Katherine, *Personality Liberation Front*, no year, no page number.
75. *Koorie* is the term for Aboriginal people in the southeast of Australia.
76. Mary, 1997:189.
77. Personal interview, Michelle.
78. Quote from http://members.ozemail.com.au/~astrogrrrl/spycore/zines.htm (Accessed July 2001). No longer available.
79. Personal interview, Michelle.
80. Personal interview, Brigette.
81. Smith, 2001.
82. Lewis, 1996:3.
83. Giroux, 1998:48.
84. Personal interview, Kylie.
85. Personal interview, Tamara, Jade and Melissa.
86. Klein, 2000:4.
87. VNS Matrix, 1996:75.
88. Fine and Weis, 1998:256.
89. However, I would suggest that when free spaces are imagined by their members as entirely separate and therefore uncorrupted, in other words, somehow structurally outside of dominant culture, their transformative qualities may indeed be questioned. This ideal image of the alternative sphere that can only provide critique as a result of its exteriority is not sustainable in a time of globalized popular cultures of bricolage and assemblage. Even so, this does not mean we should discount many young women's desire to be outside, safe, or free, even if this is only a momentary experience.
90. Fry and Lousley, 2001:151.
91. An unresolved issue is how widely accessible these spaces really are. One of the common claims of those involved in zines, comics, culture jams, and Internet communities is that anyone can participate. Integral to these cultures is a countercapitalist ethic, whereby making a difference or expressing personal and political views is not dependent on access to money or other resources. Many talk about how they finance their activities through very creative means. It remains, however, that the majority of young people do not engage in these activities, not only because they may not share this political disposition, but because they lack the economic and cultural resources to do so. Access to free photocopying at a parent's workplace, regular use of the Internet, or knowledge of webpage design may not require money, but they certainly demand other kinds of resources. It is not really surprising, then, that young women deemed at-risk are more likely to be creating spaces for themselves in more personal and local ways. Socioeconomic resources have a substantial impact on one's ability to make these spaces. This issue may ultimately be the greatest barrier to the goal of open and free participation in youth community building through border spaces.
92. Guidikova and Siurala, 2001:9.

Conclusion

1. Foucault, 1982:214, describes this as "pastoral power." He says, "This form of power cannot be exercised without knowing the insides of people's minds, without exploring their souls, without making them reveal their innermost secrets."
2. Foucault, 1982:216, continues: "The political, ethical, social, philosophical problem of our days is . . . to liberate us . . . from the type of individualization which is linked to the state."
3. The third-wave responses to this critique have been substantial and have been well elaborated elsewhere. For a summary, see Harris, 2001.
4. Felski, 1996:503.
5. Sudbury, 2002:71.
6. See Ormond, 2001.
7. Dwyer and Wyn, 2001:204.
8. See Ball, Maguire, and Macrae, 2000; Dwyer and Wyn, 2001.

9. See for example Fine and Weis, 1998, and Weis and Fine, 2000, especially their introduction.
10. Weis and Fine, 2000:xiii.
11. For example, Jay, 1994:414, suggests that Foucault overlooked the alternative meaning of "*le regard*," that is, "to pay heed to or care for someone else." Thus "caring eyes" need not be always or only disciplinary.

Appendix

1. See Johnson, 1993; Driscoll, 2002.
2. See for example Carney, 2000.
3. Driscoll, 2002:306.
4. The book draws on a diversity of empirical material, including quantitative and qualitative research about and with young women in many Western societies, as well as primary source material such as webpages and writings by young women themselves. This data has been generated by a number of different methods that provide a richness of material and variety of insights that can be more illuminating than single-method studies alone. Typically, qualitative research adds depth and quantitative research breadth, and together they can build up detailed pictures of complex environments. I include examples from research conducted by interview, questionnaire, content analysis, creative writing, participatory action, observation and large-scale statistical surveys. The aim here is not to make this material homogeneous, nor to reach the "truth" through triangulation, but to hold on to its specificity and richness. This is described by Wyn and White, 1997:3, as a "prism" approach, whereby a range of data can be used to examine central issues by turning different facets to the light.
5. Dwyer and Wyn, 2001:3.

BIBLIOGRAPHY

A New Girl Order? Young Women and the Future of Feminist Inquiry (2001), unpublished conference papers, London, Nov. 14–16.

Aapola, Sinikka (1997) "Mature Girls and Adolescent Boys? Deconstructing Discourses of Adolescence and Gender," *Young: The Nordic Journal of Youth Studies* 5, no. 4: 50–68.

Aapola, Sinikka, Tuula Gordon, and Elina Lahelma (2002) "Citizens in the Text? International Representations of Citizenship in School Textbooks," in Ari Antikainen and Carlos Torres (eds) *The International Handbook on the Sociology of Education*, Lanham, Md.: Rowman and Littlefield.

Adkins, Lisa (2002) *Revisions: Gender and Sexuality in Late Modernity*, Buckingham, U.K.: Open University Press.

Alcantara-Tan, Sabrina Sandata (1997) "A Nice Little Asian Girl," in Greene and Taormino (eds) *A Girl's Guide to Taking Over the World*, New York: St. Martin's Press.

Alder, Christine (1998) " 'Passionate and Willful' Girls' Confronting Practices," *Women and Criminal Justice* 9, no. 4: 81–101.

Alder, Christine, and Margaret Baines (eds) (1996) *And When She Was Bad?: Working with Young Women in Juvenile Justice and Related Areas*, Hobart: Australian Clearinghouse for Youth Studies.

Allatt, Pat (1997) "Conceptualising Youth: Transitions, Risk and the Public and the Private," in Bynner, Chisholm, and Furlong (eds) *Youth, Citizenship and Social Change in a European Context*, Aldershot, U.K.: Ashgate.

Angwin, Jennifer (2000) "Researching VET Pathways with Disengaged and Disadvantaged Young People," in McLeod and Malone (eds) *Researching Youth*, Hobart: Australian Clearinghouse for Youth Studies.

Archer, Louise, and Merryn Hutchings (2000) " 'Bettering Yourself'? Discourses of Risk, Cost and Benefit in Ethnically Diverse, Young Working-Class Non-Participants' Constructions of Higher Education," *British Journal of Sociology of Education* 21, no. 4: 555–74.

Ashton-Hay, Sally, and Penny McKay (1997) "Patterns of Participation in Classroom Learning: A Study of Aboriginal Girls from a Bush Setting," *Language Australia: Child ESL and Literacy Research Network Newsletter* (Queensland), *Four Queensland ESL Case Studies* (Dec.): 4–53.

Austin, Joe (1998) "Knowing Their Place: Local Knowledge, Social Prestige, and the Writing Formation in New York City," in Austin and Willard (eds) *Generations of Youth: Youth Subcultures and History in Twentieth-Century America*, New York: New York University Press.

Austin, Joe, and Michael Nevin Willard (eds) (1998) *Generations of Youth: Youth Subcultures and History in Twentieth-Century America*, New York: New York University Press.

Austin, Tony (1991) " 'A Chance to Be Decent': Northern Territory Half-Caste' Girls in Service in South Australia 1916–1939," *Labour History: A Journal of Labour and Social History* 60 (May): 51–65.

Australian Commonwealth Government Department of Education, Science and Training. www.curriculum.edu.au/democracy/biographies/tanle.htm? (Accessed May 2003).

Australian Defence Force (1999) *Australian Defence Force 1999 Census Public Report*, Canberra: Australian Government Publishing Services.

Baines, Margaret and Christine Alder (1996) "When She Was Bad She Was Horrid," in Alder and Baines (eds) *And When She Was Bad?: Working with Young Women in Juvenile Justice and Related Areas*, Hobart: Australian Clearinghouse for Youth Studies.

Ball, Stephen J., Meg Maguire, and Sheila Macrae (2000) *Choice, Pathways and Transitions Post-16: New Youth, New Economies in the Global City*, London: RoutledgeFalmer.

Banks, Cara (2001) "Desperately Seeking Sisterhood," in Mitchell, Rundle and Karaian (eds) *Turbo Chicks: Talking Young Feminisms*, Toronto: Sumach Press.

Barwick, Sandra (2001) "Sex, Boys and Make-Up: Is This What Tweenie Girls Want?" *Daily Telegraph*, Feb. 8.

Basit, Tehmina N. (1996) " 'I'd Hate to Be Just a Housewife': Career Aspirations of British Muslim Girls," *British Journal of Guidance and Counselling* 24, no. 2: 227–42.

Bates, Inge (1993) "A Job Which Is 'Right for Me'? Social Class, Gender and Individualization," in Inge Bates and George Riseborough (eds) *Youth and Inequality*, Buckingham, U.K.: Open University Press.

Baumgardner, Jennifer, and Amy Richards (2001) *Manifesta: Young Women, Feminism and the Future*, New York: Farrar, Straus and Giroux.

Beck, Ulrich (1992) *Risk Society: Towards a New Modernity*, trans. Mark Ritter, London: Sage.

Beikoff, Leanne (1996) "Queensland's Juvenile Justice System: Equity, Access and Justice for Young Women?" in Alder and Baines (eds) *And When She Was Bad?: Working with Young Women in Juvenile Justice and Related Areas*, Hobart: Australian Clearinghouse for Youth Studies.

Beroff Art, and T. R. Adams (2000) *How to Be a Teenage Millionaire*, Waterloo: Entrepreneurship Institute of Canada.

Bertram, Corinne (2001) "Enduring Impermanence: A Neighbourhood Contra (Counter)-versy (Against Verse)," in Fine and Harris (eds) *Under the Covers: Theorising the Politics of Counter Stories*, Special Issue of *International Journal of Critical Psychology* 4: 123–31.

Bessant, Judith (1993) "A Patchwork: The Life Worlds and 'Cultures' of Young Australians 1900–1950," in Rob White (ed.) *Youth Subcultures: Theory, History and the Australian Experience*, Hobart: Australian Clearinghouse for Youth Studies.

Blackmore, Jill (2001) "Achieving More in Education but Earning Less in Work: Girls, Boys and Gender Equality in Schooling," *Discourse: Studies in the Cultural Politics of Education* 22, no. 1: 123–29.

Blake, Meredith (1995–1996) "Welfare and Coerced Contraception: Morality Implications of State-Sponsored Reproductive Control," *University of Louisville Journal of Family Law* 34, no. 2 (Spring): 311–44.

Bloustien, Gerry (2000) "Teddy Bear Chains and Violent Femmes: Play, Video Cameras and the Negotiation of (Gendered) Space" in McLeod and Malone (eds) *Researching Youth*, Hobart: Australian Clearinghouse for Youth Studies.

Booth, Anna (2001) "Private Places/Public Spaces," unpublished paper presented at *Whose Place?*, Western Sydney Regional Organisation of Councils conference, Sydney, March 6–7.

Bordo, Susan (1995) *Unbearable Weight: Feminism, Western Culture and the Body*, Berkeley: University of California Press.

Bottrell, Dorothy (2000) "Optimism: Against the Odds," unpublished paper presented at *Education Research: Towards an Optimistic Future*, Australian Association for Research in Education conference, University of Sydney, Dec. 4.

———— (2001) "Breaking the Rules, Breaking the Law: Continuities in Girls' Resistances as Identity Work," in M. O'Loughlin (ed.) *Change Monograph*, Sydney: Faculty of Education and Social Work, University of Sydney.

Bowlby, Sophie, Sally Lloyd Evans, and Robina Mohammad (1998) "The Workplace. Becoming a Paid Worker: Images and Identity" in Skelton and Valentine (eds) *Cool Places: Geographies of Youth Cultures*, London: Routledge.

Boyte, Harry C., and Sara M. Evans (1992) *Free Spaces: The Sources of Democratic Change in America*, rev. ed, Chicago: University of Chicago Press.

Breitbart, Myrna Margulies (1998) " 'Dana's Mystical Tunnel': Young People's Designs for Survival and Change in the City," in Skelton and Valentine (eds) *Cool Places: Geographies of Youth Cultures*, London: Routledge.

Bridger, Sue, and Rebecca Kay (1996) "Gender and Generation in the New Russian Labour Market," in Hilary Pilkington (ed.) *Gender, Generation and Identity in Contemporary Russia*, London: Routledge.

Brown, Lyn Mikel (1998) *Raising Their Voices: The Politics of Girls' Anger*, Cambridge, Mass.: Harvard University Press.

Brown, Maggie (2000) "Give Us the Pocket Money," *Guardian*, May 29.

Brown, Wendy, Karen Ball, and Jenny Powers (1998) "Is Life a Party for Young Women?," *The ACHPER Healthy Lifestyles Journal* 45, no. 3: 21–26.

Buckingham, David (2000) *The Making of Citizens: Young People, News and Politics*, London: Routledge.

Bulbeck, Chilla (2001) "Young Women's Imagined Lives in 1970 and 2000," unpublished paper presented at *Casting New Shadows*, Australian Women's Studies Association conference, Institute for Women's Studies, Macquarie University, Sydney, Jan. 31–Feb. 2.

Bussemaker, Jet, and Rian Voet (1998) "Introduction," in Jet Bussemaker and Rian Voet (eds) *Gender, Participation and Citizenship in the Netherlands*, Aldershot, U.K.: Ashgate.

Bynner, John, Lynne Chisholm, and Andy Furlong (eds) (1997) *Youth, Citizenship and Social Change in a European Context*, Aldershot, U.K.: Ashgate.

Cahill, Caitlin (2000) "Street Literacy: Urban Teenagers' Strategies for Negotiating their Neighbourhood," *Journal of Youth Studies* 3, no. 3: 251–77.

Carland, Tammy Rae (1997) "Reflections of a Stupid Slut," in Greene and Taormino (eds) *A Girl's Guide to Taking Over the World: Writings from the Girl Zine Revolution*, New York: St. Martin's Press.

Carlip, Hilary (1995) *Girlpower: Young Women Speak Out*, New York: Warner Books.

Carney, Sarah K. (2000) "Body Work on Ice: The Ironies of Femininity and Sport," in Weis and Fine (eds) *Construction Sites: Excavating Race, Class and Gender Amongst Urban Youth*, New York: Teachers College Press.

——— (2001) "Analysing Master Narratives and Counter Stories in Legal Settings: Cases of Maternal Failure-to-Protect," in Fine and Harris (eds) *Under the Covers: Theorising the Politics of Counter Stories*, Special Issue of *International Journal of Critical Psychology* 4: 61–76.

Carrington, Kerry (1993) *Offending Girls: Sex, Youth and Justice*, St. Leonards, Australia: Allen and Unwin.

——— (1996) "Offending Girls: Rethinking Intervention Regimes," in Alder and Baines (eds) *And When She Was Bad?: Working with Young Women in Juvenile Justice and Related Areas*, Hobart: Australian Clearinghouse for Youth Studies.

Chesler, Phyllis (1997) *Letters to a Young Feminist*, New York: Four Walls Eight Windows.

Chisholm, Lynne (1997) "Sensibilities and Occlusions: Vulnerable Youth Between Social Change and Cultural Context," in Bynner, Chisholm, and Furlong (eds) *Youth, Citizenship and Change in a European Context*, Aldershot, U.K.: Ashgate.

Chisholm, Lynne, Peter Büchner, Heinz-Hermann Krüger, and Manuela du Bois-Reymond (eds) (1995) *Growing Up in Europe: Contemporary Horizons in Childhood and Youth Studies*, Berlin: Walter de Gruyter.

Clark, B. R. (1961) "The 'Cooling Out' Function in Higher Education," in A. H. Halsey, Jean Floud, and C. Arnold Anderson (eds) *Education, Economy and Society*, Glencoe, Ill.: The Free Press.

Cohen, Stan (1972) *Folk Devils and Moral Panics: The Creation of the Mods and the Rockers*, Oxford: Basil Blackwell.

Collins, Patricia Hill (1998) *Fighting Words: Black Women and the Search for Justice*, Minneapolis: University of Minnesota Press.

Cook, Sandy, and Sue Davies (1999) "Will Anyone Ever Listen? An Introductory Note," in Sandy Cook and Sue Davies (eds) *Harsh Punishment: International Experiences of Women's Imprisonment*, Boston: Northeastern University Press.

Cooper, Glenda (1998) "Girl Violence on the Increase," *The Independent* (London), July 22, 3.

Côté, James E., and Anton L. Allahar (1996) *Generation On Hold: Coming of Age in the Late Twentieth Century*, New York: New York University Press.

Cox, Kate (2000) "Girls Just Wanna Shop," *Sun-Herald* (Sydney), July 16, 14.

Craig, Stephen C., and Stephen Earl Bennett (eds) (1997) *After the Boom: The Politics of Generation X*, Lanham, Md.: Rowman and Littlefield.

Cross, Rosie (1996) "Geekgirl: Why Grrrls Need Modems," in Kathy Bail (ed.) *DIY Feminism*, St. Leonards, Australia: Allen and Unwin.

Cummings, Joan Grant (2001) "From Natty Dreads to Grey Ponytails: The Revolution is Multi-generational," in Mitchell, Rundle, and Karaian (eds) *Turbo Chicks: Talking Young Feminisms*, Toronto: Sumach Press.

Cuneo, Alice (2002) "Affiliation Targets Youngest Female Consumers," *AdAge*, Aug. 27.

Dahlström, Margareta (1996) "Young Women in a Male Periphery: Experiences from the Scandinavian North," *Journal of Rural Studies* 12, no. 3: 259–71.

Davies, Bronwyn (1993) *Shards of Glass: Children Reading and Writing beyond Gendered Identities*, St. Leonards, Australia: Allen and Unwin.

Davis, Mark (1999) *Gangland: Cultural Elites and the New Generationalism*, St. Leonards, Australia: Allen and Unwin.

De Almeida, Joao Vale (2001) "Keynote Address," unpublished paper presented at *Youth—Actor of Social Change?* symposium, Strasbourg, Dec. 12–14.

Dean, Hartley (1997) "Underclassed or Undermined? Young People and Social Citizenship," in Robert MacDonald (ed.) *Youth, the "Underclass" and Social Exclusion*, London: Routledge.

Deegan, Liz (1997) "Girls with the World at Their Feet," *The Sunday Mail* (Adelaide), Oct. 19, 157.

www.defencejobs.gov.au/CAMPAIGN/Army/Reserves/Jump/ARMYRESJump.htm (Accessed May 2003.

Defense Manpower Data Center (2002) *Defense Manpower Data Center Report No. 2002–021*, December, Arlington, Va.: Defense Manpower Data Center.

Devaney, Julie (2001) "Burning for a Revolution," in Mitchell, Rundle, and Karaian (eds) *Turbo Chicks: Talking Young Feminisms*, Toronto: Sumach Press.

Driscoll, Catherine (1999) "Girl Culture, Revenge and Global Capitalism: Cybergirls, Riot Grrls, Spice Girls," *Australian Feminist Studies* 14, no. 29: 173–93.

——— (2002) *Girls: Feminine Adolescence in Popular Culture and Cultural Theory*, New York: Columbia University Press.

Du Bois-Reymond, Manuela (1998) " 'I Don't Want to Commit Myself Yet': Young People's Life Concepts," *Journal of Youth Studies* 1, no. 1: 63–80.

Duncombe, Stephen (1998) *Notes from Underground: Zines and the Politics of Alternative Culture*, London: Verso.

Dwyer, Peter, and Johanna Wyn (2001) *Youth, Education and Risk: Facing the Future*, London: RoutledgeFalmer.

Edwards, Jan (2001) "Weaving Webs of Obligation: Working Class Young Women and Welfare Reform in Australia," unpublished paper presented at *A New Girl Order?* conference, London, Nov. 14–16.

Ehmke, Ellen (2001) "Personal, Institutional and Socio-Cultural Barriers to Participation," unpublished paper presented at *Youth—Actor of Social Change?* symposium, Strasbourg, Dec. 12–14.

Else-Mitchell, Rosamund, and Naomi Flutter (1998) *Talking Up: Young Women's Take on Feminism*, North Melbourne, Australia: Spinifex.

Epstein, Debbie, and Richard Johnson (1998) *Schooling Sexualities*, Buckingham, U.K.: Open University Press.

Erkut, Sumru, et al. (1996) "Diversity in Girls' Experiences: Feeling Good about Who You Are," in Leadbeater and Way (eds) *Urban Girls: Resisting Stereotypes, Creating Identities*, New York: New York University Press.

Espin, Oliva (1995) " 'Race,' Racism and Sexuality in the Life Narratives of Immigrant Women," *Feminism and Psychology* 5: 223–38.

European Group for Integrated Social Research (2001) "Misleading Trajectories: Transition Dilemmas of Young Adults in Europe," *Journal of Youth Studies* 4, no. 1: 101–18.

Facer, Keri, and Ruth Furlong (2001) "Beyond the Myth of the 'Cyberkid': Young People at the Margins of the Information Revolution," *Journal of Youth Studies*, 4 no. 4: 451–69.

Faust, Beatrice (1996) "Time You Grew Up Little Sister," *The Australian*, Oct. 12–13, 23.

Felski, Rita (1996) "Modern Girls," *Cultural Studies* 10, no. 3: 498–505.

"Female Offenders: An Emerging Crisis" (2001) *Juvenile Justice Magazine* 5, no. 1 (February/ March): 2–7.

Ferris, Melanie A. (2001) "Resisting Mainstream Media: Girls and the Act of Making Zines," *Young Women: Feminists, Activists, Grrrls*, 20/21 (4/1): 51–56.

Findlen, Barbara (1995) *Listen Up: Voices from the Next Feminist Generation*, Seattle: Seal.

Fine, Michelle, and April Burns (forthcoming) "Class Notes: Towards a Critical Psychology of Class and Schooling," *International Journal of Social Issues*.

Fine, Michelle, and Anita Harris (eds) (2001) *Under the Covers: Theorising the Politics of Counter Stories*, Special Issue of *International Journal of Critical Psychology* 4.

Fine, Michelle, and Lois Weis (1998) *The Unknown City: Lives of Poor and Working-Class Young Adults*, Boston: Beacon Press.

Fine, Michelle, personal communication, 2003

Folds, Ralph (1987) *Whitefella School: Education and Aboriginal Resistance*, Sydney: Allen and Unwin.

Fordham, Signithia (1996) *Blacked Out: Dilemmas of Race, Identity and Success at Capital High*, Chicago: University of Chicago Press.

———— (1997) "Those Loud Black Girls," in Maxine Seller and Lois Weis (eds) *Beyond Black and White*, Albany: State University of New York Press.

Foucault, Michel (1980a) *The History of Sexuality*, New York: Vintage.

———— (1980b) "Two Lectures," in Colin Gordon (ed. and trans.) *Power/Knowledge: Selected Interviews and Other Writings, 1972–1977*, New York: Pantheon.

———— (1982) "The Subject and Power," in Hubert L. Dreyfus and Paul Rabinow, *Michel Foucault: Beyond Structuralism and Hermeneutics*, Brighton: Harvester Press.

France, Alan (1998) " 'Why Should We Care?' Young People, Citizenship and Questions of Social Responsibility," *Journal of Youth Studies* 1, no. 1: 97–112.

Frith, Simon (1984) *The Sociology of Youth*, Causeway, U.K.: Ormskirk.

Frønes, Ivar (2001) "Revolution without Rebels: Gender, Generation and Social Change" in Furlong and Guidikova (eds) *Transitions of Youth Citizenship in Europe: Culture, Subculture and Identity*, Strasbourg: Council of Europe Publishing.

Fry, Kimberley, and Cheryl Lousley (2001) "Green Grrrl Power," *Young Women: Feminists, Activists, Grrrls*, 20/21 (4/1): 148–51.

Furlong, Andy, and Fred Cartmel (1997) *Young People and Social Change: Individualisation and Risk in Late Modernity*, Buckingham, U.K.: Open University Press.

Furlong, Andy, and Irena Guidikova (eds) (2001) *Transitions of Youth Citizenship in Europe: Culture, Subculture and Identity*, Strasbourg: Council of Europe Publishing.

Furstenburg, Frank F., Thomas D. Cook, Jacqueline Eccles, Glen H. Elder, and Arnold Sameroof (1999) *Managing to Make It: Urban Families and Adolescent Success*, Chicago: University of Chicago Press.

Future Exchange Forum (1999) "Dissent, Debate and the Internet: Crash the System," unpublished roundtable debate, *National Young Writers Festival*, Newcastle, Australia: Oct. 3.

Galland, Olivier (1995) "Changing Family Transitions: Young People and New Ways of Life in France," in Chisholm et al. *Growing Up in Europe: Contemporary Horizons in Childhood and Youth Studies*, Berlin: Walter de Gruyter.

Ganetz, Hillevi (1995) "The Shop, the Home and Femininity as a Masquerade," in Johan Fornäs and Göran Bolin (eds) *Youth Culture in Late Modernity*, London: Sage.

Garner, Helen (1995) *The First Stone: Some Questions about Sex and Power*, Sydney: Pan Macmillan.

Gaunt, Kyra D. (1998) "Dancin' in the Street to a Black Girl's Beat: Music, Gender and the Ins and Outs of Double-Dutch" in Austin and Willard (eds) *Generations of Youth: Youth Subcultures and History in Twentieth-Century America*, New York: New York University Press.

Giddens, Anthony (1991) *Modernity and Self-Identity: Self and Society in the Late Modern Age*, Cambridge: Polity Press.

Gilbert, Pam, and Sandra Taylor (1991) *Fashioning the Feminine: Girls, Popular Culture and Schooling*, Sydney: Allen and Unwin.

Gill, Rosalind (2001) "From Sex Object to Desiring Sexual Subject: A Step Forward for Media Representation of Young Women?," unpublished paper presented at *A New Girl Order?* conference, London, Nov. 14–16.

Gilligan, Carol, Nona P. Lyons, and Trudy J. Hanmer (1990) *Making Connections: The Relational Worlds of Adolescent Girls at the Emma Willard School*, Cambridge, Mass.: Harvard University Press.

www.girlpower.gov/girlarea/books/enterpreneurs.htm (Accessed May 2003).

Girls in Space Consortia (1997) *Phase 1 Report for the Girls in Space Consortia Research: A Project Investigating Young Women's Relationships to Public Space in Brisbane*, Brisbane, Australia: Backbone Youth Arts Inc.

Giroux, Henry (1996) *Fugitive Cultures: Race, Violence and Youth*, London: Routledge.

——— (1998) "Teenage Sexuality, Body Politics and the Pedagogy of Display" in Jonathon Epstein (ed.) *Youth Culture: Identity in a Postmodern World*, Malden, U.K.: Blackwell.

www.goarmyreserve.com/index02.htm (Accessed May 2003).

Gonick, Marnina (2000) "Canadian = Blonde, English, White: Theorizing Race, Language and Nation," *Atlantis* 24, no. 2 (Spring/Summer): 93–104.

——— (2003) *Between Femininities: Ambivalence, Identity and the Education of Girls*, Albany: State University of New York Press.

Gottlieb, Joanne, and Gayle Wald (1994) "Smells Like Teen Spirit: Riot Grrrls, Revolution and Women in Independent Rock," in Ross and Rose (eds) *Microphone Fiends: Youth Music and Youth Culture*, New York: Routledge.

Grace, Julie (1994) "A Future of Hope? Or Lost Dreams? The Life of Young Women in a Rural and Isolated Community," *Transitions: The Journal of the Youth Affairs Network of Queensland Incorporated* (Fortitude Valley) 4, no. 1 (March—June): 58–59.

Grant, Chris (2001) "Young People and Shopping Centres; A Legal Perspective," unpublished paper presented at *Whose Place?* conference, Western Sydney Regional Organisation of Councils, Sydney, March 6–7.

Greene, Karen, and Tristan Taormino (eds) (1997) *A Girl's Guide to Taking Over the World: Writings from the Girl Zine Revolution*, New York: St. Martin's Press.

Greer, Germaine (1999) *The Whole Woman*, London: Transworld Publishers.

Gregory, Esther (1993) *Taking a Step towards Employment*, Melbourne: Ethnic Youth Issues Network.

Griffin, Christine (1985) *Typical Girls? Young Women from School to the Job Market*, London: Routledge and Kegan Paul.

——— (1993) *Representations of Youth: The Study of Youth and Adolescence in Britain and America*, Cambridge: Polity Press.

——— (1997) "Troubled Teens: Managing Disorders of Transition and Consumption," *Feminist Review* 55: 4–21.

——— (2001a) "Good Girls, Bad Girls: Anglo-Centrism and Diversity in the Constitution of Contemporary Girlhood," unpublished paper presented at *A New Girl Order?* conference, London, Nov. 14–16.

——— (2001b) " 'The Young Women Are Having a Great Time': Representations of Young Women and Feminism," *Feminism and Psychology* 11, no. 2: 182–86.

Griffin, Cynthia E. (2001) "Girl School," *Entrepreneur* (June): 32.

Griffin, Michelle (2003) "Wonder Woman's Fashion Emergency," *The Age*, March 30, Agenda, 3.

Guidikova, Irena, and Lasse Siurala (2001) "Introduction: A Weird, Wired, Winsome Generation—Across Contemporary Discourses on Subculture and Citizenship," in Furlong and Guidikova (eds) *Transitions of Youth Citizenship in Europe: Culture, Subculture and Identity*, Strasbourg: Council of Europe Publishing.

Hahn, Carole L. (1998) *Becoming Political: Comparative Perspectives on Citizenship Education*, Albany: State University of New York Press.

Hakim, Catherine (1991) "Grateful Slaves and Self-Made Women: Fact and Fantasy in Women's Work Orientations," *European Sociological Review* 7: 101–21.

Hall, G. Stanley (1904) *Adolescence*, New York: D. Appleton.

Hall, Stuart, and Tony Jefferson (1976) (eds) *Resistance through Rituals*, London: Hutchinson.

Hall, Stuart et al. (1979) *Policing the Crisis: Mugging, the State, and Law and Order*, London: Macmillan.

Hall, Tom, Amanda Coffey, and Howard Williamson (1999) "Self, Space and Place: Youth Identities and Citizenship," *British Journal of Sociology of Education* 20, no. 4: 501–13.

Hall, Tom, Howard Williamson, and Amanda Coffey (2000) "Young People, Citizenship and the Third Way: A Role for the Youth Service?," *Journal of Youth Studies* 3, no. 4 (Dec.): 461–75.

Harris, Anita (1999a) "Everything a Teenage Girl Should Know: Adolescence and the Production of Femininity," *Women's Studies Journal* 15, no. 2 (Spring): 111–24.

——— (1999b) "Is DIY DOA? Zines and the Revolution, Grrrl-Style," in Rob White (ed.) *Australian Youth Subcultures: On the Margins and in the Mainstream*, Hobart: Australian Clearinghouse for Youth Studies.

——— (2001) "Not Drowning or Waving: Young Feminism and the Limits of the Third Wave Debate," *Outskirts* 8 (May). www.chloe.uwa.edu.au/outskirts/ (Accessed May 2003).

Heath, Sue (1999a) "Watching the Backlash: The Problematisation of Young Women's Academic Success in 1990s Britain," *Discourse: Studies in the Cultural Politics of Education* 20, no. 2: 249–66.

——— (1999b) "Young Adults and Household Formation in the 1990s," *British Journal of Sociology of Education* 20, no. 4: 545–61.

Heinz, Walter R. (1995) "Access to Working Life in Germany and Britain," in Alessandro Cavalli and Olivier Galland (eds) *Youth in Europe*, London: Pinter.

Helve, Helena (1997) "Perspectives on Social Exclusion, Citizenship and Youth," in Bynner, Chisholm, and Furlong (eds) *Youth, Citizenship and Change in a European Context*, Aldershot, U.K.: Ashgate.

——— (2002) "The Situation of Girls and Young Women," unpublished paper presented at United Nations Youth Unit *Expert Meeting on Global Priorities for Youth, Helsinki*, Oct. 6–10. www.un.org/esa/socdev/unyin/helsinki/finland_report.pdf (Accessed May 2003).

Henderson, Sheila, Rebecca Taylor, and Rachel Thomson (2002) "In Touch: Young People, Communication and Technologies," *Information, Communication and Society* 5, no. 4: 494–512.

Herrmann, Mareike (1998) "Feeling Better with BRAVO: German Girls and Their Popular Youth Magazine," in Sherrie Inness (ed.) *Millennium Girls: Today's Girls Around the World*, Lanham, Md.: Rowman and Littlefield.

Hetherington, Kevin (1998) *Expressions of Identity: Space, Performance and Politics*, London: Sage.

Hey, Valerie (1997) *The Company She Keeps: An Ethnography of Girls' Friendship*, Buckingham, U.K.: Open University Press.

——— (2001) "Beacon Girls: The Moral High Ground and Managing Aspiration in Public and Private Lives; Some Feminist Reflections," unpublished paper presented at *A New Girl Order?* conference, London, Nov. 14–16.

Hillier, Lynne (2001) " 'I'm Wasting Away on Unrequited Love': Gendering Same Sex Attracted Young Women's Love, Sex and Desire," *Hecate* 27, no. 1: 119–27.

Hillier, Lynne et al. (1998) *Writing Themselves In: A National Report on the Sexuality, Health and Well-Being of Same Sex Attracted Young People*, Carlton, Australia: National Centre in HIV Social Research.

Holdsworth, Roger (2000) "Education in Asia: Schools That Create Real Roles of Value for Young People," *Prospects* 30, no. 3 (Sept.): 349–62.

Holmes, Janelle, and Eliane Leslau Silverman (1992) *We're Here, Listen to Us!: A Survey of Young Women*, Ottawa: Canadian Advisory Council on the Status of Women.

Holsinger, K. (2000) "Feminist Perspectives on Female Offending: Examining Real Girls' Lives," *Women and Criminal Justice* 12, no. 1: 23–51.

Hopkins, Susan (1999) "The Art of 'Girl Power': Femininity, Feminism and Youth Culture in the 1990s" in Rob White (ed.) *Australian Youth Subcultures: On the Margins and in the Mainstream*, Hobart: Australian Clearinghouse for Youth Studies.

——— (2002a) *Girl Heroes: The New Force in Popular Culture*, Sydney: Pluto Press.

——— (2002b) "Power Undressing," *The Age*, Aug. 22, The Culture, 1.

Hughes-Bond, Linda (1998) "Standing Alone, Working Together: Tensions Surrounding Young Canadian Women's Views of the Workplace," *Gender and Education* 10, no. 3: 281–97.

Human Rights and Equal Opportunity Commission (1991) *Report on the National Inquiry into Racist Violence in Australia*, Canberra: Australian Government Publishing Service.

Hunter, Ernest, Patricia Fagan, and Tiffany Wilkes (1998) "Bama Wadu Wadu Mara Mara—Young Aboriginal Men and Women," *Aboriginal and Islander Health Worker Journal* 22, no. 2 (March–April): 12–18.

Huq, Rupa (2001) "Rap à la française: Hip Hop as Youth Culture in Contemporary Post-Colonial France," in Furlong and Guidikova (eds) *Transitions of Youth Citizenship in Europe: Culture, Subculture and Identity*, Strasbourg: Council of Europe Publishing.

Ige, Barbara Kaoru (1998) "For Sale: A Girl's Life in the Global Economy," in Sherrie A. Inness (ed.) *Millennium Girls: Today's Girls around the World*, Lanham, Md.: Rowman and Littlefield.

Jacobi, Juliane (1995) "Are Girls Less Political Than Boys? Research Strategies and Concepts for Gender Studies on 9–12 Year Olds," in Georg Neubauer and Klaus Hurrelmann (eds) *Individualization in Childhood and Adolescence*, Berlin: Walter de Gruyter.

Järvinen, Tero, and Markku Vanttaja (2001) "Young People, Education and Work: Trends and Changes in Finland in the 1990s," *Journal of Youth Studies* 4, no. 2: 195–207.

Jay, Martin (1994) *Downcast Eyes: The Denigration of Vision in Twentieth-Century French Thought*, Berkeley: University of California Press.

Jenkins, Kuni, and Kay Morris Matthews (1995) *Hukarere and the Politics of Maori Girls' Schooling 1875–1995*, Palmerston North, New Zealand: Dunmore Press.

Johnson, Jennifer (2002) *Getting By on the Minimum: The Lives of Working-Class Women*, New York: Routledge.

Johnson, Lesley (1993) *The Modern Girl: Girlhood and Growing Up*, St. Leonards, Australia: Allen and Unwin.

Jones, Alison (1991) *"At School I've Got a Chance": Culture/Privilege: Pacific Islands and Pakeha Girls at School*, Palmerston North, New Zealand: Dunmore Press.

Jones, Gill (1995) *Leaving Home*, Buckingham, U.K.: Open University Press.

Jones, Gill, and Wallace, Claire (1992) *Youth, Family and Citizenship*, Buckingham, U.K.: Open University Press.

Joseph Rowntree Foundation www.jrf.org.uk/knowledge/findings/socialpolicy/520.asp (Accessed May 2003).

Kaplan, Nancy, and Eva Farrell (1994) "Weavers of Webs: A Portrait of Young Women on the Web," *The Arachnet Electronic Journal on Virtual Culture* 2, no. 3 (July 26). www.monash.edu.au/journals/ejvc/kaplan.v2n3 (Accessed May 2003).

Karnes, Frances A., and Suzanne M. Bean (1997) *Girls and Young Women Entrepreneurs: True Stories about Starting and Running a Business Plus How You Can Do It Yourself*, Madison: Turtleback Books.

Kasesniemi, Eija-Liisa (2001) "Finnish Teenagers and Mobile Communication: Chatting and Storytelling in Text Messages," in Furlong and Guidikova (eds) *Transitions of Youth Citizenship in Europe: Culture, Subculture and Identity*, Strasbourg: Council of Europe Publishing.

Katz, Adrienne (1997) *The Can-Do Girls: A Barometer of Change*, Oxford: Department of Applied Social Studies and Social Research, Oxford University.

Katz, Cindi (1998) "Disintegrating Developments. Global Economic Restructuring and the Eroding of Ecologies of Youth," in Skelton and Valentine (eds) *Cool Places: Geographies of Youth Cultures*, London: Routledge.

Kelly, Paula (1986) "The Double-Bind: The Educational Dilemmas of Young Women From Indo-China," *Youth Studies Australia* 5, no. 2 (Aug.): 24–27.

Kelly, Peter (2000) "Youth as an Artefact of Expertise," in McLeod and Malone (eds) *Researching Youth*, Hobart: Australian Clearinghouse for Youth Studies.

——— (2001) "Youth at Risk: Processes of Individualisation and Responsibilisation in the Risk Society," *Discourse: Studies in the Cultural Politics of Education* 22, no. 1: 23–33.

Kenway, Jane (1990) "Privileged Girls, Private Schools and the Culture of 'Success,' " in Kenway and Willis (eds) *Hearts and Minds: Self-Esteem and the Schooling of Girls*, London: Falmer.

Kenway, Jane, and Sue Willis (eds) (1990) *Hearts and Minds: Self-Esteem and the Schooling of Girls*, London: Falmer.

Klawitter, Marieka, Robert D. Plotnick, and Mark Evan Edwards (2000) "Determinants of Initial Entry onto Welfare by Young Women," *Journal of Policy Analysis and Management* 19, no. 4: 527–46.

Klein, Naomi (2000) "The Vision Thing," *The Nation*, July 10.

——— (2001) *No Logo: No Space, No Choice, No Jobs. Taking Aim at the Brand Bullies*, London: Flamingo.

Krüger, Helga (1990) "The Shifting Sands of the Social Contract: Young People in the Transition from School to Work," in Lynne Chisholm, Peter Büchner, Heinz-Hermann Krüger, and Phil Brown (eds) *Childhood, Youth and Social Change: A Comparative Perspective*, London: Falmer.

Kuo, Lenore (1998) "Secondary Discrimination as a Standard for Feminist Social Policy: Norplant and Probation, a Case Study," *Signs* 23, no. 4 (Summer): 907–44.

Kushell, Jennifer (1999) *The Young Entrepreneur's Edge: Using Your Ambition, Independence, and Youth to Launch a Successful Business*, New York: Random House.

Laflin, Melanie (1996) "Girl Gangs: The Dangers of Female Gang Delinquency Should Not Be Underestimated," *Law and Order* 44, no. 3: 87–89.

Lagos, Marta, and Richard Rose (1999) *Young People in Politics: A Multicontinental Study*, Studies in Public Policy Number 316, Glasgow: Centre for the Study of Public Policy, University of Strathclyde.

Lagree, Jean-Charles (1995) "Young People and Employment in the European Community: Convergence or Divergence?" in Chisholm et al. (eds) *Growing Up in Europe: Contemporary Horizons in Childhood and Youth Studies*, Berlin: Walter de Gruyter.

Lahteenmaa, Jaana (1995) "Youth Culture in Transition to Post-Modernity: Finland," in Chisholm et al. (eds) *Growing Up in Europe: Contemporary Horizons in Childhood and Youth Studies*, Berlin: Walter de Gruyter.

Lanctot, Nadine, and Carolyn A. Smith (2001) "Sexual Activity, Pregnancy and Deviance in a Representative Urban Sample of African American Girls," *Journal of Youth and Adolescence* 30, no. 3 (June): 349–72.

Lauritzen, Peter (2001) "Introduction to the Themes of the Symposium," unpublished paper presented at *Youth—Actor of Social Change?* symposium, Strasbourg, Dec. 12–14.

Leadbeater, Bonnie J. Ross, and Niobe Way (1996) (eds) *Urban Girls: Resisting Stereotypes, Creating Identities*, New York: New York University Press.

Lees, Sue (1986) *Losing Out: Sexuality and Adolescent Girls*, London: Hutchinson.

Leonard, Marion (1997) " 'Rebel Girl, You Are the Queen of My World': Feminism, 'Subculture' and Grrrl Power," in Sheila Whiteley (ed.) *Sexing the Groove: Popular Music and Gender*, London: Routledge.

—— (1998) "Paper Planes: Travelling The New Grrrl Geographies," in Skelton and Valentine (eds) *Cool Places: Geographies of Youth Culture*, London: Routledge.

Lesko, Nancy (1988) "The Curriculum of the Body: Lessons from a Catholic High School," in Leslie Roman and Linda Christian-Smith (eds) *Becoming Feminine*, London: Falmer.

—— (2001) *Act Your Age! A Cultural Construction of Adolescence*, New York: Routledge-Falmer.

Lewis, Magda (1996) *Without a Word: Teaching beyond Women's Silence*, New York: Routledge.

Lipsitz, George (1994) "We Know What Time It Is: Race, Class and Youth Culture in the Nineties," in Ross and Rose (eds) *Microphone Fiends: Youth Music and Youth Culture*, New York: Routledge.

Lister, Ruth (1997) *Citizenship: Feminist Perspectives*, London: Macmillan.

Looker, E. Dianne, and Peter Dwyer (1998) "Education and Negotiated Reality: Complexities Facing Rural Youth in the 1990s," *Journal of Youth Studies* 1, no. 1: 5–22.

Looker, E. Dianne, and Pamela Magee (2000) "Gender and Work: The Occupational Expectations of Young Women and Men in the 1990s," *Gender Issues* 18, no. 2 (Spring): 74–88.

Lopez, Nancy (2003) *Hopeful Girls, Troubled Boys: Race and Gender Disparity in Urban Education*, New York: Routledge.

Lowe, Sue (2003) "For Young Women, Mobiles Replace Chocolate," *The Age*, March 15.

Lucas, Shelley (2000) "Nike's Commercial Solution: Girls, Sneakers, and Salvation," *International Review for the Sociology of Sport* 35, no. 2: 149–64.

Luker, Kristin (1996) *Dubious Conceptions: The Politics of Teenage Pregnancy*, Cambridge, Mass.: Harvard University Press.

McClelland, Alison, Helen MacDonald, and Fiona Macdonald (1998) "Young People and Labour Market Disadvantage: The Situation of Young People not in Education or Full Time Work," in *Australia's Youth: Reality and Risk*, Sydney: Dusseldorp Skills Forum.

McCormick, Jennifer (2000) "Aesthetic Safety Zones: Surveillance and Sanctuary in Poetry by Young Women," in Weis and Fine (eds) *Construction Sites: Excavating Race, Class and Gender amongst Urban Youth*, New York: Teachers College Press.

McDonald, Kevin (1999) *Struggles for Subjectivity: Identity, Action and Youth Experience*, Cambridge: Cambridge University Press.

McIvor, Gill (2000) "Exploring Diversity: Understanding and Responding to Offending among Young Women and Girls," in Monica Barry, Olwyn Burke, Joe Connolly, and Joe Curran (eds) *Children, Young People and Crime in Britain and Ireland: From Exclusion to Inclusion*, Edinburgh: Scottish Executive Central Research Unit.

McLeod, Julie (2001) "Subjectivity and Schooling in a Longitudinal Study of Secondary Students," *British Journal of Sociology of Education* 21, no. 4: 501–21.

McLeod, Julie, and Karen Malone (eds) (2000) *Researching Youth*, Hobart: Australian Clearinghouse for Youth Studies.

McNamee, Sara (1998) "The Home. Youth, Gender and Video Games: Power and Control in the Home," in Skelton and Valentine (eds) *Cool Places: Geographies of Youth Culture*, London: Routledge.

McRobbie, Angela (1997) "*More!* New Sexualities in Girls' and Women's Magazines," in Angela McRobbie (ed.) *Back to Reality? Social Experience and Cultural Studies*, Manchester: Manchester University Press.

—— (2000) *Feminism and Youth Culture*, rev. edn, London: Macmillan.

—— (2001) "Good Girls, Bad Girls? Female Success and the New Meritocracy," unpublished keynote address presented at *A New Girl Order?* conference, London, Nov. 14–16.

McRobbie, Angela, and Jenny Garber (1976) "Girls and Subcultures," in Stuart Hall and Tony Jefferson (eds) *Resistance through Rituals*, London: Hutchinson.

Maffesoli, Michel (1996) *The Time of the Tribes*, London: Sage.

Mahoney, Maureen (1996) "The Problem of Silence in Feminist Psychology," *Feminist Studies* 22, no. 3 (Fall): 603–26.

Males, Mike A. (1996) *The Scapegoat Generation: America's War on Adolescents*, Monroe, Me.: Common Courage Press.

—— (1999) *Framing Youth: Ten Myths about the Next Generation*, Monroe, Me.: Common Courage Press.

Malone, Karen (2000) "Dangerous Youth: Youth Geographies in a Climate of Fear," in McLeod and Malone (eds) *Researching Youth*, Hobart: Australian Clearinghouse for Youth Studies.

Mann, Judy (1994) *The Difference: Growing Up Female in America*, New York: Warner Books.

Manne, Anne (2002) "My Childless Career," *Sydney Morning Herald*, June 1.

Marshall, Harriette, and Anjum Yazdani (1999) "Locating Culture in Accounting for Self-Harm amongst Asian Young Women," *Journal of Community and Applied Social Psychology* 9: 413–33.

Marshall, T. H. (1950) *Citizenship and Social Class*, Cambridge: Cambridge University Press.

Martin, Yvonne (1998) "Young Girl Thugs Bash for the Thrill of It," *The Dominion* (Wellington), Apr. 8, 2.

Mary (1997) "things I'm gonna stop doing with my white privilege," in Green and Taormino (eds) *A Girl's Guide to Taking Over the World: Writings from the Girl Zine Revolution*, New York: St. Martin's Press.

Matthews, Julie (2002) "Racialised Schooling, 'Ethnic Success' and Asian-Australian Students," *British Journal of Sociology of Education* 23, no. 2: 193–207.

Melucci, Alberto (1996) *Challenging Codes: Collective Action in the Information Age*, Cambridge: Cambridge University Press.

Mendoza-Denton, Norma (1996) " 'Muy Mucha': Gender and Ideology in Gang-Girls' Discourse about Makeup," *Ethnos* 61, nos. 1–2: 47–63.

Mickelburough, Peter (1999) "Girl Danger: Attacks Rise on Modern Power Teens," *Herald Sun* (Melbourne), Dec. 6, 1, 4.

Miles, Steven (2000) *Youth Lifestyles in a Changing World*, Buckingham, U.K.: Open University Press.

Miller, Jody (1996) "An Examination of Disposition Decision-Making for Delinquent Girls," in Martin D. Schwartz and Dragan Milovanovic (eds) *Race, Gender and Class in Criminology: The Intersection*, New York: Garland.

Milligan, Sandra, Karen Thomson, and Ashenden and Associates (1992) *Listening to Girls*, Carlton, Australia: Australian Education Council.

Mirza, Heidi Safia (1992) *Young, Female and Black*, London: Routledge.

Mitchell, Allyson (2001) "The Writing's on the Wall: Feminist and Lesbian Graffiti as Cultural Production," in Mitchell, Rundle, and Karaian (eds) *Turbo Chicks: Talking Young Feminisms*, Toronto: Sumach Press.

Mitchell, Allyson, Lisa Bryn Rundle, and Lara Karaian (eds) (2001) *Turbo Chicks: Talking Young Feminisms*, Toronto: Sumach Press.

Mizen, Phillip, Angela Bolton, and Christopher Pole (1999) "School Age Workers: The Paid Employment of Children in Britain," *Work, Employment and Society* 13, no. 3: 423–38.

Morrison, Tina-Marie (1996) "Teen Angels Bite Back," *The Dominion*, May 12.

Munk, Nina (1997) "Girl Power," *Fortune* 136, no. 11: (Dec. 8): 133–36.

Murdocca, Carmela (2001) "Her HOME/S.ca: Feminist Post-ings On-line," in Mitchell, Rundle, and Karaian (eds) *Turbo Chicks: Talking Young Feminisms*, Toronto: Sumach Press.

Nagel, Ulrike, and Claire Wallace (1997) "Participation and Identification in Risk Societies: European Perspectives," in Bynner, Chisholm, and Furlong (eds) *Youth, Citizenship and Social Change in a European Context*, Aldershot, U.K.: Ashgate.

Nava, Mica (1992) *Changing Cultures: Feminism, Youth and Consumerism*, London: Sage.

Nielsen, Harriet Bjerrum (1999) "Gender, Love and Education in Three Generations," in Vesa Puuronen (ed.) *Youth in Everyday Life Contexts*, Joensuu, Finland: University of Joensuu.

Nikas, Catherine (1998) "The Power of Girls," *Ragtrader* (Apr. 3–16): 20–21.

Nutter, Steve (1997) "The Structure and Growth of the Los Angeles Garment Industry," in Andrew Ross (ed.) *No Sweat: Fashion, Free Trade, and the Rights of Garment Workers*, London: Verso.

O'Neil, Mary Lou (2002) "Youth Curfews in the United States: The Creation of Public Spheres for Some Young People," *Journal of Youth Studies* 5, no. 1: 49–67.

Ormond, Adreanne (2001) "Voice of Maori Youth: The Other Side of Silence," in Fine and Harris (eds) *Under the Covers: Theorising the Politics of Counter Stories*, Special Issue of *International Journal of Critical Psychology* 4: 49–60.

Palmer, Dave and Collard, Len (1998) " '. . . We Cleared and Built all that Run": Nyungars, Work and Cultural Incorporation', in Judith Bessant and Sandy Cook (eds) *Against the Odds: Young People and Work in Australia*, Hobart: Australian Clearinghouse for Youth Studies.

Panelli, Ruth, Karen Nairn, Nicola Atwool, and Jaleh McCormack (2002) " 'Hanging Out': Print Media Constructions of Young People in 'Public Space,' " *Childrenz Issues* 6, no. 1: 23–30.

Pastor, Jennifer, Jennifer McCormick and Michelle Fine (1996) "Makin' Homes: An Urban Girl Thing" in Leadbeater and Way (eds) *Urban Girls: Resisting Stereotypes, Creating Identities*, New York: New York University Press.

Penn, Roger (2000) "British Population and Society in 2025: Some Conjectures," *Sociology* 34, no. 1: 5–18.

Peterson, Abby (2001) "Youth and Political Militancy," unpublished paper presented at *Youth— Actor of Social Change?* symposium, Strasbourg, Dec. 12–14.

Phoenix, Ann (1991) *Young Mothers?* Oxford: Polity Press.

Pilkington, Hilary (1996) "Introduction," in Hilary Pilkington (ed.) *Gender, Generation and Identity in Contemporary Russia*, London: Routledge.

Pipher, Mary (1994) *Reviving Ophelia: Saving the Selves of Adolescent Girls*: New York: Grosset/Putnam.

Probert, Belinda, and Fiona Macdonald (1999) *Young Women: Poles of Experience in Work and Parenting*, Melbourne: Brotherhood of St. Laurence.

Proweller, Amira (1998) *Constructing Female Identities: Meaning Making in an Upper Middle Class Youth Culture*, Albany: State University of New York Press.

——— (2000) "Re-Writing/-Righting Lives: Voices of Pregnant and Parenting Teenagers in an Alternative School," in Weis and Fine (eds) *Construction Sites: Excavating Race, Class and Gender amongst Urban Youth*, New York: Teachers College Press.

Räthzel, Nora (2000) "Living Differences: Ethnicity and Fearless Girls in Public Spaces," *Social Identities* 6, no. 2: 119–42.

Rattansi, Ali, and Ann Phoenix (1997) "Rethinking Youth Identities: Modernist and Postmodernist Frameworks," in Bynner, Chisholm, and Furlong (eds) *Youth, Citizenship and Change in a European Context*, Aldershot, U.K.: Ashgate.

Redhead, Steve, with Derek Wynne and Justin O'Connor (1997) *The Clubcultures Reader: Readings in Popular Cultural Studies*, Oxford: Blackwell.

Reich, Stephanie (1999) "Norplant for Schoolgirls: Panacea or Paradox? A Case Study of the Decision-Making Process of the Baltimore Norplant Initiative," unpublished PhD thesis, Brandeis University.

"Review of *Gutsy Girls: Young Women Who Dare*" (2001) *Adolescence* 36, no. 141 (Spring): 176–77.

Riepl, Barbara, and Helmut Wintersberger (1999) "Towards a Typology of Political Participation of Young People," in Barbara Riepl and Helmut Wintersberger (eds) *Political Participation of Youth below Voting Age*, Vienna: European Centre for Social Welfare Policy and Research.

Rimmerman, Craig A. (1997) *The New Citizenship: Unconventional Politics, Activism and Service*, Boulder, Colo.: Westview Press.

Roberts, Ken et al. (2001) "The Monetarisation and Privatisation of Daily Life, and the Depoliticisation of Youth in Former Communist Countries," unpublished paper presented at *Youth—Actor of Social Change?* symposium, Strasbourg, Dec. 12–14.

Roker, Debra (1993) "Gaining the Edge: Girls at a Private School," in Inge Bates and George Riseborough (eds) *Youth and Inequality*, Buckingham, U.K.: Open University Press.

Rose, Nikolas (1990) *Governing the Soul: The Shaping of the Private Self*, London: Routledge.

Ross, Andrew (1994) "Introduction," in Ross and Rose (eds) *Microphone Fiends: Youth Music and Youth Culture*, New York: Routledge.

Ross, Andrew, and Tricia Rose (eds) (1994) *Microphone Fiends: Youth Music and Youth Culture*, New York: Routledge.

Rudd, Peter and Karen Evans (1998) "Structure and Agency in Youth Transitions: Student Experiences of Vocational Further Education," *Journal of Youth Studies* 1, no. 1: 39–62.

Rumack, Leah (2001) "Lipstick," in Mitchell, Rundle and Karaian (eds) *Turbo Chicks: Talking Young Feminisms*, Toronto: Sumach Press.

Ryan, Denise (2002) "Why X is the Unknown for a Generation," *The Age*, Feb. 16, 1, 8–9.

Saltau, Chloe, and Melissa Ryan (2000) "A New Glass Ceiling," *The Age*, May 9, 13.

Schneider, Barbara, and David Stevenson (1999) *The Ambitious Generation: America's Teenagers, Motivated but Directionless*, New Haven: Yale University Press.

Schubert, Misha (2001) "Teenager's Vision of a Grown-Up Republic," *The Australian*, May 10, 5.

Schultz, Katherine (1996). "Between School and Work: The Literacies of Urban Adolescent Females," *Anthropology and Education Quarterly* 27, no. 4: 517–44.

———— (1999) "Identity Narratives: Stories from the Lives of Urban Adolescent Females," *The Urban Review* 31, no. 1: 79–106.

Shah, Sonia (2001) "The Celebrated Immigrant," *Z Magazine*, April. www.zmag.org (Accessed May 2003).

Shandler, Sara (1999) *Ophelia Speaks: Adolescent Girls Write about Their Search for Self*, New York: Harper Perennial.

Siurala, Lasse (2000) "Changing Forms of Participation," unpublished paper presented at Council of Europe *New Forms of Youth Participation Round Table*, Biel (Switzerland), May 4–6, 2000. Summary at http://younet.ch/v4/e/table-ronde/page1.html (Accessed May 2003).

Skelton, Tracey, and Gill Valentine (eds) (1998) *Cool Places: Geographies of Youth Cultures*, London: Routledge.

Smith, Linda Tuhiwai (2001) "Troubling Spaces," in Fine and Harris (eds) *Under the Covers: Theorising the Politics of Counter Stories*, Special Issue of *International Journal of Critical Psychology* 4: 167–82.

Smith, Linda Tuhiwai, Graham H. Smith, Megan Boler, Margaret Kempton, Adreanne Ormond, Ho-Chia Chueh, and Rona Waetford (2002) " 'Do You Guys Hate Aucklanders Too?' Youth: Voicing Difference from the Rural Heartland," *Journal of Rural Issues* 18: 169–78.

Spierings, John (1999) "A Crucial Point in Life: Learning, Work and Young Adults," in *Australia's Young Adults: The Deepening Divide*, Sydney: Dusseldorp Skills Forum.

Springhall, John (1986) *Coming of Age: Adolescence in Britain 1860–1960*, Dublin: Gill and Macmillan.

Stevenson, Robert B., and Jeanne Ellsworth (1993) "Dropouts and the Silencing of Critical Voices" in Lois Weis and Michelle Fine (eds) *Beyond Silenced Voices: Class, Race and Gender in United States Schools*, Albany: State University of New York Press.

"Students: We Don't Want Vote" (2002) *Port Phillip Leader*, June 10, 22.

Sudbury, Julia (2002) "Celling Black Bodies: Black Women in the Global Prison Industrial Complex," *Feminist Review* 70: 57–74.

Summers, Anne (1994) "The Future of Feminism—A Letter to the Next Generation," preface to *Damned Whores and God's Police*, Harmondsworth, U.K.: Penguin.

Sweet, Richard (1998) "Youth: The Rhetoric and Reality of the 1990s," in *Australia's Youth: Reality and Risk*, Sydney: Dusseldorp Skills Forum.

Taft, Jessica (2001) "Girl Power Politics: Pop Culture Barriers and Organizational Resistance," unpublished paper presented at *A New Girl Order?* conference, London, Nov. 14–16.

Takayoshi, Pamela, Emily Huot, and Meghan Huot (1999) "No Boys Allowed: The World Wide Web as a Clubhouse for Girls," *Computers and Consumption* 16: 89–106.

Taylor, Jill MacLean, Carol Gilligan, and Amy M. Sullivan (1995) *Between Voice and Silence: Women and Girls, Race and Relationship*, Cambridge, Mass.: Harvard University Press.

Thomson, Pat, and Roger Holdsworth (2002) "Options within the Regulation and Containment of 'Student Voice' and/or Students Researching and Acting for Change: Australian Experiences," unpublished paper presented at *Student Voice*, American Educational Research Association conference, New Orleans, April 1–5.

Torney-Purta, Judith, Rainer Lehmann, Hans Oswald, and Wolfram Schulz (2001) *Citizenship and Education in Twenty-Eight Countries: Civic Knowledge and Engagement at Age Fourteen*, Amsterdam: International Association for the Evaluation of Educational Achievement.

Torre, María Elena, and April Burns (2001) "Calling All Girls: A Study of Urban Girls and Communications Technologies," unpublished paper presented at *A New Girl Order?* conference, London, Nov. 14–16.

Torre, María Elena, Michelle Fine, Kathy Boudin, Iris Bowen, Judith Clark, Donna Hylton, Migdalia "Missy" Martinez, Rosemarie A. Roberts, Pamela Smart, and Deborah Upegui (2001) "A Space for Co-Constructing Counter Stories under Surveillance," Fine and Harris (eds) *Under the Covers: Theorising the Politics of Counter Stories*, Special Issue of *International Journal of Critical Psychology* 4: 133–66.

Trioli, Virginia (1996) *Generation f: Sex, Power and the Young Feminist*, Melbourne: Minerva.

———— (2003) "C u @ raly :)—A Generation Speaks," *The Age*, March 29, Insight, 2.

Ule, Mirjana, and Tanja Rener (2001) "The Deconstruction of Youth," in Furlong and Guidikova (eds) *Transitions of Youth Citizenship in Europe: Culture, Subculture and Identity*, Strasbourg: Council of Europe Publishing.

Valdez, Al (1997) "Girls in the Hood: Dangerous Liaisons," *Police: The Law Enforcement Magazine* 21, no. 9: 40–41.

Valentine, Gill, Tracey Skelton, and Deborah Chambers (1998) "Cool Places: An Introduction to Youth and Youth Cultures," in Skelton and Valentine (eds) *Cool Places: Geographies of Youth Cultures*, London: Routledge.

Van Drenth, Annemieke (1998) "Citizenship, Participation and the Social Policy on Girls in the Netherlands," in Jet Bussemaker and Rian Voet (eds) *Gender, Participation and Citizenship in the Netherlands*, Aldershot, U.K.: Ashgate.

Vis, Rachel (undated) "Mainstream Feminism and the Riot Girls," *Katpounce* 4: 25–26.

VNS Matrix (1996) "Game Girls: The War against Big Daddy Mainframe," in Kathy Bail (ed.) *DIY Feminism*, St. Leonards, Australia: Allen and Unwin.

Walker, Jim, with Christine Hunt (1988) *Louts and Legends: Male Youth Culture in an Inner-City School*, Sydney: Allen and Unwin.

Walkerdine, Valerie, Helen Lucey, and June Melody (2001) *Growing Up Girl: Psycho-Social Explorations of Gender and Class*, London: Palgrave.

Wallace, Claire (1994) "Gender and Transition," in Karen Evans and Walter K. Heinz (eds) *Becoming Adults in England and Germany*, London: Anglo-German Foundation.

Wallace, Claire, and Sijka Kovatcheva (1998) *Youth in Society: The Construction and Deconstruction of Youth in East and West Europe*, Basingstoke, U.K.: Macmillan.

Walther, Andreas (2001) "Youth Transitions, Youth Policy and Participation," unpublished paper presented at *Youth—Actor of Social Change?* symposium, Strasbourg, Dec. 12–14.

Ward, Janie Victoria (2000) "Raising Resistors: The Role of Truth Telling in the Psychological Development of African American Girls," in Weis and Fine (eds) *Construction Sites: Excavating Race, Class and Gender amongst Urban Youth*, New York: Teachers College Press.

Warner-Smith, Penny, and Christina Lee (2001) "Hopes and Fears: The Life Choices, Aspirations and Well-Being of Young Rural Women," *Youth Studies Australia* 20, no. 3: 32–37.

Warnock, Steve (1998) "Girls with Attitude and Right Hook," *Sun-Herald* (Sydney), April 19, 16.

Wearing, Stephen, and Betsy Wearing (2000) "Smoking as a Fashion Accessory in the 90s: Conspicuous Consumption, Identity and Adolescent Women's Leisure Choices," *Leisure Studies* 19, no. 1: 45–58.

Weis, Lois, and Michelle Fine (eds) (2000) *Construction Sites: Excavating Race, Class and Gender amongst Urban Youth*, New York: Teachers College Press.

Wexler, Philip (1992) *Becoming Somebody: Toward a Social Psychology of School*, London: Falmer.

White, Clarissa, Sara Bruce, and Jane Ritchie (2000) *Young People's Politics: Political Interest and Engagement Amongst 14–24 Year Olds*, Layerthorpe, U.K.: York Publishing Services.

White, Rob (1998) *Public Spaces for Young People: A Guide to Creative Projects and Positive Strategies*, Sydney: The Australian Youth Foundation.

——— (ed.) (1999) *Australian Youth Subcultures: On the Margins and in the Mainstream*, Hobart: Australian Clearinghouse for Youth Studies.

White, Rob, Megan Aumair, Anita Harris, and Liz McDonnell (1997) *Any Which Way You Can: Youth Livelihood, Community Resources and Crime*, Sydney: The Australian Youth Foundation.

Whyte, William F. (1943) *Street Corner Society: The Social Construction of an Italian Slum*, Chicago: University of Chicago Press.

Wicks, Deirdre, and Gita Mishra (1998) "Young Australian Women and Their Aspirations for Work, Education and Relationships," in Edgar Carson, Adam Jamrozicz, and Tony Winefield (eds) *Unemployment: Economic Promise and Political Will*, Brisbane: Australian Academic Press.

Wilkinson, Helen, and Geoff Mulgan (1995) *Freedom's Children: Work, Relationships and Politics for 18–34 Year Olds in Britain Today*, London: Demos.

Williamson, Howard (1997) "Youth Work and Citizenship," in Bynner, Chisholm, and Furlong (eds) *Youth, Citizenship and Social Change in a European Context*, Aldershot, U.K.: Ashgate.

——— (2001) "Reaching and Researching the 'Hard to Reach' (Young People on the Margins): Methodological and Ethical Questions," in Irena Guidikova and Howard Williamson (eds) *Youth Research in Europe: The Next Generation: Perspectives on Transitions, Identities and Citizenship*, Strasbourg: Council of Europe Publishing.

Willie, Sarah Susannah (2003) *Acting Black: College, Identity, and the Performance of Race*, New York: Routledge.

Willis, Paul (1979) *Learning to Labour: How Working Class Kids Get Working Class Jobs*, Aldershot, U.K.: Saxon House.

Willis, Susan (1998) "Teens at Work: Negotiating the Jobless Future," in Austin and Willard (eds) *Generations of Youth: Youth Subcultures and History in Twentieth-Century America*, New York: New York University Press.

Withers, Graeme, and Margaret Batten (1995) *Programs for At-Risk Youth: A Review of American, Canadian and British Literature Since 1984*, Melbourne: Australian Council for Educational Research.

Wooden, Mark (1998) "The Labour Market for Young Australians," in *Australia's Youth: Reality and Risk*, Sydney: Dusseldorp Skills Forum.

Wooden, Mark, and Adriana VanDenHeuvel (1999) "The Labour Market for Young Adults," in *Australia's Young Adults: The Deepening Divide*, Sydney: Dusseldorp Skills Forum.

www.woodhull.org/about/index.html (Accessed May 2003).

www.worldywca.org/campaign/en/overview (Accessed May 2003).

Wyn, Johanna (1990) "Working Class Girls and Educational Outcomes: Is Self Esteem an Issue?" in Kenway and Willis (eds) *Hearts and Minds: Self-Esteem and the Schooling of Girls*, London: Falmer.

——— (1998) "Young People and the Transition from School to Work: New Agendas in Post-Compulsory Education and Training," in Judith Bessant and Sandy Cook (eds) *Against the Odds: Young People and Work*, Hobart: Australian Clearinghouse for Youth Studies.

——— (2000) "The Postmodern Girl: Education, 'Success' and the Construction of Girls' Identities," in McLeod and Malone (eds) *Researching Youth*, Hobart: Australian Clearinghouse for Youth Studies.

——— (2001) "What Are Young Women Getting Out of Education? A Perspective on Young Women's Outcomes Ten Years After Leaving School," unpublished paper presented at *New Directions in Feminist Youth Research* conference, Monash University, Clayton, Australia, May 17.

——— (2002) "Leisure Time Activities," paper presented at United Nations Youth Unit *Expert Meeting on Global Priorities for Youth, Helsinki,* Oct. 6–10. www.un.org./esa/socdev/unyin/helsinki/finland_report.pdf (Accessed May 2003).

Wyn, Johanna, and White, Rob (1997) *Re-thinking Youth,* London: Sage.

Yates, Lyn (2000) "Representing 'Class' in Qualitative Research," in McLeod and Malone (eds) *Researching Youth,* Hobart: Australian Clearinghouse for Youth Studies.

Young Women: Feminists, Activists, Grrrls (2001), Spring issue of *Canadian Woman Studies* 20/21 (4/1).

Young Women Connect (2001) "Young Women Connect: Racism, Violence, Poverty. Got Something to Say?" *Young Women: Feminists, Activists, Grrrls* 20/21 (4/1): 168.

Youth—Actor of Social Change? (2001) Symposium, Council of Europe, Strasbourg, Dec. 12–14.

Yuval-Davis, Nira (1992) *Nationalism, Racism and Gender Relations,* The Hague: Institute of Social Studies.

SUBJECT INDEX

activism, 9, 11, 134, 137, 139, 149, 152,
    157–159, 164–165, 169, 174–177,
    180–182, 185–188, 204 n33, 204 n50,
    205 n73; *see also* culture jamming,
    feminism, globalization, networks,
    politics
adolescence, 1, 2
    nineteenth century, 1, 2, 5, 8, 15
    theories of female development, 15,
    191–192
African-American girls, 23, 34, 82, 107,
    113–114, 117, 120, 131, 142, 157,
    170–171
Afro-Caribbean girls, 108, 193
ambassadress, girls as, 10, 71, 79, 85–91, 94,
    165, 174–176
art, youth projects, 154, 165–182
Asian girls, 34, 43, 52, 87, 90, 112, 162,
    175–176
at-risk, 13, 25–28, 34–35, 55, 90, 97,
    108–110, 115–117, 131, 153, 165–172

bedrooms, 100, 129–130
Black youth, 15, 30, 34, 51, 87, 90, 108, 117,
    142, 172, 178; *see also* African-
    American girls, Afro-Caribbean girls
body image, 20, 86, 91, 129, 131, 166, 189
boys, 13, 41, 101, 102, 103, 104, 108, 109,
    116

cell phones, 119, 129–130, 145, 156

choice biography, 8, 37, 39, 54, 74
citizenship, 2, 6, 10, 14, 28, 58, 63–91,
    94–96, 132–136, 139, 143, 145–146,
    150, 152, 155, 165, 172–173, 177,
    179–182, 185, 187–190
    citizen mothers, 72–74
    consumer citizenship, 69–70, 88–94,
    121–123, 143–149, 173–174
    employment and, 66–67, 71–73
    responsibility and, 67–68
class, 7, 9, 35, 44–45, 60–61
    middle-class girls, 7, 15, 23, 33–34,
    42–43, 46–51, 105–106, 111, 192
    working-class girls, 15, 51–59, 107, 154
colonization, 15, 85, 103, 107, 174, 176
consumption, 7, 20–22, 28–30, 111,
    121–123, 146–149, 166–168, 172–
    174
contraception, 23–24, 31
crime, 28–30, 31, 34, 58–59, 115–118,
    131–132
culture jamming, 172–173

deindustrialization, 3, 38–39, 43, 48, 54, 60,
    65
delinquency, 15, 28, 116; *see also* crime
diaries, 83, 114–115, 131, 156, 161
disability, 91, 158, 166, 181, 204 n33
discourse, 10, 11, 13, 17, 26, 35–37, 39–40,
    43–44, 46–47, 53–54, 60, 62, 64, 66,
    70–71, 79, 82, 91, 99, 100, 105, 107,

Author Index